THE HISTORY OF
THE ENGLISH NOVEL

THE HISTORY OF
THE ENGLISH NOVEL

By Ernest A. Baker, D. Lit., M.A.

THE HISTORY
OF THE
ENGLISH NOVEL

By Ernest A. Baker, D. Lit., M.A.

Volume VI

Edgeworth, Austen, Scott

New York
BARNES & NOBLE, INC.

First published 1929
Reprinted 1967 by special arrangement with
H. F. & G. WITHERBY, LTD.
326 High Holborn, London, W. C. 1

Printed in the United States of America

27412

PREFACE

AT first I intended to end this volume with the group of native Irish writers who came after Miss Edgeworth, and the historical novelists who followed Scott. But it then appeared that if I carried on my survey from Lady Morgan and the Banims to Lover and Lever, I should find myself outrunning the first thirty years of last century by several decades, and that similar chronological difficulties would arise in the other case. These two groups have, accordingly, been deferred to the next volume, which will probably begin with Peacock and end with Dickens and Thackeray. In an attempt at history, rather than chronicling, in which the question of family relationships is more important even than that of criticism, there must be these little difficulties at the beginning and the end of a volume. I had hoped to deal much more briefly with the three great novelists forming the main subject here; but the chapters grew and grew, and seeing no hope of curtailing them, I have had to divide them into twos and threes, as the table of contents shows.

In the chapters on Maria Edgeworth, I had the great advantage of having read and being permitted to quote from *The Black Book of Edgeworthstown.* I thank the two editors, and in particular Professor H. E. Butler, Maria Edgeworth's grand-nephew, for kindly reading through this portion of my work. I also thank Miss H. Winifred Husbands, M.A., of University College, London, for her kindness in overlooking the proof-sheets.

E. A. B.

CONTENTS

EDGEWORTH, AUSTEN, SCOTT

CHAPTER I

MARIA EDGEWORTH—EARLY STORIES AND *CASTLE RACKRENT*

THANKS to a happy chronological accident, a bridge was provided *The*
from the eighteenth century to the nineteenth in the work of two *passage*
novelists, Maria Edgeworth and Jane Austen, who belonged to *from the*
both the old and the new age. Without any shock of surprise or *century to*
startling change of scenery, we gradually find that the past has *the*
been left behind and we are entering upon the present. There are *nineteenth*
still many features in the scenes brought before the eye which
are now obsolete or quaint and old-fashioned. But compare any
of their novels with *Pamela* and *Joseph Andrews*, the second
centenary of which will be celebrated a few years hence—
the Victorians hardly noticed the first. There the world
depicted is not our world; all is remote and unfamiliar, except
the general traits that are of our own race and kindred or
simply human and of all ages. It is a world seemingly more
than four times as far removed as that of Miss Edgeworth and
Miss Austen, whose early novels, nevertheless, including their
finest, were written only half-a-century later. In *Castle Rackrent*
perhaps, but certainly not in *Tales of Fashionable Life*, *Sense
and Sensibility*, or *Pride and Prejudice*, do the manners seem
strange or antiquated; still less is there in the bearing and
workmanship of the novelist that requires the reader to make
allowances.

For the differences between the two groups of novels are in *How far*
the social physiognomy rather than in the mode of portrayal. *the novels*
The fashion of the world had changed much more than the fashion *reflect*
of novel-writing. In these fifty years, there had been an un- *social*
exampled advance in order and civilization. England had never *changes*
been so quiet for so long a space, never more prosperous. The
middle classes were merging with the upper classes, in spite of the

deference and even obsequiousness paid as much as ever to rank and title; they were in possession of wealth, comfort, and leisure, and were now the most stable element in the community, the portion that was coming more and more to represent the intelligence, the morality and refinement of the nation. Incidentally, they formed the reading public, which was now large enough to make the fortune of a successful novelist. Even the minor novels that were the theme of the preceding volume show clearly the amelioration of manners, the new interests shaping life, the steady transformation of society from centre to circumference, and the gradual suppression of the differences between town and country so far as the more cultivated classes were concerned. In both Miss Edgeworth's and Miss Austen's novels, the stage is oftener a manor-house or a vicarage than the fashionable end of the metropolis, and changes of scene from London or Bath to the country are a very small change of environment. The process of rapid evolution with its reactions upon literature which can be followed in the history of fiction better than anywhere else had completed a definite stage. Actually, it was to go on at an accelerated pace throughout the nineteenth century, till now, when a state of transition seems to be the normal state of mankind. But in essentials the society that we meet in the novels of these two ladies is that of our own contemporaries.

Richardson and Fielding compared with Edgeworth and Austen It would be misleading, however, not to make large allowances for the point of view and the different radius of vision of the older and the younger novelists. Simply to contrast Fielding's and Richardson's view of the world with that of Miss Edgeworth and Miss Austen would be to exaggerate the real disparity between the two epochs. Novelists latterly had shown a tendency to confine themselves to those educated classes who read their books. These two ladies kept almost exclusively to their own class; they rarely went outside a limited sphere in which manners and morals were more refined than in any other section of society. Fielding, on the other hand, had been catholic in his range, and never afraid to tell the truth however ugly; he drew his characters from low as well as from high life, as he often stops to point out, and rivalled Hogarth in his insistence on the barbarism of the mob. Even Richardson left in his two chief novels a distorted impression

of a lawless state of society by choosing transgressions of the
established code for his dramatic material. Fanny Burney, whose
novels and letters are on the whole good evidence for the progress
of manners at a half-way stage, had for the sake of sensation given
some slight glimpses of the vice and brutality of the lower classes,
though her chief object was to make fun of the absurdities of
those who aped their betters or of the crazes and affectations
rampant in a more elevated sphere. But she could have known
very little at first hand about the lower classes; she was a woman,
like her two successors, with a woman's narrow experience.
Maria Edgeworth did not by any means overlook the poorer
classes in her Irish stories, as will be seen; but she saw them as
one of their superiors, at the best as a charitable observer, not
as one who could even in imagination make herself one of them.
All three, in short, gave the feminine view of life; they were
not qualified to do more, and their delicacy would have shrunk
from a candid treatment of many things that could not escape
their notice. It needed a man, a Walter Scott, with an eye like
Fielding's for all sorts and conditions, to restore the balance, as
he did in the novels of his own day or of his yesterday which are
the nearest approach to the broad survey of his predecessor. And
even Scott is to be read as an historian of society only if some
correction is applied for the romantic bias even in his semi-
contemporary pictures. He was determined to entertain and
enthral, no matter if the exact truth of his version of reality
suffered.[1] Thus a great many disturbing factors have to be taken
into account if a register of the changes of the last fifty years is
sought in the novels.

Miss Edgeworth and Miss Austen found their right medium in *The
domestic novel*
the domestic novel, that form of the novel of manners the general
scheme of which had evolved and come into chief favour during
the last half-century. Fielding's vivid rendering of life as it goes
quietly or impetuously on was here applied to a narrower expanse,
and was blended as occasion served with Richardson's closer

---

[1] Scott in the anonymous review of his own *Tales of my Landlord* (*Quarterly*,
1816) protested against the " slovenly indifference " (*i.e.* his own) which
" sacrificed probability and perspicuity to the desire of producing effect." He says
in the *Journal* : " I only made that which I was actually writing diverting and
interesting, leaving the rest to fate."

scrutiny of the heart and with his systematic moralism.   Both
were clear-headed enough to avoid the uncertainty of aim and
halting craftsmanship which had rendered the majority of recent
novels so glaringly inferior to the pattern set by the illustrious
four.   They recovered the lost ground.   For there was no affectation of any kind in either of them.   They wrote simply and
sincerely, with a definite and consistent attitude of mind that
kept them to the point.   Both were writers because they had to
be, and were not, as too many of the literary tribe, mercenaries,
gushing amateurs, propagandists in disguise, or mere charlatans.
Jane Austen wrote to amuse herself; Maria Edgeworth
as a practical teacher, whose strong sense of responsibility
impelled her to correct and advise the rash and erring.   To
her, fiction was one of the useful arts; only once did she
yield to the joy of unfettered creation, when she bent the inner
ear to listen to old Thady " dictating " the history of Castle
Rackrent.

Both were   Both were writing in the period of the Romantic movement;
unaffected   but they were both untouched by it, and no doubt were unaware
by the   that any such thing as an important literary revolution was going
Romantic   on.   Both were well read in English literature, but their culture
movement   was that of the eighteenth century.   They knew there was a poet
named Wordsworth; he visited the Edgeworths in Ireland; but
their acquaintance with his poetry was evidently very slight, and
neither had an inkling of his inner meaning.   Coleridge they had
hardly heard of, and Keats and Shelley never appeared on the
horizon even to Maria Edgeworth, who outlived these younger
poets.   Crabbe was much more to their taste, as to that of most
readers in what we now call the age of romance.   Miss Edgeworth
was more interested in people than in books, and among the
writers whom she loved not many were poets.   She read Scott's
lays and novels with enthusiasm, very different from Jane Austen's
lukewarm appreciation of the first Waverley novels, the only ones
she lived to read.[1]   But Scott was romantic without participating

---

[1] " Walter Scott has no business to write novels, especially good ones.—It is
not fair.—He has Fame and Profit enough as a Poet, and should not be taking the
bread out of other people's mouths.—I do not like him, and do not mean to like
Waverley if I can help it—but fear I must " (*Letters*, ed. R. W. Chapman, 1932,
28th September 1814, p. 404).

in the new romanticism ; and it was his rich humanity, the truth
and splendour of his dramatization of both present and past, and
his discovery " that facts are better than fiction, that there is no
romance like the romance of real life,"[1] that fascinated Maria
Edgeworth. She herself had a weakness for romance of the old
stamp, in spite of her ridicule of sentimentalism and of Gothic and
other extravagances. The truth is that the deeper romanticism,
the romanticism of Wordsworth and his fellows, did not enter
fully into English fiction until the time of the Brontë sisters, with
their deep-rooted sense of a material world transfused with spirit.
Those novelists who were the contemporaries of Wordsworth
and Coleridge, Shelley and Keats, reveal not the slightest consciousness of that awakening of the soul and imagination which
was of its very essence.

Maria Edgeworth (1767-1849) has some affinity with the *Maria*
school of Bage, Holcroft, and Godwin, in that she embodied a *Edgeworth*
social philosophy in a series of novels and tales ; she might almost *and the*
be considered as the last and best of that group. But she was not, *reason*
like them, speculative and polemical ; and she was not in the habit
of talking at large about the abstract principles which she applied
to the daily predicaments of practical life. As to political questions, she left them to other people. Her own mind was made up.
In truth, she was not a profound thinker : but she was an intelligent
woman, the daughter of an able man, Richard Lovell Edgeworth,
and the friend of Ricardo and of Étienne Dumont, colleague and
expositor of Jeremy Bentham.[2] On the whole, she had a clearer
and more consistent view of the social order than was attained by
the revolutionary school in all their exposures of injustice, their
sentimental contrasts of selfishness and virtue, and their incessant
discussions of ethical and political problems in the light of soaring
but ill-defined ideals. Whilst they harped upon the rights of man,
she and her father were content to point out his duties. Bentham,
it will be remembered, likewise denied that the individual had
inherent rights, even the right to equality. In effect, their insistence

[1] William Hazlitt (*The Spirit of the Age*, " Sir Walter Scott ").
[2] M. Dumont is often mentioned with respect in her letters, and in her last
novel, *Helen*, Lady Davenant speaks of him more than once as a man and a writer
whose criticism and counsel were fearless and far-sighted. Maria Edgeworth
always accepted his criticisms of her own work with deference, and probably
benefited by them.

on what every man owes to the community, his obligation to make himself useful to his fellows, is nothing else than Bentham's utilitarianism, the doctrine of the greatest good of the greatest number, of the subservience of each to all, the identification of doing right with social service.

The new conception of the individual For it would be illusory to suppose that Maria Edgeworth had already grasped the modern conception of the individual as a member of the human family, a function in a living organism, the idea that was soon to displace the mechanical notion which had dominated the minds and circumscribed the imagination both of novelists and of politicians and social reformers. If she ever caught glimpses of this deeper view, its full significance had not dawned upon her. The eighteenth century beheld society merely as a vast aggregation of similar individuals, the arithmetical sum of many equal units, whose position in the social scheme was settled for them, not by personal differences, but by the external accidents of rank, property, privilege, or the inferior lot inherited by the majority.[1] This basic assumption had become instinctive; this was how men thought, how they looked at the world, until the end of the eighteenth century. Defoe and Richardson would have the individual accept resignedly his subjection to the appointed order; the revolutionary novelists would have him rebel and assert his claim to freedom and happiness. Both parties, nevertheless, acquiesced in the same fundamental axiom of the relation of the one to the many.

It is impossible to say at what precise date novelists and others began to think in different terms, though it can be safely asserted that the new view did not become general in fiction until romanticism came in with the Brontës. Then it is that characters are overheard demanding: "What was I created for? What is my place in the world?"[2] It is the view which has prevailed until the eve of the present day, when it is being challenged as an inadequate scheme for the realization of a complete personal life, and its corollary, progress, for every progress, is seen to be mean-

[1] Professor J. Macmurray dates this conception from the Cartesian affirmation of self-consciousness as the reality from which all belief and all theory have their starting-point. " Cogito ergo sum " was at once the foundation-stone of rationalism and the declaration of rights of the individual (" The Unity of Modern Problems," in *Journal of Philosophical Studies*, iv. 14, 1928).

[2] *Shirley.*

ingless. To-day personality is felt to be a higher object than any social organization, and it is being recognized that all institutions, including the State itself, exist for the service of personality. Yet Burke's prescient vision of the nation as a living structure,[1] ever developing, and not a mere mechanical sum of identical units, was fruitful in giving a deeper significance to history, as well as a warning to such rash reformers as thought it an easy task to overthrow the fabric and rebuild it from the foundations up. The full conception of the social system as an organism, and of the individual members as each exercising a vital function in the general service, was animating to the sociologist, the moral philosopher, and the novelist. Virtue, integrity, and happiness were thus seen to correspond to the fulfilment of that for which each was fitted; vice was failure and disobedience. Towards some such answer to the social enigma Bage, Holcroft, and Godwin had striven according to their lights; but they were more troubled by the breakdown of the old philosophy than ready with a comprehensive and satisfactory one to put in its place, in spite of the genial optimism of the first two and the perfectibilian theories of the last. They complacently responded to the revolutionary cry of liberty, equality, fraternity, though it was only a sentimental expression of the old individualism.

If Maria Edgeworth was too conservative to be prepared to see men and women all as organs of the body politic, with functions to perform for the common good, she had at any rate a healthy conviction of their duties and responsibilities. She herself belonged to the ruling classes, the classes which up to the time of her entry upon middle age were in Ireland unmistakably rulers. She never divested herself of some prejudices in regard to rank and station, and often in her edifying tales for children seems to be simply bidding them do that which is proper to the state of life to which Providence has called them. But her utilitarianism was an adequate working plan. She was not an unenlightened person, and had a right apprehension of the good of society as a whole. The general

Maria Edgeworth's utilitarian view

---

[1] "To him [Burke] a nation was a living organism, of infinitely complex structure, of intimate dependence upon the parts, and to be treated by politicians in obedience to a careful observation of the laws of its healthy development. To them [the French revolutionists] a nation was an aggregate of independent units, to be regulated by a set of absolute *a priori* maxims" (Leslie Stephen : *English Thought in the Eighteenth Century*, 1876, ii. 248-249).

happiness, social service, the call of duty rather than the assertion
of rights, are the ideas implicit in all her stories, whether nursery
fables inculcating the social virtues or full-length novels, " tales
of fashionable life," for the admonishment and education of the
adult.

Her own
mission
and how
her genius
trans-
cended it

Her own duty was evident; her function, if she had so regarded
it, had been marked out for her by her upbringing and special
abilities. As clearly as her father, she saw that the principal need
of all classes was education, with a view to the cheerful and
efficient performance of their duties in the world. Her mission
was to be a teacher, and she carried out her task with zeal and con-
scientiousness. Now and then she did still better. Moved unawares
by the impulse to express herself, to realize her personality, a
thing for which there was really no place in her philosophy, for
it was the dictate of genius which is ruled by no philosophy, she
wonderingly obeyed. She wrote *Castle Rackrent* without even
knowing how she did it. And, again, in many parts of *The Absentee*
and *Ormond* she built better than she knew. Partly, no doubt, it
was the Irish inspiration that seized her; she always wrote best
and most easily when the theme was Irish. And thus she was the
first writer to render the racial peculiarities of the Irish with the
charm of perfect comprehension, although, like Swift, Goldsmith,
and Henry Brooke, she was only an adopted child of the country.
Her first distinction is, then, to stand foremost among didactic
novelists, her second to be the author of the finest Irish story ever
written, her third to have given new shape and importance to the
short story. This had been the immemorial pattern for fiction
with a lesson to propound, and she had a recent model in the
Contes moraux of Marmontel, whose general level of accomplishment was indeed higher than hers.[1] But a comparison must not
be pressed; her aims were so different that comparison loses its
point. Among her tales for the young are many small masterpieces of neat workmanship and sympathetic imagination. The
more expansive stories of the world in which men and women live
out their destinies are not intrinsically superior, but they too

[1] Precedents for her stories for children were furnished by Madame d'Épinay,
with her *Conversations d'Émilie* (1774), Arnaud Berquin, author of *L'Ami des
Enfants* (24 vols., 1782-1783) and *Le Petit Grandison* (1807), and also Madame
de Genlis, with her *Théâtre d'Éducation*.

helped to re-establish and renovate a form of fiction in which the moderns have excelled.

The Edgeworths had come to Ireland towards the end of the *Her father* sixteenth century, and established themselves a hundred years later in County Longford at what was afterwards called Edgeworths-town. Maria was the eldest daughter of a man of considerable mark, Richard Lovell Edgeworth, and of Anna Maria Elers, with whom he eloped whilst still an undergraduate at Oxford, to the chagrin of his father, head of the family and owner of Edgeworthstown. It was not a happy marriage; the pair had very different tastes, and though there were several children the husband spent most of his time away, finding distraction in social amusements, travel at home and abroad, and experiments with mechanical contrivances, some of which turned out profitable. He went about for a while with Sir Francis Delaval, a notorious rake of whose exploits there are anecdotes in *Belinda*. A more reputable and more lasting friendship was with Thomas Day, another enthusiast for rational education. Day, whose scheme of bringing up two foundlings and marrying the one that proved suitable now looked unpromising, was with him at Lichfield, where Edgeworth had already been on a visit to Dr Erasmus Darwin and seems to have tried to flirt with Miss Seward, the famous " Swan." Both were attracted by a young lady, Miss Honora Sneyd, who refused to entertain a proposal of marriage from Day, but evidently treated his friend not quite with indiffer-ence. For when Edgeworth came home from abroad on hearing of the death of his wife, he received a letter from the magnanimous Day urging him to go at once to Lichfield and pay his now legitimate addresses to Honora. He did so, and hardly more than three months after the loss of his wife was again a husband.

The half-dozen years of this second marriage were a period of *His appeal* unalloyed happiness, spent partly at Edgeworthstown, and partly *to Maria's* in a less expensive residence at Northchurch, in Hertfordshire. *sense of re-* Honora was adored, not only by her little son and daughter, *sponsibility* but also by her stepchildren. Then she was carried off by con-sumption, and again Richard had to find himself a wife. Maria was now twelve years old, and received from her remarkable father a truly remarkable letter, in which he praised, with obvious sincerity, her "incomparable mother," besought her to emulate such an example, and informed her that the deceased had advised him to marry again, naming her own sister Elizabeth Sneyd as the likeliest woman to make him happy.[1] He knew himself to be a man of "strong passions," and Honora had seen what was good for him.[2] No one of his family or friends seems to have been disturbed by his haste to remarry on the death of the first Mrs Edgeworth; and with a little discretion he was now able to avoid any scandal when after an interval only twice as long he married Honora's sister, who as it happened had also been an object of Thomas Day's addresses. This marriage too was a very happy one, and Maria hardly needed her father's solemn injunction, "Continue, my dear daughter, the desire which you feel of becoming amiable, prudent, and of *Use*," to accept in full the responsibilities of his eldest child in the now rapidly expanding family circle, and to be the loyal and efficient helpmate of her new stepmother. Twenty years later, she was to salute as "Mamma" still another stepmother, this time her own junior [3]: and after the death of her "wonderful father" she became the mainstay of a huge household, looking after domestic affairs, even her sisters' clothes, keeping the accounts, managing the estates and tenants, who were always contented, and finding time for social enjoyments, correspondence with relations and eminent friends, and in addition to all this, and when nothing else had been neglected, writing her books. She was always working. Sending a piece of needlework to a friend, in case her friend might say, "It is a pity Miss Edgeworth should spend her time at such work!" she wrote, "Tell her that I like work very much, and that I have only done this at odd times . . . when my father reads out Pope's *Homer*, or when there are long sittings . . . it is much more agreeable to move one's fingers than to have to sit with

---

[1] Miss Emily Lawless quotes the whole letter with the exception of the important passage about his remarrying, although she assumes later on that the reader is aware the lady "advised that step" ("English Men of Letters"—*Maria Edgeworth*, 35-36).

[2] *The Black Book of Edgeworthstown*, 137.

[3] This fourth wife, *née* Beaufort, with her daughter, Harriet Edgeworth, afterwards Mrs Butler, was Richard's biographer, in the printed but unpublished *Memoir*, which is still the most important source for his life and that of his daughter, Maria Edgeworth.

hands crossed or clasped immoveably."[1] From when at the age of nine she wrote to her first stepmother, "I know that it will give you great satisfaction to know that I am a good girl," to when in everything but name she was head of the family at Edgeworthstown, she was a standing exemplar of the qualities illustrated in her Rosamund and Laura, the qualities instilled by her father, for, as two of the best-informed authorities on her life and his have put it, she was "his greatest creation."[2]

Born in England, she had spent a few months as a child in Ireland, but did not settle down there at Edgeworthstown till 1782, from which date, though she was often away on visits, and twice made a long stay in France, this remained her home for the rest of her life. Mr Edgeworth had returned to the family seat to live the life of a country gentleman, and to pursue his numerous avocations. He was still devoted to his mechanical amusements, he took a leading part in schemes for the improvement of agriculture, he was a busy magistrate, was called upon to take resolute action at the time of the French scare and the outbreak of 1798, and he sat as a member of the last Irish House of Commons, voting against the union although he remained undecided whether it was not for the good of his fellow-countrymen. In 1806, as author of such an important treatise as *Practical Education*, he was naturally put upon the new Board of Commissioners on Irish education. And whilst he was as industrious as his daughter Maria he found time to entertain the whole circle at Edgeworthstown with his readings and stories, and to take an active part in the gaieties of an extraordinarily clever and lively family. He was their idol till his death in 1817. Maria, his favourite child, was the person who had his entire confidence, his fellow-worker, and latterly his deputy in the exacting affairs of a landlord. She collaborated with him in *Practical Education* (1798); the didactic tales included in *The Parent's Assistant* and *Early Lessons*, some of them actually by him, were in large measure supplementary to that work. She

Richard Lovell Edgeworth and his daughter

---

[1] *Chosen Letters*, ed. F. V. Barry, 147.
[2] Her still surviving niece, Harriet Jessie Butler, and her grand-nephew, Harold Edgeworth Butler, in *The Black Book of Edgeworthstown*, 231.

wrote hardly anything that was not a more or less direct outcome
of the strong views on education and of the concern for moral
and social improvement which she shared with her father. The
problem of what she owed him, with the question whether, as has
been persistently alleged, her genius was thwarted by his interference, is simplified if their absolute unanimity be taken into
account. She was not merely his disciple, she was his other self.
It was almost as her own riper thoughts that she accepted his
continual advice and correction. He was an excellent story-
teller; she would have said he was the better of the two. The
gist of some of her best scenes and characters was supplied by
him. She was curiously weak in invention; this, if her own
evidence is to be accepted, was his strong point.[1] Possibly he did
not think that creative spontaneity and a didactic purpose were
incompatible; she, at any rate, did not think so. If he misled
her, it was by the whole process of the education which she
underwent, her apprenticeship in the workshop of the theorist
and reformer. After such a drilling, it is a miracle that she wrote
Castle Rackrent; and she could not have gone on writing like
that without abjuring the principles taken to heart in her work
upon *Practical Education*, and without freeing her mind from the
obsessing weight of her responsibilities. But she chose her narrow
path, and having taken this direction she could never again write
a story without an ulterior object.

So that the paternal influence upon a too receptive mind must
be dated further back, and it is evidently untrue that he interfered
with work which was going on well and spoiled what would have
been far better left alone. She inherited her genius from him;
as to that there can hardly be two opinions. He gave her mind
its initial bias and training. Even without those brilliant pages
which were actually taken down from his own words, he was in
a sense the joint author of Maria Edgeworth's novels, including
those that she wrote after his death. *Helen*, the last of all, is
typical of the work she used to submit to his critical approval;
yet it was now seventeen years since he might have interfered

---

[1] His dying mother warned him against being led astray by his " inventive
faculty " (see the entertaining *Memoirs of Richard Lovell Edgeworth*, 1820,
i. 104).

and corrected her. She was still writing, and writing as earnestly as ever, in her own chosen style.[1]

The tales collected in *The Parent's Assistant* (1796-1800), *Tales for children* which she would have preferred to call *The Parent's Friend*, and in *Early Lessons* (1801-1815), began in the " wee, wee stories "[2] written on a slate to please her sisters at Edgeworthstown, when she was about twenty. Her father and his wife Honora had started the fashion in the first twenty chapters of *Harry and Lucy*, that counterpart to his friend Day's *Sandford and Merton*. She completed *Harry and Lucy* many years afterwards, as a tribute to his memory, and also provided sequels for *Frank* and *Rosamund*. The *Early Lessons* were amplified in 1815, and stories of the same character and meant for the same plastic minds were included in *Moral Tales* (1801) and *Popular Tales* (1804). In those early days, she was already no doubt a sober, critical, and common-sense person, almost a mother to her flock of sisters and brothers, yet by no means lacking in good humour or forgetful of the joys and tragedies of childhood. And already she was proving herself to be " of use." To have to demonstrate their utility, to bear the brunt of the children's suffrages, was as wholesome for these maiden efforts as to have to undergo her father's criticism. It was like the practical Maria Edgeworth to keep up the habit, and test even the work of her maturity by the collective judgment of a family reading or a drawing-room audience.[3] Experiment was a root principle in her father's system of education, and she applied it both for her own benefit and for that of her juvenile listeners, who thus went through an admirable training in the critical appreciation of literature.[4]

Her father first encouraged her to write, and it was under his *Her supervision that most of her early work was done. She would *father's collaboration*

[1] On the inspiration and frequent collaboration enjoyed by Maria from her father, see the *Black Book*, especially pp. 203, 206 and 224-229, where she speaks of " his ready wit and infinite resource."

[2] *Black Book*, 165.

[3] See her letters to Mrs Ruxton on the performance of a little play, *The Grinding Organ* (1809), and the reading of one, *The Absentee* (1811), which Sheridan rejected and which went into the novel of that title (*Chosen Letters*, ed. F. V. Barry, 158-161).

[4] " Stories of children exercised the judgment of children, and so on in proportion to their respective ages, all giving their opinions, and trying their powers of criticism fearlessly and freely " (Maria Edgeworth's own words, quoted from the unpublished *Memoir*. See *Black Book*, 226).

make a preliminary outline; "this was always required by her father"; but she frequently altered it as she went on, *Helen*, in particular, which was written long after his death, giving her much trouble. The plan was perhaps improved by her father; then from time to time a part was sketched and shown him—"Let me see the bare skeleton," he would say. "Then he would in his own words fill up my sketch, paint the description, or represent the character intended, with such life, that I was quite convinced he not only seized the ideas, but that he saw with the prophetic eye of taste the utmost that could be made of them. . . . When he thought that there was spirit in what was written, but that it required great correction, he would say, 'Leave that to me; it is my business to cut and correct—yours to write on.'"[1] His more substantial contributions to *Patronage* and *Ormond* will be noted later, and are enough in themselves to refute the charge that he deliberately repressed her imagination—unless to do some of its work for her was to repress it. What he put into *Ormond* is of the same imaginative quality as that which shows her vision at its most infallible in *Castle Rackrent*.[2] Although he insisted on writing heavy moralizing prefaces to his daughter's tales, often giving them a formal, didactic air which they do not invariably deserve, her father had the root of the matter in him, and would have been as unwilling as she to let a story pass that was without life and charm. His own additions and subtractions to the work she submitted to his judgment were evidently all on the side of lifelikeness and liveliness rather than of doctrine.

Her stories for children

The very titles of many of these early stories are descriptive labels proclaiming their object: *Lazy Laurence, Simple Susan, Forgive and Forget, The Little Merchants, Waste not, Want not, or Two Strings to your Bow*. Industry, that cardinal virtue of the utilitarians, is extolled in *The Orphans, The White Pigeon*, and most of those just named, its opposite being suitably branded in *Lazy Laurence*. The time-worn method of contrast was always indispensable to Maria Edgeworth. There is the good, affectionate industrious boy, in *Lazy Laurence*, and the bad boy who will not do his lessons, idles away his time and falls into the snares of a

---

[1] *Black Book*, 241. A number of these first sketches are extant in the unpublished *Memoir*.
[2] *Black Book*, 225.

thorough-paced young rascal, narrowly escaping gaol. Franklin, in *The False Key*, stands out in relief against the wickedness of Corkscrew and Felix. Susan's modesty and integrity require the foil of Barbara's pride and arrogance. The contrast between the prudent and generous Laura, in *The Birthday Present*, and the vixenish Rosamond was often to be repeated in the novels; and already Miss Edgeworth identifies ill-temper and what was called sensibility, as she does later in the case of Mrs Somers, in *Emilie de Coulanges*. There is something like the modern contrast of good form and bad form in *Eton Montem*, which is thrown into the shape of a comedy, with nearly twenty dramatis personæ. The flattering, cajoling Wheeler and the plain-spoken Talbot are rivals for the captainship of the school, which carries with it the " Salt," a handsome offering towards the successful candidate's expenses at Oxford. Talbot is a " bad electioneerer "; but his truth and generosity are unexpectedly revealed by the same accidental disclosure as exposes Wheeler's mendacity and meanness. The little plot has a double catastrophe through the false report, presently corrected, that the *Bombay Castle* had been wrecked, when it was in fact the *Airly Castle*; and the purse-proud Bursals, not the Talbots, have lost their money. Maria Edgeworth never scorned these romantic surprises, though they usually added less than nothing to the ethical cogency of a story.[1] In another dramatic sketch, *Old Poz*, the contrasted pair are the crusty old Justice Headstrong, with his everlasting dictum " That's poz ! " and his coaxing daughter. In *Forgive and Forget*, it is the amiable and forbearing Maurice Grant and his opinionated father, who has an enemy too like himself in the Scot-hating Oakley. Industry, thrift, and honesty are set against laziness, extravagance, vice; good nature against selfishness and churlishness. It is the child's ethical values that are weighed up and compared : children are the most moralistic creatures alive, and sternly insist on poetic justice.

In truth, these tales for children are none the worse for the obviousness of the difference between the good characters and the bad, and all the better for the clock-like regularity with which

Her contrasts of character and her clear scale of values

[1] It is not a good piece ; the schoolboys are anything but true to life ; and compare miserably with her portraits of girls or of younger boys. But that is neither here nor there. It is the moral lesson that mattered.

conduct is rewarded according to merit. And, though every tale is based on a convention, Miss Edgeworth's is so entirely the child's point of view that she merely seems to the puzzled infant mind to be making things beautifully clear and showing exactly how it is that effects are determined by causes. Older people can read them for what they are, works of applied art, teaching their lesson with certainty and efficiency. But even the applied arts may have qualities of grace and charm; and, if the writer here is a craftsman rather than an artist, much of her efficiency is due to her most engaging delight in childhood. Why is *Simple Susan* one of the miniature but genuine classics? The sweet little cottage girl, who loves her parents and her pet lamb, and whose virtues save her father from the unscrupulous attorney; her opposite, the selfish girl with the bad manners; and, on the other side, the high-minded and discerning squire, and the tender-hearted young ladies of the great house, who make all right, distributing rewards and doing summary justice on the defaulters: why are such glaring contrasts not merely tolerable but precisely what is required? It is largely because self-consciousness is not here a virtue, as it had been in similar productions of the sentimental age. The nice people are not mere prigs or prudes, because their goodness comes natural.

And Maria Edgeworth entered into the pangs and ecstasies of the child's mind, and brought them out with a poignancy that touches even the more experienced heart. Without any affectation or condescension, she can find pathos in a guinea-hen or make tragedy centre in a pet lamb. Many critics have observed how, in that famous nursery tale, we are racked with suspense, until the butcher refuses to murder the innocent animal, who comes home in the last scene garlanded and with pipe and tabor. But to appreciate these little masterpieces to the full one must be able to recall the impression they made in childhood. The world depicted was perfectly·credible to those who had not had much experience of the problem of evil; it was an unravaged Eden, an Arcadia that was simply how things ought to and might easily be. It was a beautifully intelligible world, everything was admirably regulated. A child accepted it with unquestioning faith. Youth is naturally inclined to believe that naughtiness brings down its own punishment, and that ill feelings entail unhappiness, bad manners dislike, and negligence, idleness, and imprudence end in vice and misery. The real world is more complicated; but it is not distortion or deception to generalize on the likeliest and most frequent results of character and behaviour. After all, evil is abnormal; and Miss Edgeworth's mode of simplification was to eliminate the abnormal along with the complicated and obscure.

But it is different with the novelist, who can be narrowly *These* didactic only at a ruinous expense. Novels deal with the actual *methods not* world, which ordinary men and women know only too well; *so suitable* and it is a highly complex world, where the operation of causes is *in the novel* obscure and uncertain, and far too much at the mercy of accident. That world may be explored, and the generalizations established may be dramatized so as to interest in proportion to their truth and general import; but it cannot be reduced to such simple terms that the moral and the æsthetic satisfaction of the reader coincide so prettily as in a fable for children. When the novelist is burdened with a set of maxims to be exemplified, not only will truth be sure to suffer, but imagination and humour will also be held in check. Unfortunately, the neatly balanced situations, the types and antitypes of character, and the illustrations of various courses of action and their results, which did duty in the children's stories, are identical in essentials with those on which the novels are constructed. The majority of these are only moral tales amplified and elaborated. Not one but has its parallel in those pithy little apologues. The child, we know, is father of the man; but Maria Edgeworth made too much of that truth, not when she tried to prepare young people for the ordeal of life, but when she essayed to educate their elders by the same elementary means.

The consequence of reproducing the exact symmetries which *Didacti-* had formerly served her purpose was that too many of the figures *cism in* in her novels, and those the most prominent, are moral qualities *her novels* rather than persons. In *Ormond*, she varied her practice by putting the contrast and the contention in the mind of the chief character, instead of between different individuals; Ormond, who has to undergo his self-education in the school of experience, first takes Tom Jones as his hero, and then decides to be an Irish Sir Charles Grandison. Elsewhere, the contrast is between people differently constituted, or who take life in a different spirit. It is amusing to notice how fond Miss Edgeworth was of her grasping attorney as villain of the piece.[1] Lawyer Case in *Simple Susan* has his counterpart in old Thady's degenerate son, Jason, the tight-fisted factor, in *Castle Rackrent*; Mr Hardcastle in *Ennui* is just such another; and the whole plot of *The Absentee* hinges upon the rascalities of such agents as Mr Nicholas Garraghty, Sir Terence O'Fay's "honest Nick," who is seen at the first glance by Lord Colambre to be "an insolent, petty tyrant in office," grinding the face of the helpless tenants.

Their consequent short-comings   Thus her novels have to be judged by the same standards as the tales written for children, for only in rare cases did she allow herself all the rights of free and independent creation. The discipline of her early course in sociology and educational theory had been too severe. Her father's influence had to that extent proved detrimental. After she lost him, she had no longer the courage and confidence to follow her own path and give her genius full scope. Without his ready invention to help her out, she could only repeat herself, using the same motives, incidents, characters, over again, and, contrary to what is continually alleged, she wrote her inferior work after he was gone. The one novel of that barren period was *Helen*, *Orlandino* being a hasty trifle.[2]

"Castle Rackrent"   But in her first novel, or story of any great length, for in other respects it is not much like a regular novel, Maria Edgeworth gave imagination full fling, and did not let any idea of a purpose interfere, although the favourite moral theme is implicit, the nemesis of self-indulgence, extravagance, and folly, as it must needs be in such a register of tragedy. In *Castle Rackrent, an Hibernian Tale. Taken from facts and from the manners of the*

[1] Of course the grasping attorney was a very common specimen of the Irish fauna at that time, and as a rule the character appears only in her Irish stories. He turns up with the same regularity in Lady Morgan's novels.

[2] She wrote in 1834, in a letter discussing the art of fiction, in reply to Mrs Stark, who had sent her Colonel Stewart's long criticism of *Helen* : " My father, to whose judgment I habitually refer to help out my own judgment of myself, and who certainly must from long acquaintance, to say no more, have known my character better than any other person can, always reproached me for trusting too much to my hasty glances, *aperçus*, as he called them, of character or truths ; and often have I had, and have still (past my grand climacteric), to repent every day my mistaken conclusions and hasty jumps to conclusions " (*Chosen Letters*, 246).

Irish Squires, Before the year 1782,[1] which appeared in 1800, she wrote something intrinsically like history, the annals of an Irish family, who go, step by step, generation by generation, to the devil. She has told us exactly how she wrote it, and very rarely did she write again under the spell of unconscious creation :

The only character drawn from the life in *Castle Rackrent* is Thady himself, the teller of the story. He was an old steward (not very old, though, at that time; I added to his age, to allow him time for the generations of the family). I heard him when I first came to Ireland, and his dialect struck me, and his character; and I became so acquainted with it, that I could think and speak in it without effort; so that when, for mere amusement, without any idea of publishing, I began to write a family history as Thady would tell it, he seemed to stand beside me and dictate; and I wrote as fast as my pen would go, the characters all imaginary.[2]

Part of the note appended to the story is also worth quoting for the light it throws on her objective attitude, and her view of *Castle Rackrent* as having historical validity—she very pertinently compares it with Arthur Young's picture of Ireland :

The Editor could have readily made the catastrophe of Sir Condy's history more dramatic and more pathetic, if he thought it allowable to varnish the plain round tale of faithful Thady. He lays it before the English reader as a specimen of manners and characters which are perhaps unknown in England. Indeed, the domestic habits of no nation in Europe were less known to the English than those of their sister country, till within these few years.

It is important to remember that she did not spend her child- *Her* hood in Ireland, except for a short time when she was from six *knowledge* to eight years old.[3] She came there to live in 1782, and she was *of the* there, and suffered many alarms, during the terrifying events of *Irish* 1798. It was in acting as her father's secretary, in the management of the estate, riding about with him, and seeing things from the inside, that she gained her knowledge of the peasant. But her English education and the lateness of her intimacy with the Irish

---

[1] I have transcribed the title from the copy of the book that belonged to Richard Lovell Edgeworth.
[2] *Chosen Letters,* 243.   [3] See above, p. 21.

account for a certain aloofness, a sane and critical detachment, that compares advantageously with the violence and party spirit of some of the native novelists who followed her. She always kept her head, she was never carried away by pity or enthusiasm, although she did not shut her eyes to Irish grievances or to the finer side of the Irish character. She observed as an alien, one of another class, the English gentry settled in Ireland; at the same time ridiculing the apes of English fashion, the dandies, spend-thrifts, addle-pated sportsmen, and above all the hated absentees. To that combination of sympathy and detachment are largely due the rich humour and the subdued pathos of this first and greatest of her novels. It was all very well for her to say that Thady dictated the story; no doubt she honestly meant it. But Maria Edgeworth was never more herself than when she heard him dictating. All the understanding and tenderness and humour with which she had listened many times to his original were in the voice which she seemed to hear, and are revealed in the affectionate irony of her transcript.

Thady's narrative —the action seen through a character
She and her father had not yet published their *Essay on Irish Bulls*, famous as having been read by the secretary of the Irish Agricultural Society for hints on the breeding of cattle [1]; but she was already a connoisseur of this homely brand of humour. Thady's bulls, like the invincible loyalty to his scapegrace masters, stamp the narrative as his unvarnished own; yet no one can miss the smile in the eye of her who uses these touches of nature with such unobtrusive art. Sir Patrick, the first to bear the name of Rackrent, to whom Thady's grandfather was driver, " gave the finest entertainment that ever was heard of in the country; not a man could stand after supper but Sir Patrick himself, who could sit out the best man in Ireland, let alone the three kingdoms itself. He had his house, from one year's end to another, as full of company as ever it could hold, and fuller." Sir Murtagh succeeded, and refused to pay his father's debts of honour, because the law had been set in motion, and " there was an end of honour to be sure." " As for law, I believe no man, dead or alive, ever loved it so well as Sir Murtagh. He had once sixteen suits pending at a time, and I never saw him so much himself. . . . Out of

1 *Black Book*, 185.

forty-nine suits which he had, he never lost one but seventeen: the rest he gained with costs, double costs, treble costs sometimes; but even that did not pay. He was a very learned man in the law, and had the character of it; but how it was I can't tell, these suits that he carried cost him a power of money,"[1] and the upshot was he had to sell one of his best estates. This, he said, was only to carry on his suit with the Nugents of Carrickashaughlin. But he died before that could restore his fortunes, or, as pious Thady saw it, "things were ordered otherwise—for the best to be sure."

Then came Sir Kit, a gambler and an absentee: "money to him was no more than dirt . . . and though he had the spirit of a prince, and lived away to the honour of his country abroad, which I was proud to hear of, what were we the better for that at home?" When a merciless agent can send no more remittances, Sir Kit marries a " Jewish," who on her arrival at Castle Rackrent perceives the nakedness of the land and the object for which he had married her. She refuses to let him sell her jewels, and he locks her up, a high-handed proceeding for which Miss Edgeworth thought it advisable to cite the precedent of Lady Cathcart.[2] Thady was sorry for her; but an Irishman can run with the hare and hunt with the hounds, and he would not admit that his master was to blame.

Her diamond cross was, they say, at the bottom of it all; and it was a shame for her, being his wife, not to show more duty, and to have given it up when he condescended to ask so often for such a bit of a trifle in his distresses, especially when he all along made it no secret he married for money.[3]

Thady's muddleheadedness and repugnance to taking one side or the other comes out again in his account of the sad doings of his son Jason and the ruin of the last legitimate owner of Castle Rackrent, Sir Condy.

[1] The beauty and raciness of the Irish-English of Synge and Lady Gregory should not lead us to forget that they had a predecessor in the author of this novel and of *The Absentee* and *Ormond*.

[2] See her note (*Castle Rackrent and The Absentee*, with Introduction by Anne Thackeray Ritchie, 1895, pp. 19-20).

[3] *Ibid.*, 24.

I looked in the newspaper, but no news of my master in the House; he never spoke good or bad, but, as the butler wrote down word to my son Jason, was very ill-used by the Government about a place that was promised him and never given, after his supporting them against his conscience very honourably, and being greatly abused for it, which hurt him greatly, he having the name of a great patriot in the country before. The house and living in Dublin too were not to be had for nothing, and my son Jason said, " Sir Condy must soon be looking out for a new agent, for I've done my part and can do no more."

And the pathos of the end is intensified by the apparent artlessness.

Contrast with her other fiction   *Castle Rackrent* is probably the first novel to give the history of a family through several generations, and the impression of a long lapse of time. Another innovation is the staging of the drama in the mind of simple Thady, whose character projects itself in his comments and emotions. But Miss Edgeworth now reverted to the ordinary practice: descriptions of character, explanation of motive, reflection and adjudication on what takes place, enlivened with patches of dialogue. In *Castle Rackrent*, she had taken a holiday from her professional duties of educationist and moral reformer; now she settles down to serious work. She collected and published the first series of *Early Lessons* the same year as *Belinda* (1801), a novel to be grouped with her "Tales of Fashionable Life"; a further series came from her pen in 1815. *Moral Tales* also appeared this year, and *Popular Tales* three years later; it was after twenty more years that she completed *Frank* (1822) and *Harry and Lucy* (1825). The radical identity of her social fiction and her children's stories is confirmed by her easy resumption of the latter. Theory and instruction over-weight them all. The bearing of every incident, every impulse or resolve or failure, upon practical life had to be methodically demonstrated. She eliminates the obscure element in human character; all is in clear definition. Each is allotted his or her due proportion of goodness and badness, wisdom and weakness, and the resultant of the parallelogram of forces is not hard to predict. Whilst Fielding had kept the intellectual scaffolding of his novels in the background, in Miss Edgeworth's the whole framework is exhibited with the clearness of a diagram. She was not one of our great comic novelists. Life to her was a practical affair, and therefore moral above everything. Follies and pretences are not so much comic as absurd, unfortunate, regrettable. This is the great difference between her and Jane Austen, who is less concerned with the rightness and wrongness of what she relates, except so far as the antics of folly and self-indulgence make sanity smile.

CHAPTER II

MARIA EDGEWORTH—*BELINDA* AND OTHER NOVELS

"Belinda" THE first volume of *Belinda* promises a strength and shapeliness which is falsified by the second: Miss Edgeworth had poor staying powers. In *Castle Rackrent* the initial momentum never flags; but whenever she exceeded that brief compass she had to bring in irrelevancies to eke out the measure. The figure that rivets attention is not Belinda but Lady Delacour; readers thought her a brilliant picture of a society queen.[1] A high-spirited woman, she is married to a commonplace debauchee who neglects her, and in pride and resentment against a despicable world she vows herself to a career of dissipation and defiance of opinion. She outdoes her husband in extravagance, and the pair are saved from ruin only by timely legacies. She browbeats him from the height of her intellectual superiority; she flirts desperately, and tortures him with jealousy, without being reckless enough to forfeit her reputation. Triumphing over society, she is envied for her wit and style, without being loved by a soul, at any rate of her own sex. Then the wildest of her harum-scarum friends, the mannish Miss Freke, betrays her confidence, and one of her flirtations ends in a duel fatal to the man she really liked. This is the woman to whose care Belinda is committed by her match-making aunt; for the theme is that of *Evelina*, a girl's entry upon life, although the new Evelina is as passive and as incapable of a satirical diary as she is amiable and faultless.

The predestined lover, Clarence Hervey, affronts Belinda at the outset; prejudice has to be subdued,--if not pride. Belinda likes her hostess, but is mystified by her spasms of remorse and

---

[1] See the anecdote of an admirer who pours forth her ecstasies to Miss Edgeworth : " Lady Delacour, O ! Letters for Literary Ladies, O ! " (*Chosen Letters*, 92-94).

still more by some secret torment that seems to be driving her mad. For Lady Delacour thinks she has cancer, and is confirmed in her belief by a quack physician for his own mercenary benefit. There is a locked-up room, where neither Belinda nor the husband is admitted; it excites as much suspicion in her household and among the tattlers as the haunted chamber in any Gothic romance.[1] It is only the sanctum where she keeps her medicines, and where the quack and one confidential servant treat her for the supposed fatal complaint. But Lady Delacour is truly a wit; and as long as she remains a wicked and defiant person, a Satanic heroine with a generous heart, preyed upon by remorse, she is interesting. But, alas! not only the impeccable Belinda but Lady Delacour herself is a didactic creation : she is suddenly reformed, and so is her irreclaimable husband, who was too stupid to be worth the trouble; and with her reformation all her wit and vivacity and her splendid defiance vanish like smoke; she becomes an average estimable lady and a pattern for those who used to fear her. So the second part is an anticlimax; the drama of Lady Delacour is played out, and other interests have to be foisted in to carry on that of the ingenuous Belinda. She must not be married off too soon; delays must be contrived, and the two chief devices are out of tune as well as improbable. Hervey cannot propose, because long ago, in a fit of Rousseauish idealism, like Maria's friend Thomas Day, he undertook the education of a beautiful foundling, who now out of gratitude wants to marry him. Belinda meanwhile fancies herself in love with a temperamental young Creole. The two obstacles are at length smoothed away, and the blameless young lady marries her paragon.

Lady Delacour is vigorously drawn, and perhaps had an original among the demoralized people of fashion whom Maria Edgeworth contrasts with the ideal wife and mother, Lady Anne Perceval, and her carefully guarded little flock—a contrast more in the manner of the social reformer than of the satirist. It is a strong scene where Lady Delacour, convinced that she is dying, conscience-stricken, feared and envied but unloved, afraid that she is going out of her senses or will at least be powerless in the

Comparison with "Cecilia"

---

[1] There is even a make-believe ghost, the rantipole friend masquerading as the man shot in the duel.

hands of those who would put her into Bedlam, persuades herself that Belinda too is a deceiver, plotting to become a viscountess as soon as she is dead. The dialogue here, if not entirely unheightened, is the most natural since Richardson and Fielding, and far superior to Fanny Burney's in the emotional parts of *Cecilia*. Some of the lighter scenes sustain the comparison still better.

"Emilie de Coulanges"

Soon after, in 1803, was written a short story, or rather, like most of the others, a miniature novel, *Emilie de Coulanges*, which is put last in the second series of "Tales of Fashionable Life," *Madame de Fleury*, written two years later, preceding it. It is a concise specimen of Miss Edgeworth's system of types and anti-types. Mademoiselle de Coulanges, who has fled to England from the Revolution, is handsomely entertained by the wealthy Mrs Somers, whose generosity goes so far as to pay off the debts of Madame de Coulanges, though to do this she has to forgo the luxury of acquiring a Correggio and a Guido for her house in town. And then the too impulsive benefactress is hurt because she thinks the Coulanges are not grateful enough. She had thought Emilie " a complete angel—no angel had ever such a variety of accomplishments—none but an angel could possess such a combination of virtues." In which opinion most people would ironically agree, for it is the preterhuman characteristic of all Miss Edgeworth's heroines. But now the gentle Emilie, who differs from the others only in being still more long-suffering, is overwhelmed with reproaches and accusations of hypocrisy, which Mrs Somers retracts almost as soon as uttered. This lady reads her own character with more accuracy than judgment. " The strength of my feelings absolutely runs away with me. It is the doom of persons of great sensibility to be both unreasonable and unhappy; and often, alas! to involve in their misery those for whom they have the most enthusiastic affection. You see, my dear Emilie, the price you must pay for being my friend; but you have strength of mind joined to a feeling heart, and you will bear with my defects."

An analysis of sentiment-alism

Miss Edgeworth often exposed the falsehood of sentimentalism, but never better than in the case of Mrs Somers, a grown-up Rosamund. Another mark of the species is a complete lack of the sense of humour. Matters quickly come to a head again, and she writes an egregious letter to her bosom friend Lady Littleton, complaining that both mother and daughter have " too little sensibility." " Emilie plagues me to death with her fine feelings and her sentimentality, and all her French parade of affection, and superfluity of endearing expressions, which mean nothing, and disgust English ears." How adroit of Maria Edgeworth to make the unconscious addict to an acute form of sentimentalism criticize the immune, who, she says, " are continually afraid that they shall not be grateful enough; and so they reproach and torment themselves, and refine and *sentimentalize*,[1] till gratitude becomes burdensome." Lady Littleton, one of Miss Edgeworth's sober and sensible elderly women, sends a laconic reply, and later on gives her friend a dressing-down rich in unimpeachable moral casuistry.[2]

Emilie de Coulanges is a study of a common form of egoism, though ostensibly the story has another object; in providing a happy issue to the troubles of her titular heroine, the author shows her inability to refrain from romantic surprises. The tables are turned on the captious Mrs Somers when the Countess de Coulanges is unexpectedly restored to her wealth, Emilie becomes a more than eligible match, and the unknown with whom she had fallen in love in the terrible Abbaye turns out to be the darling son of Mrs Somers herself. So that justice is done with something over.

Leonora (1806) was read as Miss Edgeworth's retort to Madame *"Leonora"* de Staël's *Delphine*,[3] which appeared in 1802; the story being told in letters, the case against the romantic doctrine of the rights of passion can be argued point by point. Lady Leonora has the anguish of watching her excellent husband slowly succumb to the

[1] Her own verb.

[2] Perhaps her study of ill temper may profitably be compared with Balzac's in *Le Lys dans la vallée*, especially as the latter also attributes the disease to a morbid excess of sensibility. M. de Mortsauf observes : " J'ai fini par saisir les causes de la maladie, la sensibilité m'a tué." But the French novelist had studied medicine, and so he makes his patient continue : " En effet, toutes nos affections frappent sur le centre gastrique." M. de Mortsauf, his constitution warped by his sufferings as an *émigré*, is a tragic figure ; Mrs Somers is not even good comedy. True to life she may be, but she is more tiresome and absurd than comic—simply a thorn in the flesh of the insipid heroine, who is intended to monopolize attention.

[3] According to the unpublished *Memoir*, it " was written with the hope of pleasing the Chevalier Edelcrantz, the gentleman from the Court of Stockholm," with whom she was " exceedingly in love," but whom she refused, because she knew the family could not afford to lose her (see *Chosen Letters*, 118-122).

arts of one trained in this school. Worshipping " real sensibility," and scorning those of her own sex who in certain situations are incapable of " the delicate *tact* of sentiment," this young woman recognizes her own affinity in the husband. He for his part cannot help comparing the two, and easily convinces himself that his wife's affection is mere respect for the marriage bond. " Lady Leonora," he writes to a friend who had told him not to be the dupe of a " Frenchified coquette," " Leonora is calm, serene, perfectly sweet-tempered, without jealousy and without suspicion ; in one word, without love." But Olivia had at first no mischievous intentions ; and she too has her confidential friend, to whom she writes, " I meant but to satisfy an innocent curiosity, to indulge a harmless coquetry, to gratify the natural love of admiration, and to enjoy the possession of power." But she has heedlessly walked into a quicksand, and awakes to find herself hopelessly in love : " Yes, Gabrielle, this provoking, this incomprehensible, this too amiable man, has entangled your poor friend past recovery. Her sentiments and sensations must henceforward be in eternal opposition to each other. Friendship, gratitude, honour, virtue, all in tremendous array, forbid her to think of love ; but love, imperious love, will not be so defied." Leonora's husband is preparing to fly with Olivia, when some of his wife's letters to her mother are put in his hands, and his heart is wrung. " My dear friend, what injustice have I done to this admirable woman ! With what tenderness, with what delicacy has she loved me ! while I, mistaking modesty for coldness, fortitude for indifference, have neglected, injured, and abandoned her ! " He has no longer any patience for Olivia's " sentimental metaphysics," and the emancipated lady is presently left as desolate as Ariadne, to the delight of all. " Lady Olivia," writes another friend of the reunited couple, " thus unmasked by her own hand, has fled to the Continent, declaring that she will never more return to England." The " unmasking " was an unfortunate addition to a story which would have been stronger and more consistent without it, a packet of letters from the siren being discovered in which she declares that her whole design had been due to pique against Lady Leonora and thirst for revenge upon " that proudest of earthly prudes," her mother, the Duchess.

The Duchess, like Lady Davenant, Mrs Hungerford, Lady Littleton, Lady Anerly, sees through everybody, gives sound advice long before any mischief takes place, and is amply justified by the outcome of events.

The first series of " Tales of Fashionable Life " came out in 1809, and comprised *Ennui*, *The Dun*, *Manœuvring*, and *Almeria*; the second consisted of *Vivian*, *The Absentee*, *Madame de Fleury*, and *Emilie de Coulanges*, and appeared in 1812. *Ennui* was written in 1804, and broaches the question of absenteeism, with satire on dissipated people living abroad on rents exacted from peasants whom they have never seen. Two land-agents are contrasted, Hardcastle and M'Leod, the ordinary rascally extortioner, and the man of integrity, dour, but far-sighted. Characteristically, Miss Edgeworth makes Hardcastle hold forth on the policy of keeping the tenantry uneducated and resigned to their lot. But this is a side issue. The martyr to ennui is Lord Glenthorn, dissatisfied with wealth, society, luxury, because he has nothing to do. He is almost on the point of ending his tedious existence, but betakes himself instead to his castle on the west coast of Ireland, where his aged foster-mother, Ellinor, puts a little energy into him; and he meets with plenty of trials in managing his estates, in a rebel plot aiming at his own murder, and a love affair that ends in his helping the lady to marry the poor man who deserves her and whom he puts in a lucrative post. But the supreme trial is his dilemma when he learns that Ellinor is his mother, and his foster-brother, the blacksmith Christy Donoghue, is the true Lord Glenthorn. With genuine heroism he resigns his honours, and subsequently makes good as a commoner. True to her faith in education, Miss Edgeworth ignores the question of heredity, and simply shows the peasant-bred Lord Glenthorn going comfortably to the dogs, and the unintentional usurper, after his reform, winning golden opinions. M'Leod's approval is his finest reward.

The Dun is a barefaced sermon on the wickedness of extravagance and of not paying your tailor's bills, perhaps leaving a poor workman's family to starve. In *Almeria*, a young woman of no family and no culture inherits two hundred thousand pounds. Dazzled by smart society and the deceptive lure of marriage for a title, she presently finds herself left on the shelf, a snubbed and

Tales of Fashionable Life : "Ennui"

"The Dun," "Almeria," and "Manœuvring"

embittered old maid. Nor is there much less of - this dull moralization in *Manœuvring*, the "heroine "[1] of which is an "intriguess," a "policizer," a "manœuvrer."[1] She cannot be sincere and open even when nothing is to be gained by underhand dealings. She has a son and a daughter, and her neighbours the Walsinghams have a daughter and a son; the two couples are more or less consciously in love. If they married, they would inherit the fortune of the rich West Indian, Mr Palmer. But the manœuvrer tries to make her daughter marry a repulsive old baronet, who expects to come into a vast estate and a peerage; and she tries to persuade her son that he is in love with the light-headed sister of this sprig of nobility. The author calls attention to every move in her heroine's little game at the moment she plays it. Not unexpectedly, the lady outwits herself; and the result is that the young people marry as their hearts dictate, and the intriguess, seeing no other way to secure the great estate and the earldom, weds the unpleasant baronet herself, only to find that he will inherit neither.

"Vivian" and "Madame de Fleury"   *Vivian*, praised by Scott, is the life of a weak young man, whose snobbish, ambitious, and vulgar-minded mother must be held responsible for his initial mistakes. She frowns on his love for the admirable Selina Sidney, and urges him to marry one of the daughters of Lord Glistonbury. He kicks at this proposal, the only marriageable one at present being unattractive and older than himself. Vivian enters public life, and in the Commons, guided by his old tutor Russell, wins a reputation for integrity and independence. But he comes under the influence of the profligate and intriguing Wharton, and worse, falls in love with Mrs Wharton, who runs off with him. He is exonerated, partly at least, when the complicity of the two Whartons comes out; but the scandal has lost him Selina, who becomes the wife of Russell. Then, after being disappointed in a sincere passion for Lady Julia, Vivian has to fall back upon her overripe sister, the Lady Sarah whom he had once fought shy of. Even this is not the worst. Sarah, under her plain exterior, has a heart of gold, which Vivian does not discover until he has wronged her; and in a duel with the villainous Wharton he ends his sorry existence.

---

[1] These are Miss Edgeworth's own terms.

Miss Edgeworth is not above such devices as letters put into wrong envelopes, Selina getting the one meant for Mrs Wharton, and vice versa; or the compromising secret let slip by a lover in delirium, prelude to an elopement. *Madame de Fleury* is a comparative trifle, the edifying story of a charitable lady who is saved from the guillotine by people who remember how she rescued their parents from destitution.

The one big item in "Tales of Fashionable Life" was *The Absentee* (1812), a long story or short novel which she expanded out of a little play for children written the previous year. It was written quickly, to fill out the measure of a second series of these very popular tales; but it is none the worse for that, and with *Ormond* comes second or third after *Castle Rackrent*, for the freshness and truth of the Irish scenes. Miss Edgeworth when she wrote this and *Ennui* was full of the wrongs of Ireland, and in parts it reads like a tract, a frontal assault on landlordism disporting itself in London or Dublin, whilst the wretched tenantry are bullied and robbed by agents, busy feathering their own nest. Both sides are shown. The peasants, neglected and poverty-stricken, are still loyal to their distant lord, and might be industrious and happy under an honest factor, such as Mr Burke. Here we are listening to Miss Edgeworth herself. But in most of the scenes where the giddy absentees, and their mob of fops and fortune-hunters, match-making mothers, dangerous women, and hare-brained men, exhibit themselves like a troupe of performing animals, she is only a second-rate Fanny Burney.

Lord Clonbrony, the absentee, is a gambler and a spendthrift, but would have been nothing of the sort had not his silly wife, whom he married for her dower, insisted on living in " Lon'on," where her extravagance and his make him the prey of sharks and attorneys, and especially of the Jew Mordicai, whose caustic portrait was resented by the sons of Israel. His vulgar wife hates to be taken for an Irishwoman, and is blind to the humiliating snubs of the people of rank and fashion whom she courts and who mimic her Cockney speech to her face. The Clonbronys slide deeper and deeper into debt, and are saved from ruin in the sequel only by the son's union with an Irish heiress. This is not meant ironically : to Maria Edgeworth prudence was one of the cardinal virtues, and

"The Absentee"

the generous but cautious behaviour of young Lord Colambre deserves its reward, in which his parents must have their share. Her case would obviously have been strengthened if she had left them to their fate. But she was too romantic at heart to do without happy endings; in *Castle Rackrent*, something greater than herself seems to have worked out the tragedy to its natural conclusion.

A fine Irish novel, marred by didacticism The reader cannot help wondering how such a pair could have begotten such a faultless young man as Lord Colambre. At all events, he is the hero, and he has to be made happy both in fortune and in love. Before this can be brought about, he has to prove his worth, and Miss Edgeworth seizes the opportunity to send him to Ireland. He goes on a visit incognito to the Colambre and Clonbrony estates, and finds the former admirably managed by the honest agent Mr Burke, who however has been traduced to Lord Clonbrony and is under notice to quit, and the latter, comprising the bulk of his father's property, in the iniquitous hands of Mr Garraghty, who has fleeced the tenants and by manipulating the accounts has secured the whip-hand of his employer and will soon have the estate itself. The brilliant stage-stroke when Lord Colambre reveals his identity and confounds Nick Garraghty and his confederate, " St Dennis," in the very act of swindling the browbeaten tenants, was compared by Macaulay to the famous recognition scene in the *Odyssey*.[1] Probably, this central situation of a person of discreet age visiting his Irish home for the first time owes a good deal to its being parallel to Miss Edgeworth's own experience.[2] And the other Irish characters are some of her best: among the humbler, those modest, warm-hearted, confiding peasants, marked with that dignity peculiar to the race, a dignity not lacking, only turned to the grotesque, even in such a figure as Larry the drunken postilion; among the superior and more remarkable, Sir Terence O'Fay, that witty, urbane, and magnificent sponger[3]; the fine old Irish gentleman, Count O'Halloran, philosophically observing the world from his ancient castle and

[1] *Life and Letters*, xi.
[2] See above, p. 29.
[3] Sir Terence was one of those characters which she described as " likewise written off, not philosophically constructed. Whilst I was writing him, I always saw him and heard him speak; he was an individual to me " (unpublished *Memoir*, iii. 153).

the society of his eagle, his Persian goat, and his otter. Even the patterns of virtue, Sir James Brooke and Miss Nugent, have more charm and vitality than their like in the other novels, either because they are Irish or because the contrasts are not too neat. But, if the moral of the Clonbronys' history, apart from the question of absenteeism, is simply prudence, what is the moral of Lord Colambre's love story? He loves Miss Nugent, who deserves the best of husbands, and she is represented as in love with him. Yet he is prepared to jettison her happiness and his own rather than marry a woman with a stain on her parentage, not on herself. What would have happened had Miss Nugent not proved to be legitimate after all, if the marriage papers of the dead officer and the convent girl had never been traced? Would she have been mercilessly sacrificed to the proprieties? And what if she had not also unexpectedly come in for a fortune, and so been instrumental in restoring the prosperity of the Clonbrony family? To ask such questions is to put a finger on the weakness of didactic fiction, and invalidate the scale of values taken for granted in the Edgeworth novels.

Both *Patronage* (1814) and *Harrington* (1817), like *Leonora*, were written to a formula, the " original design " of the one being supplied by Richard Edgeworth,[1] its " only begetter,"[2] the other being expressly intended to make amends to the Jews, who had taken umbrage at the Shylock portrait of Mordicai in *The Absentee*. Her father had once amused his wife with a story called " The Freeman Family," and Maria wrote it out from memory under his correction. This was in 1787 [3]; and in 1793 she tells a friend, " I am scratching away very hard at the *Freeman Family*." [4] Such was the genesis of *Patronage*, which among the average professional output would be styled an able novel, but is interesting chiefly as showing what Miss Edgeworth could achieve by " scratching away very hard " when she was giving imagination a rest, or, which is much the same thing, abstaining from Irish characters.[5] A large crowd, from every walk of life, are made to

"Patron-age" and "Har-rington"

---

[1] *Black Book*, 22-25.
[2] *Ibid.*, 230.
[3] *Ibid.*, 164-165.
[4] *Chosen Letters*, 59.
[5] *Patronage* is exceptional, however, as containing many portraits from life. Members of the Edgeworth family testify that a number of the characters were drawn from the household circle at Edgeworthstown.

illustrate the evils of patronage, subservience, compared with responsibility for one's own character and career. Virtues are patiently weighed against vices, until there is hardly any residue of personality left.

Two contrasted families It is the history of two families, the Percys and the Falconers; the former are the freemen, energetic, self-reliant, honourable; the latter will get on at all costs except that of honest exertion; in short, the Falconers are born to be the creatures of patronage. One of them, Buckhurst Falconer, a well-meaning, easy-going fellow, seems to the Percys to promise well, and is even thought of as a son-in-law; but he lets himself swim with the tide, goes into the Church against his conscience, as the quickest way to get clear of monetary embarrassments, then ruins himself by fast living, and to escape a debtors' prison has to marry the lady whom he had described as " an old, ugly, cross, avaricious devil ! " Buckhurst and the dignified, magnanimous, indomitable old statesman, Lord Oldborough, a real leader of men, are the most vivid characters in the book; the rest are merely terms in a moral equation. Cunningham Falconer, master of all the arts of exploiting patronage, is only another Jason raised to a higher power; the Percys, for whom the reader's sympathies are solicited, are not much more than abstract virtues; Godfrey's cold-blooded integrity is truly formidable. There is a wise Mrs Hungerford also, who acts efficiently in the same capacity as Lady Littleton, or the Duchess in *Leonora*.[1]

The Percys meet with undeserved misfortune, and are ousted from Percy Hall through the loss of the title-deeds in a fire. The telling bit of melodrama by which they are at length reinstated is based no doubt on a home incident related in the *Black Book*. Mr Edgeworth was on the point of losing an expensive lawsuit, when Honora found the missing lease at the bottom of an old box. It was thrust into the hands of the counsel " before he had concluded his speech, was triumphantly produced, and the case was won." [2] In the novel, a missing conveyance is rediscovered;

---

[1] She had in her mind's eye a certain Lady Louisa Connolly, " one of the most respectable, amiable, and even at seventy, I may say, charming persons I ever saw or heard. . . . She is all that I could have wished to represent in Mrs Hungerford " (*Chosen Letters*, 190-191).

[2] *Black Book*, 152-153.

but the rival claimant produces what purports to be a later deed. The scene in court is as startling as the appearance of Lord Colambre in *The Absentee*. When all seems lost, Alfred Percy, who is acting as his father's counsel, asks to have the seal examined on the deed put forward by the opposite party. As a witness had sworn, there was a sixpence under the seal. But the sixpence bears a later date than that of the document. The forsworn witness is detained for perjury, the fraudulent claimant retires ignominiously, and the Percys re-enter upon their estate. Miss Edgeworth pokes fun at the sentimental young lady, Rosamond Percy—another Rosamond! But she is still more romantic in such accessories to her plot as Godfrey Percy's rencounter with the Dutch merchants whose ship had been wrecked years ago off Percy Hall, and the astonishing discovery that the estimable Mr Henry is Lord Oldborough's long-lost son. *Patronage* sold best of all Miss Edgeworth's novels, bringing her 2000 guineas. *Harrington* and *Ormond*, which came out together (1817), earned £1150.[1] The former is a mystery novel, with one exciting episode, the anti-popery riots of 1780. So far as the supposed object of the story is concerned, reparation to the Jews for an alleged libel, she gives her own case away. The heroine who has acquitted herself to everyone's satisfaction is pronounced " Not a Jewess," after all, but " a Christian—a Protestant "; so that both Semites and anti-Semites are disarmed.

Ormond is not only one of her three best novels but has unique *"Ormond"* importance for students of Miss Edgeworth in the large contributions which, as she herself proudly avowed, came from her father; they are among the finest pages in all her novels, and can stand even a comparison with *Castle Rackrent*. It is a rambling story, picaresque almost, odd incidents and eccentricities of character that she had observed or had from hearsay being tacked on to the adventures of Harry Ormond, a young fellow who has to learn wisdom in the ordeal of life. Most of her approved young men seem to be born good; he has to learn the job of being an Edgeworthian hero; but his imperfections, and still more his consciousness of them, are his saving grace. The strength of the

[1] See prices obtained for copyrights (" English Men of Letters "—*Maria Edgeworth*, 196-197).

book, however, is in those large episodes which bring on the stage such an epitome of the Irish comic genius as King Corny of the Black Isles, and his brother, almost as inimitable, that urbane and far from irredeemable cynic, Sir Ulick O'Shane. Apart from these major personages, the incalculable element in human nature, so rigorously excluded from the great majority of her characters, gives a pleasing effervescence to some who are not intrinsically very important—for instance, to Mademoiselle O'Faley, half French half Irish, who " spent above half her life in France, looking for an estate that could never be found "; and even to such racy variants of common types as Mrs M'Crule, née Black, Miss Darrell, and Lady Millicent.

Her father's contributions

Like *Castle Rackrent* and *The Absentee*, *Ormond* was written at high speed. It was the year of Mr Edgeworth's death, 1817. In February, " Maria read out to her father the first chapter of *Ormond*," in the carriage going on the last visit he ever paid. He had suggested a tale to accompany *Harrington*, " and in all her anguish of mind at his state of health, she, by a wonderful effort of affection and genius, produced these gay and brilliant pages." [1] Her father was delighted, so she went on. " The admirable characters of King Corny and Sir Ulick O'Shane, and all the wonderful scenes full of wit, humour and feeling, were written in agony of anxiety, with trembling hand and tearful eyes." [2] After his death, Maria wrote, " The following parts of *Ormond* were written for me by my dear father in his last illness. The death of King Corny . . . the whole of Moriarty's history of his escape from prison . . . also the meeting between Moriarty and his wife, when he jumps out of the carriage the moment he hears her voice." [3] The problem of what the novels gained or lost by her father's hand in them takes on a different complexion when these facts are considered. One of King Corny's most amusing exploits, the feat of lifting the roof of his mansion on the Black Islands, and " building up to it, to get attics," is founded on the doings of a Mr Corry, of Chantinee, who performed this and other extraordinary operations, and enlarged his house both skywards and downwards whilst business went on inside as usual. He lifted the roof, and kept it propped up whilst a new story was

[1] *Black Book*, 206.   [2] *Ibid.*   [3] *Ibid.*, 229.

inserted. He blasted the rocks on which the house stood in order to make a large kitchen and offices. "A gentleman who was breakfasting . . . heard one of the explosions, and starting, Mr Corry quietly said, ' It is only the blasting in the kitchen, finish your breakfast.' "[1]

In answer to a criticism of her later novel, *Helen*, Miss *Herself on* Edgeworth went into some detail upon her method. She "had *her method* often and often a suspicion " that her manner was " too Dutch, too minute "; she admired, perhaps too warmly, " the bold, grand style of the master hand and master genius," evidently Scott. But where she had erred or fallen short was not in " drawing from the life, or from individuals, or from putting together actions or sayings noted in commonplace-books from observation or hearsay in society."[2] She preferred not to draw from real characters, since she was tempted to throw in differences, which ended in making her own characters inconsistent. She instances King Corny, the first idea of whom came from an oddity who was " generous and kind-hearted, but despotic, and conceited to the most ludicrous degree "—obviously the Mr Corry alluded to above. " One after another, in working out King Corny, from the first wrong hint I was obliged to give up every fact, except that he propped up the roof of his house and built downwards, and to generalize all; to make him a man of expedients, of ingenious substitutes, such as any clever Irishman in middle age is used to. I was obliged to retain, but soften, the despotism, and exalt the generosity, to make it a character that would interest."[3] *"Helen"*

After her father's death, Miss Edgeworth, who, of course, was *and "Or-* now growing old, published only one novel full-length, *Helen* *landino"* (1833), and a tale, *Orlandino* (1847). She said of *Helen*, " there is no humour in it, and no Irish character. It is impossible to draw Ireland as she now is in a book of fiction—realities are too strong, party passions too violent to bear to see, or care to look at their faces in the looking-glass."[4] But writing at all now went against the grain. " To write a tale which was to bear comparison with *Belinda* or *Patronage* seemed to her for many years to be, without her father's encouragement, an impossibility."[5] She

---

[1] *Chosen Letters*, 154. [2] *Ibid.*, 239. [3] *Ibid.*, 242-243.
[4] *Ibid.*, 384. [5] *Memoir*, iii. 77.

often felt disheartened, and frequently altered the preliminary outline. It was not merely that she was much interrupted by household affairs and the business of the estate; "she never wrote fiction with more life and spirit than when she had been for some time completely occupied with the hard realities of life."[1] So now, without the zest that her father's inspiration used to give her, she wrote another able novel, like *Patronage*, concerned entirely with a principle of conduct, and the consequences of the most venial neglect of it in our relations with others.

Another moral problem

The points of her characters here, without exception, are moral points; each could be summed up in ethical terms, what might be called neutral idiosyncrasies being almost entirely lacking. The title should have been simply " Truth." Helen, a young woman of perfect integrity, goes to live with a friend of her girlhood, Lady Cecilia, about whose ingrained defect she has been cautioned, an inability to be absolutely truthful, honest to herself and wholly sincere with others. This infirmity sows mistrust in the mind of Granville Beauclerc, the one man worthy of Helen. But the tragic dilemma arises when a packet of love-letters Cecilia had written in old days to a woman-hunter falls into other hands, and is about to be the savoury morsel in a book of scandalous memoirs. She had assured her husband that she had never had an affair, and he is one of those who require that the wife of their bosom shall be a virgin of the spirit as well as of the flesh. On the spur of the moment, knowing it would be the ruin of their married life if it came out that she had misled him, she pretends that they are Helen's letters; and Helen is over-persuaded to acquiesce, at least not to deny the imputation. But the scandal gets wind. It is soon the talk of the town that Helen, the pattern of propriety, had been madly in love with the dead roué. Cecilia has now the most urgent reasons to dread a disclosure. On the other hand, Beauclerc inevitably hears the story, and the union of two well-matched lovers seems doomed. Miss Edgeworth has been a long time setting the stage and marshalling her performers for the conflict; but, now that the battle is joined, the mental and moral tension holds the reader down as irresistibly as in almost any novel dealing with an acute spiritual crisis.

[1] *Memoir*, iii. 77-78.

In *Helen*, more than in any other story, she brings out the collision of manners and morals between the profligate Regency set and the refined, self-respecting people whom she and Jane Austen approved. All her didactic personages are here. The middle-aged mentor is now Lady Davenant; but there is another impersonation of goodness and good sense in Miss Clarendon, and one not quite so conventional. Shreds of melodrama show that she was still not proof against the enticements of romance; for instance, the confidential letters copied and betrayed by the page Carlos; while, of course, the whole business of Lady Cecilia's compromising letters is rank melodrama. She was right to apologize for the absence of humour. There is hardly a sparkle of mirth to lighten the seriousness. Vulgarity is branded; but not as a pleasant foible, only as a moral delinquency. In short, this is an epitome of her graver novels, which are an epitome of the age of reason—in the narrowest sense. Maria Edgeworth's was a scientific scheme of morality, which provided means of reformation when people were worth reforming, and vindicated itself satisfactorily when they were not. It was a reasonable morality, not too exacting and not in any way inspiring; a table of commandments which might produce useful and respectable members of society, but not saints or heroes, nor yet such exquisite creatures as an Elizabeth Bennet or an Anne Elliot. Seeing life thus, she gave her honest, straightforward, and practical version of what she saw, unaware of the distortions due to her didactic scheming and her retributive conclusions. She was anti-romantic by conviction, and mocked at sentimentalism and affectation, not only in such a skit as *L'Amie inconnue*, [1] but whenever she came across it. Yet she tripped inadvertently herself in the instances noted and in many others. But her worst technical fault was the habit that grew upon her of prosy abstract analysis, from which *Castle Rackrent* and the best pages of *The Absentee* and *Ormond* alone are free, for the simple reason that she allowed herself to forget for a time the hampering purposes which were her justification for being a novelist.[2]

" Helen " typical of her non-Irish novels

[1] See Volume V. 226.

[2] *The Absentee* and *Ormond* are only partly free. Take this characteristic passage from the former novel. It shows her naturally clear insight so warped by her determination to bring about a *dénouement* fully in accord with her sense of

Hannah
More

Much that has been said of Maria Edgeworth could be said also of Hannah More (1745-1833), who likewise bridged the two centuries. She was the daughter of a schoolmaster and herself a teacher, a devoted philanthropist, and a practical exponent in fiction of the same utilitarian ethics more strongly tinged with Christian piety. She was the intimate friend, in the one century, of Dr Johnson, Horace Walpole, Garrick and his wife, Mrs Barbauld, Mrs Montagu, Mrs Delany, Burke, and Reynolds, and of Wilberforce and the Macaulays in the other. Garrick produced her tragedy *Percy* (1777), an early essay in Gothic romance. He died before he could produce her next, *The Fatal Falsehood* (1779); after which she refused to enter a theatre, and contented herself with publishing her *Sacred Dramas* (1782) as a book for children. Intercourse with Dr Kennicott, the Biblical scholar, Bishop Porteous, and John Newton, deepened her congenital seriousness; and from this time onwards she concentrated her splendid energies, with unflinching self-sacrifice, on the reclamation of the masses from vice and irreligion. Not that her eyes were not wide open to the shortcomings of the higher classes. *Her Thoughts on the Importance of the Manners of the Great* (1788) sold to the extent of seven large editions in a few months, and made a great sensation if it did not regenerate society. When Miss More and Mrs Sarah Trimmer, another famous labourer in the same field, called on Bishop Horsley, he observed " that he

propriety, that she makes Colambre blind to Grace Nugent's obvious affection for himself, and actually prepared to hand over the girl he passionately loves to a man they both despise. Psychological analysis of this kind would be a slovenly method of telling a story, even if the psychology were not erroneous.

" In peace !—never was our hero's mind less at peace than at this moment. The more his heart felt that it was painful, the more his reason told him it was necessary that he should part from Grace Nugent. To his union with her there was an obstacle, which his prudence told him ought to be insurmountable ; yet he felt that, during the few days he had been with her, the few hours he had been near her, he had, with his utmost power over himself, scarcely been master of his passion, or capable of concealing it from its object. It could not have been done but for her perfect simplicity and innocence. But how could this be supported on his part ? How could he venture to live with this charming girl ? How could he settle at home? What resource?

" His mind turned towards the army. . . . But his mother . . . expected him to return and live with her in Ireland. . . . He knew that she would be shocked at the bare idea of his going into the army. There was one chance—our hero tried, at this moment, to think it the best possible chance—that Miss Nugent might marry Mr Salisbury, and settle in England. On this idea he relied as the only means of extricating him from difficulties " (*Absentee*, xiv.).

was between two very singular women, one of whom had undertaken to reform all the poor, and the other all the great; but he congratulated Mrs Trimmer upon having the most hopeful subjects."[1] This pithy little work was followed by *An Estimate of the Religion of the Fashionable World* (1790). Other books show her to have been a fellow-labourer of the Edgeworths; for example, *Strictures on the Modern System of Female Education* (1799) and *Hints towards forming the Character of a Young Princess* (1805). Like them, she saw that stories enforcing practical lessons were the best auxiliary of the recognized forms of practical education, especially on the moral side.

When the ruling classes were in a state of panic at the dis- *Tales for* content and disaffection excited by the pamphlets of the English *the people* Jacobins, Mrs Hannah More and her sister, soon supported by private subscribers and voluntary committees all over the country, poured forth a stream of popular tracts, and stories which were tracts in disguise, as an antidote in kind. These were priced to undersell their competitors. The best of them, along with the more ambitious *Cœlebs in search of a Wife* (1808), are preserved in three tiny volumes, *Tales for the Common People* and *Stories for Persons of the Middle Classes*, both published in 1818 but consisting of pieces written at various dates, and a third entitled in full, *Cœlebs in Search of a Wife, comprehending Observations on Domestic Habits and Manners, Religion and Morals* (1808). The tales and the stories—note the careful distinction—belong to the borderland of practical politics rather than to literature, much more so than Miss Edgeworth's moral or popular tales. "The Shepherd of Salisbury Plain" and "Hester Wilmot," in particular, helped in their humble way to make history, and their interest now is purely historical. The stories for the middle classes, with the appended allegories, were more akin to Edgeworthian

___

[1] *Hannah More*, by Charlotte M. Yonge (1888), 73. The bishop was more serious than Horace Walpole, who told her ironically, in discussing her *Thoughts on the Great*, " that the Fourth Commandment was the most amiable and merciful law that ever was promulgated, as it entirely considers the ease and comfort of the hard-labouring poor, and beasts of burthen ; but that it was never intended for persons of fashion, who have no occasion to rest, as they never do anything on the other days ; and, indeed, at the time the law was made there were no people of fashion " (quoted by Miss Yonge, p, 74 ; it is to be hoped she was responsible for the slipshod English).

didacticism. Hannah More knew how to write down to simple minds, without their resenting it; she had force, though little charm, and sometimes writes like Bunyan, who however was no favourite of hers.

"Cœlebs" In *Cœlebs*, a young man, whom she forgets to supply with a character of his own, makes the round of various households, and interviews mothers, fathers, and their marriageable daughters, ultimately settling upon the faultless Lucilla, who had, unknown to the young pair, been destined for him by the parents on both sides.[1] Being well brought up, an orthodox Christian, and a graduate of Edinburgh, he is a severe examiner, and discovers endless moral and social defects in the homes where he is entertained. The result is a criticism of manners, of intelligence, of taste, education, and prevailing attitudes towards religion, especially cant and the effusive pietism that was devoid of earnestness of life. Sometimes, but all too rarely, as in the visit to the Ranby household, humour almost converts the pious tract into literature.

In the evening, Mrs Ranby was lamenting in general and rather customary terms, her own exceeding sinfulness. Mr Ranby said, " You accuse yourself rather too heavily, my dear, you have sins to be sure——" " And pray what sins have I, Mr Ranby? " said she, turning upon him with so much quickness that the poor man started. " Nay," said he meekly, " I did not mean to offend you : so far from it, that hearing you condemn yourself so grievously, I intended to comfort you, and to say that except a few faults——" " And pray what faults? " interrupted she, continuing to speak however, lest he should catch an interval to tell them. " I defy you, Mr Ranby, to produce one." " My dear," replied he, " as you charged yourself with all, I thought it would be letting you off cheaply by naming only two or three, such as——" Here, fearing matters would go too far, I interposed, and softening things as much as I could for the lady, said, " I conceived that Mr Ranby meant that though she partook of the general corruption——" Here Ranby interrupting me with more spirit than I thought he possessed, said : " General corruption, sir, must be the source of particular corruption. I did not mean that my wife was worse than other women." " Worse,

[1] The same piquant situation as in Congreve's *Incognita*, Sheridan's *Rivals*, and Peacock's *Nightmare Abbey*.

Mr Ranby, worse?" cried she. Ranby, for the first time in his life, not minding her went on, "As she is always insisting that the whole species is corrupt, she cannot help allowing that she herself has not quite escaped the infection. Now to be a sinner in the gross and a saint in the detail; that is, to have all sins, and no faults, is a thing I do not quite comprehend." After he had left the room, which he did as the shortest way of allaying the storm, she apologized for him, saying, " he was a well-meaning man, and acted up to the little light he had," but added, " that he was unacquainted with religious feelings, and knew little of the nature of conversion."[1]

Hannah More enjoyed Scott's novels; but, sad to relate, " She thought that, though his works were free from the coarseness of earlier writers, they were deficient in the practical precepts to be gleaned from them."[2]

Another contemporary whose novels were in great request with the serious-minded, Mary Brunton (1778-1818), was a native of the Orkneys and wife of a Scottish pastor. She had read some philosophy, chiefly of the Scottish school of common sense; and her husband said of her fiction, "To its moral usefulness she uniformly paid much more regard than to its literary character."[3] The object of *Self-Control* (1811) was " to show the power of the religious principle in bestowing self-command." The lesson of *Discipline* (1814) was "that the mind must be trained by suffering ere it can hope for usefulness or for true enjoyment."[4] *Emmeline*, which she never finished, showed what little chance there was of happiness when a divorced wife married the co-respondent. All three are of interest now chiefly as evidence of what a large section of the reading public wanted, and what a moral gulf separated that section from the frivolous people of fashion on the one side and the unreclaimed lower classes on the other. It is edifying to realize what social ostracism was the normal chastisement of such a " crime " as Emmeline's in 1819, the days of the Prince Regent.

Both *Self-Control* and *Discipline* are far too melodramatic to carry conviction, and hence far inferior as didactic stories to

Mrs Brunton

"Self-Control"

---

[1] Chap. v.
[2] *Hannah More*, by Miss Yonge, 182.
[3] Introduction to *Emmeline, with some other Pieces* (1820), xix.
[4] *Ibid.*

either Maria Edgeworth's or Hannah More's. Mrs Brunton evinced very little self-control in devising a plot to illustrate that useful quality; she exaggerated virtues and vices, went to extremes of emotionalism, and strained the probabilities to breaking-point. Her first novel, in fact, is a throw-back to the sentimental romanticism of Prévost and his reckless disciples; though she may perhaps not have gone further than Mackenzie's *Man of the World* and *Julia de Roubigné* for the scenes in the Indian backwoods and the lurid domestic drama.[1] A young Scots lady, nursed in the lap of piety and discretion, takes natural offence at the licentious behaviour of her accepted suitor, a man of higher rank, who had seemed unexceptionable and is still unsuspected by her father. But he is as profligate as Zeluco and as ungovernable in temper. Why, indeed, had Laura not found him out before? At any rate, she does not, like the other Laura, marry her black sheep; but she continues deeply in love, and allows him to curtail the two years of probation on which she had compromised. But the lover's temper does not improve, and he is unfaithful. A rival appears, whom he challenges, and finding him too virtuous to fight a duel, shoots and wounds him unarmed. When Laura shows signs of encouraging the rival, the monster has her kidnapped and abducted to Canada. She escapes from captivity among the redskins, and in an Indian canoe is swept over the falls—apparently of Montmorenci—and survives, to be brought home to Scotland and find her oppressor dead by his own hand, after he had exonerated her from any stain on her propriety. But there have to be pages and pages of explanations and protestations that her Lovelace had not been successful, before it is quite safe for her to marry the chivalrous De Courcy.

Mrs Brunton had the best intentions; but it was a mistake to leave a hard and fast moral to the chance-work of a romantic plot. A certain formalism is indispensable perhaps to the didactic novelist; at any rate, the comparison brings out the superior cogency of Maria Edgeworth's clear, almost mathematical, demonstration of the consequences of character and of the way one plays one's part. Mrs Brunton was unwise enough to gird at other novelists. It appears that *Peregrine Pickle* and other

[1] See Volume V. 106-107.

" irregular " romances, poetry, and plays, were the agencies of Hargrave's moral corruption; and she permits the light-headed Julia " in an evil hour " to open a volume of the *Nouvelle Héloïse*, and give up reading sermons for the literature of sentiment. She herself fails at the Fanny Burney touch, notably when the rich young spark Mr Warren tries to abduct the heroine in the regular Pollexfen style.

Discipline was a pendant to *Self-Control*, " the whole moral " *Dis-* and religious discipline of life being intended to form those habits *cipline* " of self-command, in which Laura excelled, and in which Ellen Percy is so miserably defective."[1] It recounts, not only the reformation, but also the conversion of this ill-conditioned and flighty girl, spoiled by a widowed father and the blandishments of society. Her faithful counsellor, Miss Mortimer, asks her, when she thinks of eloping with a fashionable rake, " You have told me that you mean one day to change your plan of life—to put away childish things—to begin your education for eternity. Is Lord Frederick well fitted to be your companion—your assistant in this mighty work? " Mrs Brunton's religious fervour is very moving, and no doubt was largely the reason for her vogue. Ellen renounces the trip to Gretna Green. Then her father is ruined, she is thrown from affluence and unlimited self-indulgence into poverty, and at length is confronted by her real self and her buried talents. In due time, she is chastened and made fit for the dour and critical but unswervingly enamoured Mr Maitland, who turns out to be somebody else and entitled to a fortune, so that she is not left unrewarded even in this world.

Her unfinished last story opens well, with the wedding morn of " *Em-* the divorced Emmeline and the rich and idolized De Clifford, *meline* " wearing the laurels of war service on his brow. The rural surroundings, as they chime or contrast with the heroine's moods, are a part of the picture. Sensibility to natural beauty is now a commonplace of fiction : " A religion of the imagination . . . is the natural inmate of every feeling and elegant mind." Tears are to be expected, for the erring lady receives no mercy from society; there is no redemption in this world for one like her. On settling down at the Cliffords' ancestral seat, she is ignored by

[1] Preface, vi.

her equals, patronized by inferiors, and treated disrespectfully even by the domestics. And the author, whilst pitying her, feels that it is a fit punishment. Had she not bowed her head in shame, she would have evinced effrontery. "Heart of iron, as well as a brow of brass, is necessary even to the worldly comfort of the infamous." Even the warm-hearted and intelligent Mrs Villiers cannot "know" Lady de Clifford; she can scarce recognize her existence when the latter has nursed her little boy after an accident which was nearly fatal. What was to have been the ultimate lot of the Magdalene we cannot know; but *Emmeline* is assuredly a document.

CHAPTER III

JANE AUSTEN—EARLY STORIES AND
SENSE AND SENSIBILITY

WHEN Jane Austen's first novel, *Sense and Sensibility*, appeared in *Jane* 1811, the two eminent women writers with whom at the hastiest *Austen* glance it was evident that she had close affinity, Fanny Burney, *and Fanny* now Madame d'Arblay, and Maria Edgeworth, were not only *and Maria* still far from the end of their literary activities but were destined *Edgeworth* to survive her, the one by more than twenty the other by more. than thirty years. For she had only six more years to live, a very brief time in which to give the world *Pride and Prejudice* (1813), *Mansfield Park* (1814), and *Emma* (1816), and to leave two shorter novels, *Northanger Abbey* and *Persuasion*, ready to be brought out after her death. Both her elders lived twice as long as she, and both had seen themselves in print very early. Madame d'Arblay belonged now to the past, but still had *The Wanderer* (1814) and the memoirs of her father (1832) to write, the great *Diary* going on regularly all the time. Maria Edgeworth was in the middle of her long course, "Tales from Fashionable Life" being still in progress; *Patronage* was to see the light almost simultaneously with *Mansfield Park* and to challenge comparisons, *Harrington* and *Ormond* in the year of Miss Austen's death, and *Helen* seventeen years later. Herself apart, these two were the most representative and most productive women novelists of Jane Austen's time, and, were there no other reason, chronology would require some comparison of their circumstances and personalities. But the three cases were parallel in so many ways that this would be pertinent even had they not been related by propinquity of time.

Jane Austen (1775-1817) was of the same social rank as the two older novelists, though she never enjoyed the same social consequence, and was never in the same sense a woman of the

world. Her father was a country clergyman, not poor nor rich,
a fine scholar himself and able to give his children a decent
education. He and his wife were both of good family, and had
two or three wealthy friends and relatives whom Jane and her
sisters visited, often for a long stay. Visits were apt to be long in
those days of slow and expensive communications. But in most
respects the life of the Austens was the life of thousands dwelling
in the depths of the country at a time when the excitements of
town were almost as remote as in the Middle Ages. The Rev.
George Austen, rector of Steventon, was a man worthily held in
high respect by all who knew him; but he was not an influential
landed proprietor, or a man of acknowledged genius, or otherwise
of such note as to be on familiar terms with the great or courted
by society. Nor, when she was an author, did fame come early
enough to his daughter to bring her the friendship of those who
were her peers in the intellectual realm.

She and her brothers and sisters were a sociable set, and
of course knew everybody in their Hampshire parish and most
people of their own level throughout a wide neighbourhood.
The isolation of a country existence threw gentlefolk on their own
resources; they had to make the most of their neighbours; and
such social events as subscription balls and private dances were
pretty frequent. Jane was fond of dancing, and her letters
show how she was always meeting the county people and those of
lesser degree at such assemblies. When she and Cassandra went
to stay at the Kentish seat of their brother Edward, adopted by
the Knights of Godmersham Park, or with the Leigh Perrots,
their rich aunt and uncle at Bath, or at Lyme or some other
watering-place in Dorset or Devon, it was the same sort of people
they met, the rural gentry and the residents at those places who
were of the same class or its satellites. For one in her position,
Jane had a wide circle of friends and acquaintances, and of those
whom she could observe without being intimate with them.
Nevertheless, the radius within which she gained her experience
and beyond which her artistic integrity never let her stray in her
portraiture of life was much more constricted than the varied
spheres in which Fanny Burney and Maria Edgeworth found
their material. Theirs was a wider commerce with the world,

and also a more active one, especially the energetic Miss Edgeworth's, the bustling head of a large household and manager of a crowd of younger folk and of the affairs of a big estate. It must go down to the credit of Jane's thoroughness that her picture of life never sins by vagueness or neglect of the solid framework, for she herself never had to cope with such practical responsibilities.

A point of exact correspondence is that they were all three *All three* members of large families—the Austens had eight children—and *members* all three keen-eyed observers of what was going on around them. *of large* Like Fanny Burney, Jane made this her quiet hobby; and long *all quiet* before she was out of her girlhood started writing down her *observers* observations, without any such prompting to tell a story and improve the shining hour as Maria Edgeworth had from her pedagogic father, with no other motive indeed than the best of all, to amuse herself. It has been recounted often enough how she used to sit for hours at her writing-desk in the general sitting-room, undisturbed by the coming and going, and would not have the creaking door at Chawton repaired because it gave notice of every arrival, and she was unwilling that anyone not belonging to the family should be too curious about what she was writing. Her life was very uneventful, if compared with that of her two predecessors, or, to put it differently, the events were on a very small scale, more intimate, more ordinary, extremely insignificant except to herself and those like Cassandra who shared her feelings and her confidences. But she made the most of her opportunities, and amassed the material she needed. The knowledge that she required was very thorough at the time she wrote her best fiction; she knew the middling classes of society through and through; and for her such a strip of society was a world in itself in the range and diversity of character that it enfolded, even though many of the types interesting to other novelists were missing. To one who was neither a social philosopher nor a romancer, but only intent on the comedy of human nature, it was a source practically inexhaustible.[1]

[1] That she confined herself " chiefly to the middling classes of society " is Scott's expression. He said : " The scenes of Miss Edgeworth are laid in higher life, varied by more romantic incident, and by her remarkable power of embodying and illustrating national character " (review of *Emma* in *Quarterly Review*, October,

Jane's
novels
reveal
more
of herself
than do
her letters

In the case of Fanny Burney and Maria Edgeworth, no one would go to the novels to find the best presentment of the author, or to get a clearer conception of a character that has been self-portrayed in letters or diary and interpreted in others' memoirs. Less biographical material exists on Jane Austen, though as much as is warranted by the little there is to relate. But even her letters, frank and intimate as they are, would leave but a faint and elusive idea of the woman if the novels were not at hand to throw a different and ampler light on many fine points. Though her art was strikingly objective and impersonal, her character shines through; and the impress of that wise, tolerant, though piercing and exigent mind never varies from one novel to another. This is among the aspects of Jane Austen that have reminded many of Shakespeare. It is curious that some have found the letters too reticent and wanting in vivacity.[1] Perhaps they have looked for

1815, reprinted by R. B. Johnson, in *Famous Reviews*). Mary Augusta Austen-Leigh, who wrote a whole book, *Personal Aspects of Jane Austen* (1920), mainly to disprove the statement that her kinswoman's experience was narrow, misunderstands the question. She points out that Jane was at Oxford at the age of six, at Southampton a little later, and then at school at Reading ; that she visited here and there, and was always coming into contact with people, the very best sort of people, of course. But all this confirms what Scott and others have always pointed out. She had a very wide experience of people ; but her experience was narrow because they were all people of one narrow class. Obviously, it is the reverse of any disparagement of her genius to remind ourselves of this fact. A more relevant question, suggested by Scott's reference to her characters from a rather lower class, is why poor people, and also servants and other dependents, make hardly any appearance in her work, a much smaller appearance than in most novels dealing with the better classes. There are no flunkeys, no faithful servants, nurses, and the like. The tradespeople of Highbury are non-existent in *Emma*, for the Coles were outsiders—the Coles, very good sort of people, but, "they were of low origin, in trade, and only moderately genteel." Jane was very kind-hearted, and good to the poor, if not fond of them. But she does not put them even into the background of her picture.

[1] See *Introductions to Jane Austen*, by John Bailey, 2-3. But here is a passage distinctly more lively than the general tenor, and of course others might be quoted : " My morning engagement was with the Cookes, & our party consisted of George & Mary, a Mr & Miss Bendish who had been with us at the Concert, & the youngest Miss Whitby ;—not Julia, we had done with her, she is very ill, but Mary ; Mary Whitby's turn is actually come to be grown up & have a fine complexion & wear great square muslin shawls. I have not expressly enummerated myself among the party, but there I was, & my cousin George was very kind & talked sense to me every now & then in the intervals of his animated fooleries with Miss Bendish, who is very young & rather handsome, & whose gracious manners, ready wit, & solid remarks put me somewhat in mind of my old acquaintance Lucy Lefroy.—There was a monstrous deal of stupid quizzing, & common-place nonsense talked, but scarcely any wit ;—all that border'd upon it, or on sense came from my Cousin George, whom altogether I like very well.— Mr Bendish seems nothing more than a tall young man.—I met Mr F. Bonham

something as amusing as the novels, and still more lively and pungent because more personal and confidential. But all who love as well as admire Jane Austen, and they are more numerous now than ever, have their own mental image of her, derived from the novels and merely confirmed by the letters. Fanny Burney's letters and diaries often read like a preliminary study for her novels, to which they are in certain ways superior. The Austen letters were not written for the purpose, direct or indirect, of entertaining anyone, or with an eye for the approval of even so kindly a judge of a telling epistolary style as Daddy Crisp. They are no rough draft for fiction, nor anything else than what they purport to be, an exchange of private news and of information that was awaited, of fond inquiries, gossip, merry tittle-tattle, and occasional foolery, highly personal observations and impromptu strokes of satire. There is much more small talk in them than in the novels, almost as much as in the delightful babble of Miss Bates. Inevitably, they shed a welcome light on the characters of the two sisters, Jane and her beloved Cassandra, and of course on others of the family and their many friends and connexions, although a number, possibly the most intimate and revealing, were destroyed by the older sister. Yet they cannot compare as revealing documents with dozens of letters in the novels, from Edmund Bertram, Mary Crawford, Isabella Thorpe, or the immortal Mr Collins, all of which Jane Austen composed with the definite object of letting the writer give away his or her secrets without intending it.

Those familiar with the novels can read the letters almost as *The world* they were read by Cassandra, who did not perceive the reticences; *in which* she had no need to have indirect meanings underlined or points of *she lived* view explained. These informal memoranda showing Jane's mind in undress do not rank with the collections of letters accepted as classics of that agreeable art. But if not literature themselves

the other day, & almost his first salutation was ' So Miss Austen your cousin is come.'—My Evening Engagement & walk was with Miss Armstrong, who had called on me the day before, & gently upbraided me in her turn with change of manners to her since she had been in Bath, or at least of late. Unlucky Me ! that my notice should be of such consequence & my Manners so bad ! " (*Letters*, ed. R. W. Chapman, i. 155-156).

A sprightly bit, but how far short of her fiction ! The difference from Fanny Burney is very perceptible.

they are the stuff of which literature is made. Read discerningly, they confirm our intuitive belief in her fidelity to what she saw and the shrewdness of her vision. We are made invisible spectators of the Steventon and Chawton households and their doings, and of all that very provincial life amid which their lot was cast. We see the material in its roughest state, material that has to undergo many processes of sifting, rearrangement, and quiet preparation in the mental studio, before it reappears transmuted into a *Pride and Prejudice* or a *Mansfield Park*. The facts are few; events are more rare and unexciting than in the quietest of the novels. Visits and journeys naturally bulk largest, being the occasion for letters; then a wedding, a dinner, new clothes, a ball, a fresh arrival, news of the absent, especially Jane's sailor brothers; there are echoes of a reckless flirtation or two, and rumours of a love affair that was supposed to be serious but came to nothing, perhaps only through the death of a gentleman who might have been an eligible mate even for Jane Austen. Fanny Burney married late in life. Maria Edgeworth had only one attachment in the smallest degree serious. So it was with Jane Austen. And yet hers was a full life, though not one of full length, and it differed intrinsically from the trivial existence of most of those around her. The beautiful relationship between her and Cassandra must have been of inestimable value to Jane, the woman and the novelist; that sisterly spirit was more to her than Mr Crisp and Mr Edgeworth had been to her two predecessors. One fact comes out repeatedly in the correspondence, the absurdity of the charge that she disliked children; the records are that she was fond of them and that they worshipped her.[1]

Her reading and its effects— Fielding and Richardson　　In the matter of their reading, historically so important, of the writers they approved and those whom they regarded as gone astray and chiefly to be laughed at, there was not much difference between Jane and the two veterans, except that she had the advantage of reading and appreciating the works of the latter and observing where the novel now stood. All three were rather

[1] Look at the pretty vignette of the Gardiner children (*Pride and Prejudice*, xlvii.), in a novel and at a moment concerned with very different matters ; or the charming little boy at the dance, in *The Watsons*. Perhaps hours when she was ailing and irritable were in mind when she wrote some scenes in *Persuasion*, which provoked John Bailey to complain a little too sweepingly (*Introductions to Jane Austen*, 102-103).

desultory, and had some odd likes and dislikes. But she was the soundest critic, with the most intelligent grasp of the aims and the capacity and limitations of fiction. No one could be less of a theorist; but she had the same intuitive hold of the principles of her art as Shakespeare had in drama, and had no call to formulate rules which she obeyed with unerring instinct. The novel was worthy to exercise " the greatest powers of the mind," she wrote in its defence against indiscriminating depreciators[1]; Fielding himself had no better-founded respect for the art of fiction.

A bare allusion to *Tom Jones* in a novel[2] and one more specific in her letters[3] are all that she allowed herself, and whether she had read Fielding through can only be surmised. That which her age deprecated as his coarseness may have given her some distaste, though she did not revile him for it. But her irony is his irony, or its feminine counterpart; in that integral component of her art she is probably his nearest analogue in the whole range of novelists. Irony is perhaps a masculine trait; there is scarcely another woman who has employed it so shrewdly and made it such a corner-stone of her very foundations. But to Jane Austen it must have been congenital; Fielding only confirmed an original bias by setting his seal upon this mode of seizing and exposing the under side of life and character. She had no need to dissemble her knowledge of Richardson; she shows by the casual reminiscence which is better than direct quotation that she was steeped in *Sir Charles Grandison*, even if she knew or remembered less of the other two novels. Once or twice in the letters she likens herself to Harriet Byron in an embarrassing situation. *Mansfield Park* is Richardsonian through and through; Sir Thomas Bertram has the unmistakable Grandisonian stamp. Darcy and Mr Knightley, in other novels, show marks of the same origin. Richardson, admittedly, would never have drawn them as they stand; they are Richardsonian with radical differences. Fielding and Richardson seem somehow to meet and blend in Jane Austen, as later in Meredith, just as the masculine and the feminine principles seem to combine in more than one great genius. She is like Richardson in her registration of the minutest details of mannerism and behaviour, and in her annotation of the scarce

[1] *Northanger Abbey*, v.   [2] *Ibid.*, vii.   [3] Chapman, i. 3.

perceptible but significant and often decisive impulses of the heart. Her scale of values might be described as Richardson's corrected by Fielding.

Essayists and poets; contemporary novelists

Goldsmith's works, the *Spectator*, and such a successor to this as Mackenzie's *Lounger*, were the sort of books she liked to browse in; but of all in that category she loved and revered Dr Johnson the best; her moral philosophy was identical with his, and so probably was her religion. Among the poets, she found the most congenial enjoyment in Cowper, but recognized an even closer artistic affinity in the inexorable truthfulness of Crabbe. As to Scott, she liked his poetry well enough; but said, only half playfully, in a letter to Anna Austen, "Walter Scott has no business to write novels, especially good ones."[1] Her obligations to Fanny Burney will have to be touched upon. She often alludes to Miss Edgeworth's novels, and *Belinda* is bracketed with *Cecilia* and *Camilla* as one of the works " in which the greatest powers of the mind are displayed."[2] Jane did not think much of Hannah More as a novelist, and smiles at the absurdities of Mrs Brunton's *Self-Control*.[3] Everyone knows what she thought of Mrs Radcliffe; and her opinion of Sir Egerton Brydges, Regina Maria Roche, and their like was not very different from that of E. S. Barrett, whose *Heroine* she speaks of as "a delightful burlesque, particularly on the Radcliffe style."[4]

Shakespeare: her genius essentially dramatic

She knew her Shakespeare well, as is obvious to the critical reader.[5] But it would be as futile to ask how much she learned from him of her insight into the workings of the mind as of the roots of the irony in which she shows her likeness to Fielding. Her genius was essentially dramatic. She is nearer akin to Congreve and Molière than to Fanny Burney and Maria Edgeworth, who

[1] Chapman, ii. 404.

[2] It is suggested by C. L. Thomson that it was Miss Edgeworth's advertisement to this novel which provoked the famous outburst, the author describing it as a "Moral Tale," and deprecating its being classed with such doubtful merchandise as novels (*Jane Austen*, 45-46).

[3] " I declare I do not know whether Laura's passage down the American river is not the most natural, possible, everyday thing she ever does " (Chapman, ii. 344, *cp.* 423).

[4] Chapman, ii. 376-377. For the object of her satire, see Volume V., " The Gothic Novel," especially p. 227.

[5] " She knew Shakespeare well, but it would not be extravagant to guess that she cared less for Shakespeare as a poet than as a revealer of human nature " ("English Men of Letters," *Jane Austen*, by F. W. Cornish, 15).

could depict characters, and contrive plots and scenes to show off idiosyncrasies, but only carried a few brilliant raids into the territory of the comedy of manners. Jane Austen was dramatic in a deeper and truer sense. Character and action are inseparable in the work of the true dramatist, whether it be staged in a novel, or designed for the platform of a theatre. She did not write for representation by actors; she was a dramatist nevertheless, sometimes in the actual manner of the stage. Her pointed dialogue, the ironical situations in which the characters would have conducted themselves so much more wisely had they only been aware of what is patent to the reader, and the scenes in which pretences and delusions are stripped away, the tables turned on humbug and folly, and the rights of common sense re-established, are theatrical as well as dramatic. But take not merely the episodes but the wholes. In every novel, wills are set in motion, something important results, and characters are tested and survive or else are dismissed with ignominy. When the goal is reached, they see themselves as they are, and not only this, they are changed by what they have gone through; they have been brought up against realities, something fundamental has happened within them. Marianne Dashwood and Elizabeth Bennet in the first, Emma Woodhouse and Anne Elliot in the last of her novels, are not the same at the end as at the beginning. That is what drama always does, whether tragic or comic. Jane Austen chose to write what is essentially comedy; she quailed at tragedy: " Let other pens dwell on guilt and misery. I quit such odious subjects as soon as I can," she wrote in an oft-quoted passage in *Mansfield Park*.[1]

The theatrical form of some of her girlish sketches and the *Little* liveliness of their dialogue and repartee are another matter, and *plays and* may well be simply the result of her reading of Sheridan, Gold- *other* smith, and others of that period, and of the amateur performances *juvenilia* of the Austens and their friends. Much of this juvenile work of hers has now been printed, and shows that as soon as she began to write she had chosen her recreation, not to say her vocation : to watch what people did and also what people wrote, and make merry with the foolish, the stilted, the extravagant. *Love and*

[1] Chap. xlviii.

Freindship, written in 1790,[1] with the pieces of rather later date that accompany it in her note-books, is perhaps the only item of much intrinsic merit, and even so was not of merit enough in her own eyes to warrant publication.   But even the light-hearted fooling and often brilliant nonsense of the heterogeneous scraps are the effervescence of a fertile and buoyant fancy promising more. It soon fastens on an object.   The merry inconsequence becomes a parody of smug self-consequence and pompous triviality; the gush and silliness are shown to be the birthmarks of half the novels in the circulating library.   But in many of these slapdash drolleries irrelevance is meant to be a virtue.   The point of the " unfinished comedy " darkly entitled " The Mystery " is that the point is so neatly omitted.   And in " The Three Sisters,"[2] a burlesque of that overworked theme, marriage to an unpleasant person who has money, the fun, such as it is, must be looked for in the caricature of novelists who make out that the bride is always unwilling.

As soon as he was gone Mary exclaimed, " Thank Heaven ! he's off at last; how I hate him ! "   It was in vain that Mama represented to her the impropriety she was guilty of in disliking him who was to be her Husband, for she persisted in declaring her aversion to him & hoping she might never see him again. What a Wedding this will be !

And of course the wedding takes place ; Mary has done her duty as a protesting heroine, but nothing in the world would prevent her marrying Mr Watts and his gorgeous house and equipage.

" *Love and Freind- ship* "   *Love and Freindship* was written before Jane was fifteen. There was good talk at Steventon, and current literature must have been pretty thoroughly dissected, for Jane to have been so right and so sure in her judgments.   It is an uproarious travesty of the average fiction of the time, sentimentalism in its flatulent decadence, crossed with the strained sublimity of Mrs Radcliffe and the wild improbabilities of the sensationalists.[3]   Jane's scorn

---

[1] *Love and Freindship, and other early Works*, with preface by G. K. Chesterton, 1922.

[2] *Volume the First*, 1933, pp. 104-130.

[3] Mrs Radcliffe's second novel, *A Sicilian Romance*, appeared in 1790 ; Miss Charlotte Smith's *Emmeline* and *Ethelinde* had preceded it, and of course the novels of Clara Reeve, Sophia Lee, Anne Fuller, and others mentioned in Volume V. (chapters vi. and vii.) were mostly still earlier.

of sentimentalism and cheap romance was more thorough than Miss Edgeworth's; she rarely if ever succumbed to the magic of coincidence and melodrama. Thus early did she repudiate the delusive principles that had blighted fiction in the last half-century. *Love and Freindship* is of no little historical importance. It was the first small block in the edifice she was to build. And her novels taken together represent the return to truth and sanity, emancipation from the shams and the glamour which had so long misled. Better than *The Rovers*, *L'Amie inconnue*, *The Heroine*, or the other regular burlesques, do they fix the date of the reaction [1]; and in them she qualified herself by critical self-orientation and correction of unwary lapses to be a sensible and truthful novelist.

The novels stigmatized were by second- and third-rate writers, Mrs Radcliffe the only one of the slightest notoriety to-day; Jane had no complaint to make against Richardson, though she had plenty against his infatuated disciples.[2]

A case as hackneyed, though the converse of that in "The Three Sisters," is prettily hit off in the sixth letter:

"My father," says the noble youth whose name was Lindsay —though for particular reasons it is to be concealed under that of Talbot, "seduced by the false glare of Fortune and the Deluding Pomp of Title, insisted on giving my hand to Lady Dorothea. No never exclaimed I. Lady Dorothea is lovely and Engaging; I prefer no woman to her; but know Sir, that I scorn to marry her in compliance with your wishes. No! Never shall it be said that I obliged my Father."
We all admired the noble Manliness of his reply. . . .
Sir Edward was surprised; he had perhaps little expected to meet with so spirited an opposition to his will. "Where, Edward, in the name of wonder" (said he), "did you pick up this unmeaning gibberish? You have been studying Novels I suspect." I scorned to answer: it would have been beneath my dignity.[3]

---

[1] See Volume V. 225-227.
[2] Through a sort of megalomania, some readers can detect parodies of Fielding as well as Richardson in some of the episodes—*e.g.* Clara Linklater Thomson (*Jane Austen*, 56-57); but it was the bad novels of her own day that were in question.
[3] *Love and Freindship*, 10.

Then the landscape mania, indulged by Charlotte Smith and ridden to death by Mrs Radcliffe, comes in pat:

As soon as we had packed up our wardrobe and valuables, we left Macdonald Hall, and after having walked about a mile and a half we sate down by the side of a clear limpid stream to refresh our exhausted limbs. A grove of full-grown Elms sheltered us from the East —. A Bed of full-grown Nettles from the West —. Before us ran the murmuring brook and behind us ran the turnpike road. We were in a mood for contemplation and in a Disposition to enjoy so beautifull a spot. A mutual silence which had for some time reigned between us, was at length broke by my exclaiming—"What a lovely scene! Alas why are not Edward and Augustus here to enjoy its Beauties with us?" [1]

This early zest for caricature and farce was abjured entirely in her serious novels.

" Lady Susan "   One other work preceding those comprised in the Austen canon must not be passed over, although it was abandoned before it had got very far, having evidently proved a false start. *Lady Susan* first appeared as an addendum to Austen Leigh's memoir of his aunt in 1871,[2] and has now been reprinted from the fair copy left by Miss Austen, which was written out in 1805 or later.[3] It was the work of some period between 1792 and 1796, earlier, that is, than *Elinor and Marianne* and *First Impressions*, the original drafts of *Sense and Sensibility* and *Pride and Prejudice*. It is the history of a woman irredeemably bad; in other words, it is an essay in what has since been called "unflinching realism." [4] Instead of adopting the ironical attitude of Fielding in *Jonathan Wild* or endowing her adventuress with the magnanimity of a Becky Sharp, Jane Austen undertook to tell impassively the plain truth and exhibit an evil-hearted being in all her enormity.

Lady Susan is a more formidable, cleverer, and more accomplished woman of the same stamp as Lucy Steele, in *Sense and Sensibility*. Without the vulgarity of that odious minx, she is

---

[1] *Love and Freindship*, 29.   [2] In the 2nd edition.   [3] 1925.
[4] It is suggested that the plot was based on the marriage of her cousin, Éliza de Feuillide, to her brother Henry, ten years her junior; the evil disposition, however, being derived from another person whose inhuman selfishness was well known to the Austens (Thomson, 71). But it was probably written too early for that.

more hateful in her cold-blooded double-dealing and her joy in mischief for its own sake. She schemes to sell her daughter Frederica, a girl of sixteen, to a wealthy rake who has made love to herself, and to entrap on her own account an ingenuous young man who is attracted by Frederica, while she herself is intriguing with a married man. Thus she has three men in leash at once. Jane Austen must soon have found herself out of her element and beyond the orbit of her own experience; the pose of heartlessness, also, must have made her uncomfortable. But it is all related efficiently, in spite of the intractable form of the novel in letters.

At present my Thoughts are fluctuating between various schemes [writes the adventuress when she finds herself in a tight corner]; I have many things to compass. I must punish Frederica, and pretty severely too, for her application to Reginald; I must punish him for receiving it so favourably, and for the rest of his conduct. I must torment my Sister-in-law for the insolent triumph of her Look and Manner since Sir James has been dismissed—for in reconciling Reginald to me, I was not able to save that ill-fated young Man—and I must make myself amends for the humiliations to which I have stooped within these few days. To effect all this I have various plans.

All this is addressed to a confidant of her own sex; and, if Lady Susan does not outrage nature in her unqualified flagitiousness, she outrages probability in this dangerous candour, and truth in her cool analysis of her own motives. Even villainy nurses some atom of self-justification. Whatever her misgivings or growing distaste, Jane Austen came to an abrupt and makeshift conclusion, as if eager to have done with a thing so repellent. But she may have foreseen that Lady Susan, if allowed the triumph which her unscrupulous arts seemed to guarantee, would be a monster; and, having tied her right hand behind her back by discarding irony, what could she have done? Out-and-out villainy was not her province.

About 1795, Jane Austen read aloud to the Steventon household a story in letters called *Elinor and Marianne*. It was put aside whilst she wrote *First Impressions*, which afterwards became *Pride and Prejudice*; but she returned to it in November 1797, and recast it in the ordinary form of a novel. After a further "*Sense and Sensibility*" revision, in 1809, it was published as *Sense and Sensibility* (1811), being the first of her works to be given to the public; and its favourable reception paved the way for *Pride and Prejudice*, which had been rejected in 1797. *Northanger Abbey*, finished in 1798, and then known as *Susan*, was revised and offered for sale in 1803, but still lay unprinted in a publisher's drawer.

Any Janeite, to use a recent mark of distinction, who was asked which is the best of her novels, might excusably fall back on the one last read. But it is improbable that, even without much thinking, he would propose *Sense and Sensibility*. A general vote would surely declare for *Pride and Prejudice*; critical as distinct from popular opinion would perhaps choose *Emma*; and those most interested in scales of values and their application to the conduct of life would undoubtedly plump for *Mansfield Park*. Then *Persuasion* has the exquisite charm of self-betrayal, the escape of a tender emotion, long repressed; and *Northanger Abbey* the appeal of youth and a captivating heroine. But *Sense and Sensibility* no one would cite as her masterpiece. Nevertheless, it is a masterpiece, and may reasonably be pronounced the finest example yet seen of one kind of realistic fiction, the Burney and Edgeworth kind, and to have all those superiorities of matter and manner which she was to exhibit later in a more mature and more exquisite degree.

Not a didactic novel
The fashion of her titles, *Love and Freindship*, *Sense and Sensibility*, *Pride and Prejudice*, *Persuasion*, sounds like an echo of the didactic school. Something seems to be hinted of the same nature as the two lines of conduct produced and contrasted by Miss Edgeworth in *Patronage*. But Jane Austen was not didactic, nor even a moralist in the way of her predecessors. She had done with all that in *Lady Susan*. The genial task she had chosen was to contemplate and disentangle the play and interplay of all the varieties of character met with in her small world, and to reproduce her mental vision, to which the darker purlieus were a closed book. If a lesson could be deduced from anything that she related, well and good; she left it to those who liked it to pick and choose. These epigrammatic titles of hers were only finger-posts; they gave the dip of a contour, the trend of an outline which had to be filled in, a suggestive point of view. But

the novel was the total result of a clear and comprehensive survey by one who loved humanity but did not take sides, unless it was with the spirit of comedy and common sense.[1] Her titles do, however, mark one new tendency. They show that novels were beginning to have specific subjects; a theme, a particular aspect, is isolated, offering a clue to the baffling confusion presented by men and women in the act of living.

" Novel of manners " is an ambiguous term, a rough and ready *A novel of* translation of *roman de mœurs*, in which manners and morals are *manners* not discriminated. It fitted the two older novelists well enough, if manners and morals are lumped together. But Jane Austen's is a novel of manners in a narrower and truer sense. She takes the morals for granted. If morality is wilfully violated, she does not dwell on the delinquency. Willoughby and Wickham's misdeeds are not part and parcel of the story, in her first two novels; they are merely unfortunate circumstances, external events which happened to have serious results for the people with whom she was directly concerned. She found enough to occupy her in characters that were never assailed by the darker temptations; in venial mistakes of judgment and their unforeseen results, in the mannerisms and eccentricities of temperament, and the contacts of heterogeneous personalities. This is the sphere of comedy; the study of moral disorder, on the other hand, leads straight to tragedy. The dramatists had usually kept these separate, as was right and proper. Richardson had done the same, *Clarissa* being all tragedy, and *Sir Charles Grandison* as nearly and as consistently like comedy as such a writer could achieve. Fanny Burney, after a brilliant success in the comic rôle, jumbled comedy and what she meant for tragedy together in *Cecilia*, with untoward consequences. Later novelists, Hawthorne and George Eliot, for instance, were apparently to succeed in driving the two steeds abreast; but this impression is due to a misunderstanding of the place of humour in their work. Humour is not incompatible with a tragic view of life; tragedy and comedy never long cohabit, even in an illicit union.[2]

---

[1] " Now Comedy is the fountain of good sense " (Meredith : *The Idea of Comedy*, 28).

[2] See Meredith's careful differentiation of the Comic, from humour, satire, etc. (*Op. cit.*, 78-80).

Let others deal with the harsh contradictions of right and wrong; Jane Austen was serenely happy in her humbler sphere, as they might consider it. The small change of social intercourse, the niceties of decorum, grace, tolerance, sympathy, self-respect, with their opposites, ill-breeding, self-deceit, egotism, affectation, were all she wanted. If these virtues and vices pertain to the realm of ethics, it is where this shades off into the æsthetic domain, where right and wrong are the beautiful and the unbeautiful.[1] Call it the higher ethics, and then she is a moralist. Hers, indeed, is a more exacting, a loftier and a finer code than that of the older novelists; it was based on a high conception of the intrinsic worth of personality. Every one of her novels is the history of a process of self-correction and self-education, with inner harmony, understanding, integrity, and self-approval as the goal.[2] The canons which she tacitly acknowledged and the conviction from which they derive, that there is nothing of higher worth, foreshadow a view which did not become prevalent in English fiction till near our own day.

The critical observer among her dramatis personæ

Jane had been studying her part for a long time, for such a young woman. In every novel there is a family, like or unlike the Austens; and in every novel, one female character in whom it is not too fanciful to recognize an impersonation of the demure observer, in the corner of the room, ticking off instances and oddities and forming judgments and conjectures. Being players themselves, with a great deal at stake, these anxious spectators do not see the whole of the game; but they see more than the other players; they read, mark, learn, for their own benefit; sometimes they also teach. In *Sense and Sensibility*, this is Elinor's part. She is not a sprightly and humorous creature, and not much

---

[1] *E.g.* " The beauty of truth and sincerity " (*Emma*, li.).

[2] " When he talked of her having such a steadiness and regularity of conduct, such a high notion of honour, and such an observance of decorum as might warrant any man in the fullest dependence on her faith and integrity, he expressed what was inspired by the knowledge of her being well principled and religious " (*Mansfield Park*, xxx.). " The only source whence anything like consolation or composure could be drawn was in the resolution of her own better conduct, and the hope that, however inferior in spirit and gaiety might be the following and every future winter of her life to the past, it would yet find her more rational, more acquainted with herself, and leave her less to regret when it were gone " (*Emma*, xlviii.). Such passages call to mind the Greek idea of measure and balance. Yet the reliance on an inner source rather than a rule imposed from without is a distinct mark of the individualism of the Romantic age.

like Jane Austen, except in her good sense and clear insight. She is much more like the sensible but reserved Cassandra. This sedate lady has finished her education, and looks at the weaknesses and errors of her fellow-beings with regretful forbearance, and with a tender solicitude for those who are her nearest and dearest. Elizabeth Bennet, in the next novel, and Anne Elliot, in the last, who are the closest likenesses in character to Jane Austen herself, seem to have least of this particular duty allotted them. They are in such ticklish situations themselves that their part as critical observers is not so much to the fore. But none is a better mouthpiece of Jane Austen's caustic reflections than Elizabeth; and in Anne she lays bare more of her heart and lets out more of her inmost thoughts than she permitted herself elsewhere, even in the characters she loved best. Fanny Price, in *Mansfield Park*, is a different type; but as a simple young thing watching intently and learning to fit herself into a society entirely new and strange, she has a similar function. Catherine Morland, in *Northanger Abbey*, is another neophyte, bewildered by her first experiences, who is taught sense by a series of misadventures and disillusionments. As a girl making her debut, she is obviously like Fanny Burney's Evelina, the ingenuous diarist. Emma Woodhouse, in the novel called by her first name, with mental powers not inferior to Elizabeth Bennet's, has to be schooled by an arduous course of blunders and humiliations, due to misconceptions of what is going on under her eyes. Only after many reverses and some bitter pangs do these characters attain to anything like the novelist's omniscience. The reader sees far more than they can, and is invited to smile at their aberrations. But they are placed at the centre, they are obliged by their situation to be watchful and critical. The story in each case shows them assimilating experience, acquiring tact and judgment, and adjusting themselves with more or less pain and difficulty to their circumstances and obligations; and it is largely through their eyes that the story in all its bearings grows clear to the reader.

Sense and Sensibility was by the young woman who a few years earlier had written *Love and Freindship*, and a little later was to write *Susan*, the original sketch for *Northanger Abbey*. Jane

" Sense and Sensibility" in origin a skit on contemporary romances

Austen never minded confessing that her family were omnivorous novel readers. No doubt, there was great merriment among the Steventon girls when Mrs Radcliffe's *Sicilian Romance* and *Romance of the Forest* were far outdone by *The Mysteries of Udolpho*, the great event of 1794. Here was another exquisitely sensitive heroine, ignorant as a new-born babe of the wickedness of the world, preserving in the most terrifying situations her faith in the constancy and prowess of her lover, who is not less refined than herself, and shares all her raptures for scenery, music, and poetry. *Elinor and Marianne* has disappeared, and we can only conjecture what it was like; but we are probably not far from the truth in supposing it to have been a simple contrast between a young lady, as innocent and as fervid and trustful as Mrs Radcliffe's Adeline or Emily,[1] and her wiser sister, and between their histories, the result of these contrary dispositions. "Sense," the young lady who behaves rationally, would have her trials, but would surmount them and have nothing to complain about in fortune; whilst the foolish virgin would meet with nothing but trouble. Precisely how much of the touching relations between the sisters and of the comedy of the family history of the Dashwoods was introduced when the novel in letters came to be recast, can never be known. But it is not illegitimate to suppose that the points in which this comes closest of all Jane's novels to *Cecilia*, her favourite among Fanny Burney's novels, date from the first draft. The book went through two revisions, before it appeared at last in 1811, and of course it must be judged by this final shape.

Parallel history of the two sisters

The formality remained: the two heroines, the antithesis of disposition and attitude, and the dual plot, for both sisters have their ordeals to go through, the parallel furnishing excellent openings for Jane Austen's irony. In the final version, at any rate, the character who engages the warmest sympathies is the erring Marianne. If there was at first any caricature in this gentle figure, it has been completely expunged. Extravagant she is; but her very extravagance is appealing, it is so entirely devoid of affectation and even of self-love. It is less the wrong to herself

---

[1] See Volume V. 194-199. For quiet raillery of the craze for ruins, blasted trees, and similar constituents of romantic scenery, see in particular Edward's conversation with Marianne at the beginning of chapter xviii. (*Sense and Sensibility*).

that distresses her than her lover's baseness, the overthrow of her
faith in all that she holds sacred. Not a word of resentment, only
of lamentation. And who was to blame? Why, her mother, who
had not brought her up properly: "Mrs Dashwood entered into
all their feelings with a warmth which left her no inclination for
checking this excessive display of them. To her it was but the
natural consequence of a strong affection in a young and ardent
mind."[1] Elinor knew too well "that what Marianne and her
mother conjectured one moment, they believed the next—that
with them, to wish was to hope, and to hope was to expect."[2]

Both sisters have heroic qualities; each has precisely those
which the other lacks; each is half a heroine.[3] Elinor's superlative virtues are intelligence and self-control; she has so much
of the latter that she runs some risk of forfeiting the reader's
esteem by her extreme patience and submissiveness towards the
unhappy lover tied to a designing woman whom he has never
loved. Edward Ferrars comes off better than he deserves; or, to
put it otherwise, Jane does not go deep enough into the original
business of his entanglement with Lucy to exonerate him from
the charge of exceeding foolishness. It is difficult to rehabilitate
a dupe. And Lucy Steele is such a horrid minx! Did Jane think
more of Elinor than the fastidious reader possibly can? It is
disconcerting to find her writing to Cassandra, when the book
had just come out, referring to their friend Mrs Knatchbull, "I
think she will like my Elinor, but cannot build on anything else."[4]
For a certain flatness in the Elinor-Edward business can only
be condoned on the assumption that it is subservient to the more
interesting theme, the misfortunes of Marianne. That this was
meant to be central is clearly shown by the summing up towards
the end:

Marianne Dashwood was born to an extraordinary fate. She
was born to discover the falsehood of her own opinions, and to
counteract, by her conduct, her most favourite maxims. She was

---

[1] Chap. xi.   [2] Chap. iv.

[3] It is amusing to notice that Jane Austen thought it necessary to state that her
older heroine, Elinor, at the dreadful moment when Lucy Steele slyly lets out the
fact of her engagement to Edward Ferrars, "stood firm in incredulity, and felt
in no danger of an hysterical fit, or swoon" (chap xxii.).

[4] Chapman, ii. 273.

born to overcome an affection formed so late in life as at seventeen, and with no sentiment superior to strong esteem and lively friendship, voluntarily to give her hand to another!—and *that* other, a man who had suffered no less than herself under the event of a former attachment, whom, two years before, she had considered too old to be married,—and who still sought the constitutional safeguard of a flannel waistcoat![1]

Jane Austen must have changed her point of view considerably in the fifteen years between *Elinor and Marianne* and *Sense and Sensibility*, to account for these small discrepancies. But a more serious blot is the perfunctory characterization of Willoughby, who is unanimously regarded as a very inadequate occasioner of so much disturbance. As already suggested, Willoughby is a figure of melodrama, and does not fit in properly.[2] Marianne's transports seem to be mere infatuation for a worthless object. And then Jane Austen was always coy over love scenes, and so failed to make good either the personal fascination of Willoughby or the ardour which swept Marianne off her feet.

The other Dashwoods must have been brought in at a latish stage. The Steele girls, the bluff, jolly, tactless Sir John Middleton, and that polite nonentity his wife; Mrs Ferrars, a vinegarish cartoon for the future Lady Catherine de Bourgh; and even Mrs Jennings, with her cheerful impertinence, jovial indelicacy, and real tenderness of heart, could have been invented if not fully developed by the pupil of Fanny Burney. But the John Dashwoods, the brother and sister-in-law of Elinor and Marianne, are a subtler creation, with the mint-marks of Jane's ripest art. None but a practised novelist could have written the dialogue in the second chapter between that well-matched couple, sprinkling it with such tell-tale clues to the whole personality of these two worthies, on the question what they are called upon to do for the mother and sisters who have been left with no share in the entailed estate except what John Dashwood may allow them, to fulfil the promise made to his dying father. The least he felt he could do was to give them three thousand pounds. But how could they so reduce the fortune of their dear little boy? So it comes down by degrees to a present of " fish or game, and so forth, when they are

[1] Chap. l.   [2] See above, p. 71.

in season," and an offer of help in moving their things. It is the classic anatomy of meanness, and a masterpiece of Jane's irony.

Traces of when she was less experienced may be discerned in the alternations of irony with direct statement, or of the under-meaning that hardly ripples the surface with the more elementary *Jane Austen's irony* sarcasm of a descriptive phrase or a bit of analysis, often in antitheses echoing her revered Dr Johnson. Elinor's anguish on her sister's account finds a happy relief in Lady Middleton's polite unconcern, when the meddlesome attentions of the others only rasp her sensibilities.

> Every qualification is raised at times, by the circumstances of the moment, to more than its real value; and she was sometimes worried by officious condolence to rate good-breeding as more indispensable to comfort than good-nature.[1]

This falls flat in comparison with those passages in which characters betray the very motives they would fain conceal, or the baseness of which they are not even aware. John Dashwood's talk with his sister Elinor, when he explains how hard it is to meet all the demands upon his large income, is almost as good as the famous debate with his wife already cited.

> "We must live at a great expense while we are here." He paused for her assent and compassion; and she forced herself to say—"Your expenses both in town and country must certainly be considerable; but your income is a large one."
>
> "Not so large, I daresay, as many people suppose. I do not mean to complain, however: it is undoubtedly a comfortable one, and I hope will in time be better. The enclosure of Norland Common, now carrying on, is a most serious drain. And then I have made a little purchase within this half-year; East Kingham Farm, you must remember the place, where old Gibson used to live. The land was so very desirable for me in every respect, so immediately adjoining my own property, that I felt it my duty to buy it. I could not have answered it to my conscience to let it fall into other hands. A man must pay for his convenience; and it *has* cost me a vast deal of money."
>
> "More than you think it really and intrinsically worth?"
>
> "Why, I hope not that. I might have sold it again, the next

[1] Chap. xxxiii.

day, for more than I gave; but, with regard to the purchase money, I might have been very unfortunate indeed; for the stocks were, at that time, so low, that if I had not happened to have the necessary sum in my banker's hands, I must have sold out to very great loss."

Elinor could only smile.[1]

Not less fatuous is his certainty that Elinor is going to make a match of it with Colonel Brandon and his two thousand a year —" I wish with all my heart it were *twice* as much "—Colonel Brandon who is Marianne's suitor ! His bland obtuseness to everything but the net profits, and the avidity of his wife, which turns to a cold spite when her schemes for feathering the family nest do not prosper, are stripped of disguise with the same deadly serenity.

There are many little episodes that would go brilliantly on the stage.   Elinor is the bearer to Edward Ferrars, whom she loves and who she is convinced loves her, of Colonel Brandon's offer of a living, to enable him to marry Lucy Steele, whose clutches he sees no hope of escaping.   The unblushing Mrs Jennings eavesdrops, and amiably congratulates Elinor on what she thought was a handsome offer of marriage.[2]   For more serious comedy nothing could be finer than the scene in which the author manages to shepherd into the same room four such unpropitious companions as Elinor and Lucy Steele, Edward Ferrars and Marianne.   First, Elinor has to endure with a cheerful countenance Lucy's ill-founded ecstasies at the affable reception which she has had from the redoubtable Mrs Ferrars, her mother-in-law presumptive.   They are interrupted by the entry of Edward, who is speechless with confusion at such a meeting, and then of Marianne, still unshaken in the belief that he is her sister's suitor and most anxious to see the back of Miss Steele.   The reader knows exactly how much each knows, and can appreciate at ease all the fine shades of covert humour.[3]   On the other hand, the irony becomes tragic in Marianne's " Happy, happy Elinor, *you* cannot have an idea of what I suffer," to her whom she fondly thinks providentially immune from the miseries of her own lot.[4]

[1] Chap. xxxiii.
[3] Chap. xxxv.
[2] Chap. xl.
[4] Chap. xxix.

When Elinor's false situation as the beloved but not the betrothed of Edward, and the bleeding heart that she has been nursing through all Marianne's woes, may no longer be hid, Jane Austen can hardly bring herself to write more than a line or two of dialogue:

"Four months! Have you known of this for four months?" Elinor confirmed it. "What! while attending me in all my misery, has this been on your heart? and I have reproached you for being happy!" [1]

And then she falls back on cold prose.

The weakest joint in the structure of *Sense and Sensibility* is the forced solution of Edward's dilemma; it assuredly does not cause the surprise which gradually changes to conviction, the regular test of originality. Edward has the satisfaction of being deprived of Lucy, the millstone round his neck, by that man of straw his brother Robert; she contrives to let him cut Edward out. Edward is accordingly free to marry Elinor. Elinor hears with resignation that Lucy is now Mrs Ferrars, and then with stupefaction that she is Mrs Robert Ferrars, not Edward's wife at all. The world goes upside down for her when she realizes that Edward is not lost to her for ever. Not a hint has been dropped to prepare either the reader or the lovers for such a contingency. The retrospective explanation is lame and impotent. It is all more arbitrary even than the surprising conduct of Willoughby and the secret history of that gentleman which comes out also after the fact. Otherwise, the story ends in a manner characteristic of Jane Austen. Not for her the conventional winding up with rewards strictly graduated according to deserts. She ignores the money prizes, which in this case go to the vicious Lucy and Robert, Edward not even regaining the rights of the eldest son, and the usurpers continuing to be the favourites of Mrs Ferrars. Warm family affection, tenderness and perfect agreement between husband and wife, and the sense of having preserved one's soul inviolate, are an infinitely more desirable quittance. Marianne shares in this, for there was nothing ignoble in her romantic excesses. As to poetic justice, all that Jane ever insists upon is

Defects of plot (marginal note)

[1] Chap. xxxvii.

the flouting of such self-appointed guardians of society as Mrs Ferrars in this novel and Lady Catherine de Bourgh in the next; theirs was an order of values which she repudiated.

Jane Austen and Fanny Burney The difference between Jane Austen and Fanny Burney is easy to gauge from a comparison of the brilliant chapter in *Cecilia*,[1] in which four incompatible and mutually incomprehensible old men discomfit each other with their absurdities, and the quadruple scene referred to on a preceding page. It is the difference between comedy so broad as to be scarce distinguishable from farce and caricature, and the subtle comedy of the moral and temperamental reactions between characters who are each other's opposites. Jane, surely, did not write this in her inexperienced youth. But there are similarities that leap to the eye to both *Cecilia* and the earlier *Evelina*. The eccentric Mr Palmer, for whom Jane actually apologizes,[2] is obviously suggested by Mr Meadows, Fanny Burney's Insensibilist in *Cecilia*.[3] Listen to him paying his silly wife a few inattentions:

" Oh, my love," cried Mrs Palmer to her husband, who just then entered the room, " you must help me to persuade the Miss Dashwoods to go to town this winter."

Her love made no answer; and after slightly bowing to the ladies, began complaining of the weather.

" How horrid all this is ! " said he. " Such weather makes everything and everybody disgusting. Dulness is as much produced within doors as without by rain. It makes one detest all one's acquaintance. What the devil does Sir John mean by not having a billiard-room in his house ? How few people know what comfort is ! Sir John is as stupid as the weather." [4]

Just as indubitably are the Steele sisters Fanny's Miss Branghtons come to life again, along with their accomplished retainer Mr Smith, reduced considerably in stature, however, in Mr Rose, " a prodigious smart young man, quite a beau, clerk to Mr

---

[1] See Volume V. 169.

[2] "Elinor was not inclined, after a little observation, to give him credit for being so genuinely and unaffectedly ill-natured or ill-bred as he wished to appear. . . . It was rather a wish of distinction, she believed, which produced his contemptuous treatment of everybody, and his general abuse of everything before him. It was the desire of appearing superior to other people " (chap. xx.).

[3] See Volume V. 167-168.

[4] Chap. xx. John Bailey called Mr Palmer " a rude beginning of Mr Bennet " (*Introductions*, 32).

Simpson, you know, and yet if you do but meet him of a morning, he is not fit to be seen." The Steeles are the Branghton sisters touched with a sharper malice: vulgar and illiterate, they are also base and cringing; sycophants, crawling intriguers, with venom for anyone who steps on them. Listening at keyholes is one of their more venial foibles. Their address is Bartlett's Buildings, Holborn, so that they are almost next-door neighbours to their originals; and, like them, they are related to more stylish people who live nearer the haunts of fashion. Their talk about beaux, the coyness of the simpering Miss Steele, and the sly cattishness of her sister, who entrapped Edward Ferrars when he was her uncle's pupil at Longstaple, are perhaps a blot upon the novel. Satire does not mix with pure comedy; the rawness and bluntness of this does not go well with the fineness of the rest of the book. Jane Austen's urbanity afterwards kept clear of matters that make the reader feel uncomfortable—from the realism which reviewers call "unpleasant." The portrait of Mrs Ferrars in such company has a spiteful look, as if she were deliberately gibbeted:

A little, thin woman, upright, even to formality, in her figure, and serious, even to sourness, in her aspect. Her complexion was sallow, and her features small, without beauty, and naturally without expression; but a lucky contraction of the brow had rescued her countenance from the disgrace of insipidity, by giving it the strong characters of pride and ill-nature.[1]

[1] Chap. xxxiv.

CHAPTER IV

PRIDE AND PREJUDICE AND NORTHANGER ABBEY

"*Pride and Pre-judice*"

THE theme and the actual title of *Pride and Prejudice* (1813) were suggested by Fanny Burney, whose *Cecilia* was a history of the bitter opposition and sufferings which were " the result of Pride and Prejudice," as the worthy Dr Lyster summarizes it in the last chapter.[1] *First Impressions*, the early novel forming the original draft of *Pride and Prejudice*, was probably written between October 1796 and August 1797, and was offered to the publisher Cadell, and immediately refused, in November of that year.[2] Egerton, who had published *Sense and Sensibility*, was very willing to accept a second novel, towards the end of 1812, and brought it out in January. Little is known of the extent to which *First Impressions* was revised, and it would be venturesome to try to determine this by internal evidence. Jane Austen was capable later of finer workmanship; but *Pride and Prejudice* remains her most brilliant novel, the one with the most exciting story, the wittiest and most spirited heroine, and her two most magnificent grotesques, the egregious Mr Collins and his worthy patroness Lady Catherine de Bourgh.[3]

Superiority at all points to " Sense and Sensibility "

If the imperfections of a first draft were not entirely removed in *Sense and Sensibility*, it would be difficult to find any such traces of *First Impressions* in *Pride and Prejudice*. The story runs limpidly, unclogged either by mismanaged situations or by

[1] See synopsis of *Cecilia* (Volume V. 164-166). It has been pointed out that the phrase " pride and prejudice " had been used before—*e.g.* by Gibbon (*Times Lit. Suppt.*, 22nd August 1929) ; in a sense it was a cliché ; but no doubt Jane took the title from a novel which we know she admired.

[2] *Memoir*, 47.

[3] Elizabeth Bennet was her own favourite among her creations. " I must confess that I think her as delightful a creature as ever appeared in print," she wrote, " and how I shall be able to tolerate those who do not like *her* at least I do not know " (Chapman, ii. 297).

patches of analysis and cautious explanation of motive. The discussions on ethical points that sometimes occur and Darcy's lectures on the casuistry of etiquette are a different matter, on which something will be said later. What goes on before the eyes is made to tell its own story, with a minimum of parenthetical direction. The range of character is wider. The whole gamut of Jane's command of human nature is brought into play, with such creatures of instinct as Mrs Bennet and her skittish younger daughters at one end and the more finely compounded Mr and Mrs Gardiner and the complex Darcy and Elizabeth Bennet at the other. If *First Impressions* underwent any drastic revision, this must have been done at Chawton, where the Austens had settled down in 1809 after their eight years at Bath and Southampton; but the general picture of the rural society at Longbourn must have been painted from the time at Steventon. Jane Austen did not draw individuals straight from life[1]; but she would not describe places that she did not know or anything she did not properly understand, and she was just as conscientious in her more extraordinary creations. Mr Collins and Lady Catherine de Bourgh do exceed the modesty of nature; but they never contradict nature, though such modesty as they possess is a spurious alloy. Between the Austens and the Bennets or the Dashwoods there was doubtless only the general likeness of any domestic interiors of gentry of moderate means in a village at that time. Jane and Elizabeth Bennet are not Cassandra and Jane Austen; but internal and external evidence agrees that Elizabeth displays more of her author's own mentality and disposition than any other personage in the novels; and the bond between the two elder sisters, here as in the previous novel, is the counterpart of that subsisting between herself and Cassandra. The scene in the first was Devon, and in this second Hertfordshire; but it might equally well have been Jane Austen's own Hampshire, so insignificant is the difference in the local circumstances and the lie of the land. And it would be useless to identify such places as Longbourn or Meryton even were it possible; almost any group of inhabited spots in the southern counties would have served just as well.

[1] " It is a thoroughly attested fact that in no single instance did she ever draw one of the figures in her novels straight from life " (Walter Herries Pollock : *Jane Austen : her Contemporaries and Herself*, 9).

A dramatic story

Why this is the most exciting of all Jane's stories is because of the strength and wit of the leading characters, especially the heroine, and the formidable nature of the obstacles to be overcome, so that hope is ever contending with anxiety, before the happy ending comes in sight—a dramatic subject, treated dramatically. The initial position has to be reversed. Pride and prejudice have to be subdued, and the tenderest and most perfect understanding put in their place. This entails a change of heart in the two principals, a change going very deep in one of them, and a change subtly and unobtrusively echoed in the shock even to the cherished imperturbability of Mr Bennet. The merely sardonic view will not do in the long run for a responsible actor in the human drama. " For what do we live, but to make sport for our neighbours, and laugh at them in our turn? "[1] Jane herself may have said so once upon a time. But Mr Bennet has had his lesson, and Jane's best-loved heroine now feels, " It was necessary to laugh when she would rather have cried." Mrs Bennet and her like stand where they were; she is irreclaimable; but various others are chastened, if not, like Darcy, changed almost out of knowledge. A novel is not a play, and should never pretend to be a play. Literature always simplifies, and drama carries the process to the farthest lengths, making an abstraction from reality. Fiction, however, is no mere abstract, it is a representation of reality, a more or less full representation of a segment of life. Hence the qualifications already stated if any parallel is drawn between novel and play.[2] Here, at all events, Jane Austen was necessarily most dramatic, even approximating to the stage in her preference to description and analysis of that which is infinitely more telling, that which goes on before our eyes and ears, the human drama in action. Just as the playwright drops at times into makeshift soliloquy, she may write out the whole of her heroine's meditations[3] at a crucial juncture. But for the most part she lets the scene proceed without interference. And in the present case she was so dramatic that it is tempting to divide the narrative into the five acts of high comedy.

That which may be taken as the first act opens briskly, and

[1] Chap. lvii.   [2] See above, pp. 64-65.
[3] *E.g.*, after Darcy's letter (chap. xxxvi.) or after she has told him the news of Lydia's elopement (chap. xlvi.).

with the arresting first sentence introduces the Longbourn people, *" Pride*
hitting off their leading traits, foibles, and prejudices with such *and*
dexterity that a closer acquaintance can only deepen the first *Preju-*
impression. Elizabeth and Darcy meet, and affect each other so *five acts*
unfavourably that nothing seems more remote than the possibility
of a warm attachment between such predestined foes. But
presently it is evident that, if this is dislike, it is not indifference ;
so far from it that Darcy " feels the danger of paying Elizabeth
too much attention," whilst she is puzzled by a gallantry which
belies his former arrogance. Along with these hints of future
developments, the sub-plot also begins to outline itself, in the
mutual attraction of Darcy's friend Bingley and Elizabeth's sister
Jane. Both affairs come to an apparent end with the departure
of the two girls from Netherfield, and Bingley's silence. The
heart-burnings are entirely on Jane's side, Elizabeth's disappointment is only for her sister. Such is the posture of affairs at the
beginning of the second act, in which the plot stands almost
still or dallies for a while with other matters, matters not so
irrelevant as they seem. It is largely taken up with the absurd
antics of Mr Collins, who is refused by Elizabeth and marries her
less squeamish friend Charlotte Lucas. Elizabeth flirts with the
handsome scapegrace Wickham, but remains heart-whole, though
his airs of injured innocence and his mendacious revelations set
her inflexibly against Darcy. That gentleman continues to be
fascinated by Elizabeth, but is still more repelled by the follies of
the Bennet family. A master-stroke of irony is preparing, however, throughout this act, as telling as the spontaneous antagonism
of the future lovers in the first ; for Mr Collins and Wickham
are both to be instrumental in bringing about a most unexpected
result, the complete reconciliation of Elizabeth and Darcy. That
is still hid in the future ; but there is another stroke which the
reader must note, the irony of Darcy's interference between
Jane and Bingley, since what he has deliberately done now will
have to be deliberately undone later.

The turning-point of the story is in act three. Still indifferent *The*
to Darcy, in fact still more prejudiced against him, Elizabeth *critical*
goes on a visit to the Collinses, and at Lady Catherine de Bourgh's *third act*
meets Darcy and his friend Colonel Fitzwilliam. Darcy surprises

her, and perhaps the reader, with a proposal of marriage, which she rejects, stigmatizing his pride and the alleged wrongs done to Wickham. His long letter of exculpation gives her food for thought, and may be regarded as of decisive moment in the drama. She sees that there is another side to the case put by Wickham; Colonel Fitzwilliam's talk about Darcy sinks in, and combined with other facts tends to open her eyes. Things begin to move decisively in the fourth act, of which the big event·is the visit to Pemberley. Whilst Elizabeth and her fellow-tourists the Gardiners are being shown round this famous mansion, they are astonished and she is much embarrassed by the arrival of its owner, who pays them such pointed attentions that the Gardiners are inclined to suspect a more than ordinary intimacy between him and her. Is Darcy still in love? Elizabeth cannot help thinking so, and she feels her resistance melting away. But when a fresh proposal seems imminent from Darcy, all such ideas are turned to derision by the terrible news that her sister Lydia has eloped with Wickham. Obviously, Darcy's pride, however much he may be in love, will never stoop to an alliance with a family so disgraced. Elizabeth's distress, sharpened by remorse for her lack of prudence in not warning her family against Wickham, is further embittered by the sense that she could have loved Darcy now, "when all love must be vain."

The climax   But now comes the final act, with one surprise following fast upon another. Elizabeth's father and her excellent uncle Mr Gardiner are in quest of the runaways in London ; and before long news arrives that the pair have been traced, and that pressure has been put upon Wickham and the wherewithal provided to induce him to make Lydia an honest woman. Mr Gardiner is supposed to have done all this; but the giddy Lydia coming home un-abashed with her husband lets out that Darcy had been present at the wedding. What can it mean? Lizzie writes off at once to inquire of her aunt, and learns by return of post that the person who had taken the chief part in rescuing her sister was no other than Darcy. He pretended to have done it because he held himself responsible for the mischief done by Wickham. But was there not a more powerful motive? Elizabeth cannot be sure. The situation is still an enigma. It is not cleared up even by

Darcy's reappearance at Longbourn, along with his friend Bingley. And even when the latter renews his addresses to Jane, and is accepted, Elizabeth's gladness on her sister's account is not yet enhanced by any ray of hope for herself. Of course, the reader has recognized the sterling nature of Darcy's character long before this becomes manifest to Elizabeth, and standing on one side has marked the dramatic change that has taken place within him. It is the spectator that sees most of the game. But as yet both parties are tormented with doubts and hesitations. Neither can forget that Darcy had once been rejected contumeliously by Elizabeth. Only some happy accident can now break down the barriers and make plain speaking possible. The accident occurs. A visitor who came to intimidate chances to be the agent of Elizabeth's happiness. There is no more brilliant scene in fiction than the duel of wit and aristocratic insolence when Lady Catherine de Bourgh, in presuming to browbeat Elizabeth Bennet, manages to ensure the event which she is most anxious to avert. Darcy, who arrives shortly after, confesses that he had not allowed himself to hope till now. But till his arrival Elizabeth still did not permit herself to hope, and her father's ironical compliments on the receipt of a letter of remonstrance from Lady Catherine's toady, Mr Collins, while it hurts her to be reminded of her former abuse of Darcy, renews her misgivings :

Her father had most cruelly mortified her by what he said of Mr Darcy's indifference; and she could do nothing but wonder at such a want of penetration, or fear that, perhaps, instead of his seeing too *little*, she might have fancied too *much*.[1]

But the lovers meet, and it does not take long for two such intelligent and sensitive persons to make sure that pride and prejudice are at length beaten.

They have, however, not yet done with the irony that has *Pervasive* dogged them from the beginning. They still have to explain *irony* themselves to their sceptical friends and relations. The reader has learned to look out for irony in every twist of the story, and particularly in the speeches, many of which have had to be unsaid by the speakers, or wished unsaid, not least by Elizabeth. It

[1] Chap. lvii.

penetrates the whole structure of the novel. Observe how skilfully Wickham's rascality is made the chief agency in the reconciliation of Elizabeth and Darcy, providing a signal occasion for Darcy's magnanimity to transpire. Note how the pompous stupidity of Mr Collins's proposal to Elizabeth, the crowning example in fiction of pertinacious and unacceptable addresses, softens by contrast the infatuated assurance of Darcy's, which speedily follows. Jane Austen herself pauses to count the nails which Miss Bingley hammers into her own coffin when she teases Elizabeth, in Darcy's presence, about the departure of the officers, including Wickham, little aware of the pain she is inflicting by reminding him of Wickham's nearly successful attempt to run off with his sister Georgiana.[1] It is Darcy, his solemnity gone now that he is an accepted lover, who points out the irony of his aunt's intervention; " Lady Catherine has been of infinite use, which ought to make her happy, for she loves to be of use." [2] Elizabeth, with her formidable wit, can hold her own with anyone ; she can also be humorous about herself, as when she answers Jane's inquiry when did she first find out that she loved Darcy, " It has been coming on so gradually, that I hardly know when it began ; but "—and this is only half raillery—" I believe I must date it from my first seeing his beautiful grounds at Pemberley." It was not the grounds that were the grounds for the change, but she was right about the date.[3] Irony is the soul of Jane Austen's comedy ; the comic aspects of life are the ironical aspects, visible to good sense in its contemplation of erroneous judgments and bigoted or merely indolent persistence in error, of the contradiction between our desires and the good that we desire.[4] Mrs Gardiner was not far wrong about Darcy, who is a comic figure along with the rest of them, when she remarked,

---

[1] Chap. xlv.   [2] Chap. lx.
[3] It is odd to find Scott writing of Elizabeth : " The lady . . . refuses the hand which he ungraciously offers, and does not perceive that she has done a foolish thing until she accidentally visits a very handsome seat and grounds belonging to her admirer " (quoted by R. Brimley Johnson in *Famous Reviews*, 217—" Sir Walter Scott on Jane Austen ").
[4] Meredith said : " Those who detect irony in Comedy do so because they choose to see it in life " (*The Idea of Comedy*, 86). Meredith seems to narrow unduly the significance of irony, which he merely distinguishes from satire, as stinging someone " under a semi-caress, by which he shall in his anguish be rendered dubious whether indeed anything has hurt him " (*Ibid.*, 79).

" I fancy, Lizzie, that obstinacy is the real defect of his character, after all." [1]

It was Jane Austen's habit to leave didacticism, the practice *Discussions* of edification, to certain chosen characters. It was one of their *of manners* idiosyncrasies, sometimes a virtue, more often a vice. Elinor, *and morals* in the previous novel, was a little too prone to it; but no one could say the same of Henry Tilney, in *Northanger Abbey*, his correction of the innocent heroine being so gently done and so necessary for her redemption, which is the whole upshot of the comedy. One of the ironies of the present novel is that the persons most given to the moral instruction of their fellow-beings are the most absurd; they are Mr Collins and Lady Catherine de Bourgh. The only plausible excuse for the existence of such a character as Elizabeth's sister Mary, who anyhow was a missfire, is that she was meant as a sly poke at the heavy school of moralistic novelists. This young woman was always " deep in the study of thorough bass and human nature," and stupefies Elizabeth with her threadbare morality at the harrowing moment when there is every reason to fear the worst of Lydia's escapade with Wickham.

" This is a most unfortunate affair, and will probably be much talked of. But we must stem the tide of malice, and pour into the wounded bosoms of each other the balm of sisterly consolation." And she goes on :—" Loss of virtue in a female is irretrievable . . . one false step involves her in endless ruin . . . her reputation is no less brittle than it is beautiful." And more in the same strain.

Taken ironically, as she is intended, Mary does provide some amusement, and the satire was probably clear enough to con-temporary readers. In those days, moralization was a prevalent social infirmity. People were addicted to the public discussion of such questions as a certain class of novelist seemed to regard as the sole justification for writing about human nature. There are many such conversations in Jane Austen's novels; and in *Pride and Prejudice*, where they are usually provoked by the behaviour or some observation of Darcy, they are thoroughly in character. In nothing is that gentleman more Grandisonian than in his conscious pursuit of personal excellence; and it was

---

[1] Her letter to Elizabeth (chap. lii.).

natural for him to expound himself to Elizabeth, with whom he is in love long before he declares himself, before he is even fully aware of it.

" It has been the study of my life to avoid those weaknesses which often expose a strong understanding to ridicule."
" Such as vanity and pride."
" Yes, vanity is a weakness indeed. But pride—where there is a real superiority of mind—pride will always be under good regulation."
Elizabeth turned away to hide a smile.
" Your examination of Mr Darcy is over, I presume," said Miss Bingley; " and pray what is the result? "
" I am perfectly convinced by it that Mr Darcy has no defect. He owns it himself without disguise." [1]

Elizabeth's wit must not blind us to the fact that she is a little too hard on Darcy, as her creator meant her to be. Elizabeth Bennet also has almost as much pride in her as prejudice; and in both her and Darcy, Jane Austen can be seen between the lines championing the cause of honesty and self-respect at the risk of condoning pride. Though for a long while Elizabeth does not give Darcy a chance, she is usually both sane and fair-minded, and her attitude is a contrast to her father's indolent cynicism. Like other clear-sighted critics of the human scene, like Fielding for instance,[2] she had her fits of disillusionment. There is a passage in which she eloquently compares the angelic sweetness and disinterestedness of her sister Jane, cheerfully bearing up against the pain of Bingley's desertion, with her own instinctive distrust of the motives of others.

" *You* wish to think all the world respectable, and are hurt if I speak ill of anybody. *I* only want to think *you* perfect, and you set yourself against it. Do not be afraid of my running into any excess, of my encroaching on your privilege of universal goodwill. You need not. There are few people whom I really love, and still fewer of whom I think well. The more I see of the world, the more am I dissatisfied with it; and every day confirms my belief of the inconsistency of all human characters, and of the little dependence that can be placed on the appearance of either merit or sense." [3]

[1] Chap. xi.   [2] See Volume IV. 187.   [3] Chap. xxiv.

One feels intuitively that it is Miss Austen speaking for herself:
Elizabeth Bennet is so like her. Another trait, of a different
significance, comes out in the visit to Pemberley, where there are
many good paintings : "but Elizabeth knew nothing of the art,"
and was interested only in the portrait of Darcy and some efforts
by his sister.[1] Writing to Cassandra about a visit to the Liverpool
Museum and the British Gallery, Jane said : " I had some amusement at each, tho' my preference for Men and Women always
inclines me to attend more to the company than the sight." [2]

Darcy is at his worst for Elizabeth in his low opinion of the *The minor*
Longbourn people, the Bennets, the Lucas and Philips families; *characters*
not less so because he is manifestly right. Given his intellectual
and moral superiority, Darcy's struggle with himself was bound
to be acute, and he holds the reader's sympathies not less than
Elizabeth, at any rate on a second perusal of the book. Jane
Austen puts in one for herself in a speech that must be credited
to Elizabeth, though who was the speaker is left to the reader's
intelligence. The talk is about those intricate characters who
are " the *most* amusing "; and Darcy observes, " The country can
in general supply but few subjects for such a study. In a country
neighbourhood you move in a very confined and unvarying
society." This irritates Mrs Bennet, who is entirely incapable
of understanding him. " I assure you there is quite as much of
that going on in the country as in town," she foolishly remarks.
It must be Elizabeth Bennet who corrects Darcy's generalization,
" But people themselves alter so much, that there is something
new to be observed in them for ever." Else Jane Austen's novels
would never have been written. For it is not only the protagonists
that engross interest, the minor characters are as perfectly studied,
in their due perspective. Leaving Mr Collins and Lady Catherine
out of account, not as extraneous, however, for together they
provide a magnificent comic pendant to the more intense drama
of Elizabeth and Darcy, look at the others. The Bennets are a
comedy in themselves, and Mary is a failure only because she
remains an unfinished sketch. But the two elder sisters, so finely
contrasted, and the pair of hoydens, the empty-headed, flirting
Lydia, and Kitty who so narrowly escapes the same fate; and

[1] Chap. xliii.   [2] Chapman, ii. 267.

their friends, the over-genial, babbling Sir William Lucas, so uplifted with his knighthood; his womenfolk, and the officers from Meryton; every one is individualized with masterly precision.[1] With such figures may be coupled that amiable, colourless young fellow Bingley, and his insincere sister, and the easy-going scamp Wickham, whose worst faults are left unprobed. Mrs Bennet is a comic production of high order. Silly, incredibly ignorant, and irresponsible, she was a dreadful infliction for those who were in any way dependent upon her. She alone would justify all Darcy's strictures upon the Bennet family, and what a thorn in the flesh she must have been to Elizabeth! Yet she is never made an object of satire. On the contrary, it is an exquisitely kind touch on Jane Austen's part when her namesake, who has regained the laggard Bingley, will not lose a moment before consoling her mother with the glad news. Elizabeth, with less tenderness if equal affection, thinks first of her father, when Darcy's suit is in question, and the interview is one to be read with mixed feelings. In drawing the hare-brained, vulgar, incontinent Lydia, Jane seems at times to be trembling on the verge of some personal resentment. Regarded less indulgently, Lydia would be a terrible example of moral and mental recklessness, and can be made to point the lesson which it is easy to draw from this history, that education, discipline, and self-control are all-important, and that parental Laodiceanism bears pernicious fruits. Her father and mother are another Mr and Mrs Shandy. He has cultivated impassivity as an antidote to his wife's shallow effusiveness, and the attitude has set. Lizzie, the only member of the family who inherits his sense of humour, comprehends him; to his wife he is as inscrutable as Mr Shandy was to his better half.[2] Sterne was one of the classic authors whom Jane Austen knew well enough to quote from.

Jane Austen was not a pedagogic novelist like Maria Edgeworth; she did not make it her business to preach a doctrine or

---

[1] "She stands alone in that Shakesperian gift and practice of being always true to nature, to the nature of each and every personage of her creation, clever or stupid, agreeable or disagreeable " (W. H. Pollock, *op. cit.*, 30).

[2] "Mr Bennet was so odd a mixture of quick parts, sarcastic humour, reserve, and caprice, that the experience of three-and-twenty years had been insufficient to make his wife understand his character " (chap. i.).

illustrate some moral theorem by devising a conclusive chain of *Her irony* events. She saw herself, rather, as a critical observer, an inter- *and her* preter of what actually goes on; and she adopted the comic *idealism* view as the most illuminating as well as the one that appealed to her humour. But there are passages in which she summarizes the history enacted, or in which one of her more thoughtful characters formulates his reflections; and what she made of it all is perfectly clear. The idea which detaches itself from almost every novel, giving the story point and coherence, is that life is a process of education. Experience such as Elinor's and Marianne's teaches how to live wisely and temperately, and therefore well, and therefore, too, happily. Happiness comes of internal harmony and harmony with the rest of the world. She was a religious woman; but except as a personal quality, reverence, and as a moral sanction, religion is not an active element in the life she portrayed. It is not recorded that Wordsworth and Coleridge were among the poets she read. She was no transcendentalist, but keenly interested in every phase of the life going on around her. The value she set upon a fine personality was no doubt intuitive. Human beings have their duty to others, to society, but especially to themselves. It is through their manner of fulfilling their duties that they show what they are, and what they are is the important matter. In this profound sense of the value of personality she forestalls philosophies of life that more recent novelists and others have thought out more rigorously. *Pride and Prejudice* also is an educational novel; but more specifically than its predecessor is it concerned with the problem of achieving a perfect marriage, chief among the personal relations in which the individual asserts and at the same time develops personality. Her irony was far removed from either cynicism or satire; it was conformable with what the average respectable citizen would regard as pure idealism. Jane Austen was, in fact, as good an idealist as her romantic fellow-novelists, or a better. But she was a practical idealist. Her lucid scheme of order and a personal life worth living was one that could be carried out. Everyone has commented on this preoccupation of hers with the subject of love and marriage, and the importance that she ascribes to suitable mating among the supreme things in this earthly existence. She never married; how realize a union that would have come up to her idea? But she thought about loving and marrying as intensely as the sentimental enthusiasts whom she laughed at. Her conception of a genuine union was a loftier one than theirs. They either romanticized love, glorifying it with ecstatic emotionalism, or like Fanny Burney sedately followed the match-making tradition to the conventional goal, a handsome husband, satisfactory marriage settlements, and a happy and elegant home. They were not even serious enough to regard marriage as a serious vocation for women. The conclusions of Jane Austen's novels are always the achievement of self-knowledge, self-control, and self-respect, and a principal means of such an achievement is a league of perfect sympathy with another who is one's spiritual counterpart. She had the felicity of such a fusion of herself with her sister Cassandra; but her Elizabeth was able to improve upon sisterly affection and unanimity, beautiful as that was. A perfect marriage, in short, is fundamentally a perfect friendship. It is the theme which, conceived transcendentally, was to inspire the Brontës to more poetic flights, in verse and in romantic fiction. Maria Edgeworth would have subscribed to it in theory, but in practice she did not refine much upon the conventional endings of the generality of novelists.

"*North-anger Abbey*" In its origin, *Northanger Abbey* (1818), which Jane left ready for the press, with a preface written in 1816, to be published with *Persuasion* after her death, dates back to the time of *Love and Freindship*, and is another scoff at the romanticists, especially Mrs Radcliffe. In its first form it was written in 1797-1798, and in 1803 the manuscript, with the title *Susan*, was sold for ten pounds to a publisher in London, who failed to bring it out, but allowed Jane's brother to have it back for the same money in 1816. By that time she thought the satire out of date, and wrote an apologetic advertisement, explaining that many things had happened in these thirteen years and that parts of the novel were "comparatively obsolete." When it was first written, Mrs Radcliffe was at the height of her vogue; *The Mysteries of Udolpho* had appeared in 1794 and *The Italian* came out in 1797. It is the former which is closely parodied in certain chapters; though, as in *Sense and Sensibility*, the reader of romances rather than the writer is made a laughing-stock. Possibly, the cautious publisher held up the book out of fear of affronting the thousands of readers who idolized Mrs Radcliffe; he may even have been loath to hurt that amiable lady's feelings. But Jane probably exaggerated the extent to which Mrs Radcliffe had been forgotten in 1816; for it was only three years ago that Barrett had published *The Heroine*,[1] a pleasantry which she read with enjoyment, and only six since Sarah Green's *Romance Readers and Romance Writers*, not to mention the lines in *The Borough* where Crabbe alludes to his own early addiction to such literary dram-drinking:

> And to the heroine's soul-distracting fears
> I early gave my sixpences and tears.

Internal evidence would argue this to have been the least *Early* altered of the three revised novels. There are marks of the *work not* inexperienced writer in the free and easy, girlish burlesque, *much* troubling little about verisimilitude; in the working out of the *altered* initial situation, the romantic young lady prepared to adopt any delusion at the bidding of Mrs Radcliffe; in the impossible General Tilney, a crude sort of Mr Delvile, or " Don Pedigree," whom she takes for another Montoni, and the son who is only amused and takes no offence at the supposition that his father was guilty of putting his mother out of the way. Jane forgot to give anything in the shape of a character to her heroine's brother, James Morland, whilst John Thorpe, with his horse and gig, is only excellent farce. All this must indeed be read as farce, and then can be gratefully accepted: the hulking young Oxford man, who " seemed fearful of being too handsome unless he wore the dress of a groom, and too much like a gentleman unless he were easy where he ought to be civil, and impudent where he might be allowed to be easy," who drives " with all the vehemence that could most fitly endanger the lives of himself, his companion, and his horse," is first-rate caricature; though there is an unexaggerated touch of nature in John's sheepish love-making.

[1] See Volume V. 227. The opening passage of *Northanger Abbey* ironically describing Catherine Morland as destined to be a heroine sounds almost like an echo of Barrett. It is possible, though somewhat unlikely, that this was one of the parts touched up in 1816.

" Did you ever hear the old song, ' Going to one wedding brings on another ' ? I say, you will come to Belle's wedding, I hope."

" Yes, I have promised your sister to be with her, if possible."

" And then, you know "—twisting himself about, and forcing a foolish laugh—" I say, then you know, we may try the truth of this same old song." [1]

Captain Tilney, again, whose sole function is to make Isabella Thorpe think him head over ears in love and jilt James Morland, must be counted among the stage figures that speak their part and then are done with.

The irony, too, is of an elementary cast; and, very different from Jane's later subtlety, it is carefully underlined.   John Thorpe's critique of Fanny Burney will do for another instance :

" I suppose you mean *Camilla* ? "

" Yes, that's the book; such unnatural stuff !—An old man playing at see-saw; I took up the first volume once, and looked it over, but I soon found it would not do; indeed, I guessed what sort of stuff it must be before I saw it; as soon as I heard she had married an emigrant, I was sure I should never be able to get through it."

" I have never read it."

" You had no loss, I assure you; it is the horridest nonsense you can imagine; there is nothing in the world in it but an old man's playing at see-saw and learning Latin; upon my soul, there is not." [2]

Or take Catherine's meditations in the ball-room when neither Tilney nor John make an appearance and she is left without a partner : " To be disgraced in the eye of the world, to wear the appearance of infamy while her heart is all purity, her actions all innocence, and the misconduct of another the true source of her debasement, is one of those circumstances which peculiarly belong to the heroine's life, and her fortitude under it what particularly dignifies her character." [3]   This should be compared with Henry Tilney's remark when Catherine is disgusted with the fickle Isabella's letter : " Your mind is warped by an innate principle of general integrity, and therefore inaccessible to the

[1] Chap. xv.   [2] Chap. vii.   [3] Chap. viii.

cool reasonings of family partiality, or a desire of revenge," [1] or with that letter itself, which gives the writer away so completely. It is among the best by a past master of this insidious art of self-betrayal. Could it have been penned in 1797 or 1798, or was it not rather one of the strokes by an older hand put in about 1803 or, still more likely, 1816? It is surely not the new-fledged humour of *Love and Freindship*.

The view commonly accepted that Jane started to write a skit, *The mock-heroine turns into an Evelina* and then fell in love with her heroine and could not help expanding the skit into a novel, is better founded than the legend of Fielding's similar change of purpose in writing *Joseph Andrews*.[2] She was apparently in two minds about Catherine. This innocent, impulsive girl, with her ingenuous faith in the romantic version of life, would make a very good mock-heroine, in the style of Mrs Lennox's Arabella or Jane's own Marianne. But the shocks and misadventures the bashful maiden would have to face in her premature introduction to society would naturally tend to a story like *Evelina*. The burlesque of *Udolpho* was clearly part of the original design; but the culminating episode, Catherine's stay at the abbey and her wild idea that the tyrannical general, like the marquess in Mrs Radcliffe's novel, had murdered his wife or that his victim was languishing in some obscure dungeon, had to be deferred till all the preparations were complete. This, and the curing of her infatuation by the sage and mildly caustic Henry Tilney, though they are the main points of the satire, do not come in therefore till near the end. Thus Catherine enters upon the scene as another Evelina, a still more delicate sketch of shy, developing girlhood; and the incidents of her bashful debut are similar with characteristic differences. The scene at the Upper Rooms calls up Evelina's rude experiences at her first ball; and the embarrassing intimacy into which Catherine is thrown with John and Isabella Thorpe, two different types of vulgarians, is a variation of the Branghton episodes. The gushing Isabella with her eye for the main chance would have been an unexceptionable member of that family. Henry Tilney is a much more lifelike being than the stilted Lord Orville; in fact, all this outshines Fanny Burney in truth and insight. There is an obvious

[1] Chap. xxvii.   [2] See Volume IV. 88.

resemblance also between the two stories in the course of education and initiation into the rude realities of life; and, although Catherine Morland is not her own historian, she serves her creator's purpose in much the same way as Evelina, as an eager observer. Fanny Burney was much in Jane Austen's mind when *Northanger Abbey* was being written, as many allusions show besides those quoted.[1]

"The Watsons"   From the time when the Austens left Steventon in 1801 to some eighteen months after they settled down at Chawton in 1809, Jane seems to have written nothing, except perhaps to revise some of her early work and certainly to begin a novel, now known as *The Watsons*, which she never finished. This was in 1804 or 1805, when the Austens were at Bath. There is nothing to wonder at in her silence. *First Impressions* had been rejected, and *Susan* remained unpublished. What was the use of writing? This fragment of a novel, the very title of which had to be supplied by Austen Leigh, her biographer, was published with *Lady Susan* and another unfinished story as a supplement to the *Memoir* (1871). In length it amounts to four or five chapters of such a work as *Mansfield Park*. Jane is said to have abandoned it because she had " placed her heroine too low," though it was not in a humbler position than that of Fanny Price, the poor cousin adopted by the Bertrams. Perhaps the story came too near home, her heroine, Emma Watson—note that she did not waste the name " Emma "—being one of a family of sisters in monetary circumstances much like those of the Austens after the death of their father, in January 1805. At all events, it could not have been thrown up out of mere dissatisfaction. The opening pages show Emma on her way to her first ball. The Watson sisters will have to marry or put up with privations. Hence some poignancy in the chat with the older sister who is driving her, on the odiousness of marrying without love.

"To be so bent on marriage—to pursue a man merely for the sake of situation, is a sort of thing that shocks me; I cannot

[1] The seven obscure sensation-novels recommended to Catherine by Isabella Thorpe, in chapter vi., as agreeably horrid have all been identified by Mr Michael Sadleir (*The Northanger Novels : a Footnote to Jane Austen*, 1927) ; and though a bibliographer, he appears to have read them. It is not known whether Miss Austen performed that feat. They all appeared from 1793 to 1798.

understand it. Poverty is a great evil; but to a woman of education and feeling it ought not, it cannot be the greatest. I would rather be teacher at a school (and I can think of nothing worse), than marry a man I did not like."

" I would rather do anything than be teacher at a school," said her sister. " *I* have been at school, Emma, and know what a life they lead; *you* never have. I should not like marrying a disagreeable man any more than yourself; but I do not think there *are* many very disagreeable men; I think I could like any good-humoured man with a comfortable income."

This older sister is an honest and sound-hearted woman, who can still think kindly of her other sister, Penelope, who ruined her own chances of happy wedlock. Emma has unexpected success at the ball, although her party are cold-shouldered by the stylish Osbornes and their friends. But the good-natured girl chances to attract attention without in the least intending it by going to the rescue of a little boy, who had been disappointed of a dance with Miss Osborne. Her good looks do the rest. Lord Osborne's own chaplain and tutor, the worthy Mr Howard, solicits a dance, and also Tom Musgrave, whom she had been warned against as a dangerous flirt. His lordship wants to follow suit. It is something like the opening of *Pride and Prejudice*; though Emma was not intended to marry the great man. She was to refuse Lord Osborne and accept Mr Howard. For the plot was confided to Cassandra, who after Jane's death used to read the fragment to her nieces and tell them how it was to have ended. A sister-in-law of Emma's who comes on the scene before the story breaks off might have been a preliminary study for the ill-bred Mrs Elton, in *Emma*. The small talk is excellent, though without the pungency of riper days. Otherwise, the style is not much more than simple reporting; but, it must be remembered, this was only a first draft.

CHAPTER V

MANSFIELD PARK, EMMA AND PERSUASION

"Mans-field Park": a change of tone

AFTER the years of silence, a change of mood seems to have come over Jane Austen; she writes in a sadder or at any rate a graver frame of mind. There is as much difference between the sobriety of tone that sets in with *Mansfield Park* and the sprightliness of *Pride and Prejudice* as between *Sense and Sensibility* and the careless levity of the trifles that amused her sister at Steventon. *Mansfield Park* is the one among her novels which can be very closely compared with the didactic fiction of Miss Edgeworth; the practical lesson is not entirely resolved into comedy. But the two ensuing novels are not less serious in their general drift, although they do not slip so often into explicit moralization. Jane Austen was nearing the forties when she commenced *Mansfield Park* in 1811; she was not only older but she had had personal sorrows, in the loss of her father and of others among her relations or friends. Some have thought that she must have been touched by the wave of evangelicalism that swept over England in those years, carrying away such writers as Hannah More and Sarah Brunton. It is certainly curious that in *Mansfield Park* she singles out for the honour of "my Fanny's" hand a young man one of whose chief claims to the suffrages of readers is that he has a proper sense of the responsibilities of a clergyman and a firm resolve to live up to them. Some sarcasm at the expense of a more phlegmatic dignitary suggests that he was meant as a foil to this worthy young candidate for holy orders.[1] Jane had not always paid such respect to the cloth. Mr Collins was a caricature, and was not meant to be taken as a fair specimen of his profession; but she did not do it any credit by making her most ludicrous character a clergyman. The most respectable

---

[1] Dr Grant, " through an interest on which he had almost ceased to form hopes," leaves Mansfield for a stall at Westminster, and brings on apoplexy and death by three great institutionary dinners in one week (last chapter).

people in her earlier novels regard a living as simply a living, a welcome resource for those without independent means, the assurance of a house and income and some moderate social advantages, perhaps with other amenities if the parish was in a sporting county. But as to the duties and responsibilities involved in the care of souls, Edmund Bertram is the first person who takes them very seriously. This is but one instance of a new earnestness and gravity that did not, however, affect her art, except in betraying her into sundry passages of undisguised edification, and inclining her to be unfair to such a kind-hearted worldling as Mary Crawford, to the detriment of sound character-drawing. But, although she allowed the desire to point a moral to warp her judgment, and took upon her to condemn instead of being content to understand and interpret, her insight was as clear as ever, for Mary lives and charms in spite of her creator's bias. It was an odd coincidence that *Mansfield Park* and Maria Edgeworth's *Patronage* appeared the same year (1814); both are family histories, though the formal comparison between the Percys and the Falconers is not on all fours with Jane Austen's unemphatic contrast of the Bertrams and Prices or the Bertrams and Crawfords; and amateur theatricals form a large episode in each case.[1] The play is merely a prominent incident in Miss Edgeworth's story; in Jane Austen's it is a chief act in the comedy, it is catastrophic in its immediate and its ultimate effects. Like the ball or the Pemberley scene in *Pride and Prejudice*, or the Box-Hill picnic in *Emma*, it is the episode that stands out in our recollections of *Mansfield Park*. For she deliberately made it the occasion for bringing the contradictions of character and the strife of motives to a crisis.

Sensibility is not an object of satire in *Mansfield Park*; on the contrary, spontaneous good feeling is rewarded in Fanny Price, a heroine, like one of Maria Edgeworth's good little girls, who, if not too spotless, too unselfish, is so self-effacing as almost to sink her own personality, and have nothing to show for herself but an obstinate resistance to the wiles of the frivolous. Sometimes, in involuntary revulsion, the reader will prefer the worldly,

Sensibility sympathetically treated

[1] See the elaborate comparison of their different handling of the play business, much to the disadvantage of Miss Edgeworth, by W. H. Pollock (*op. cit.*, 60-79 —two chapters).

flippant, but humorous and not cold-hearted Mary Crawford, though the author clearly did not mean this to happen. But that is unfair; Fanny is really the only one among the contemporary faultless heroines who is a living creature, and the only one that never or very seldom irritates with her perfections. Henry Crawford thinks that even his uncle the Admiral, who hates marriage, and thinks " it never pardonable in a young man of independent fortune," will dote on Fanny : " She is exactly such a woman as he thinks does not exist in the world. She is the very impossibility he would describe," if he had to show how impossible it was to provide a reasonable man with a tolerable mate. Feeling in Fanny has its opposites in the meanness and privy spite of Mrs Norris and the indifference of Mary Crawford. She is put in the centre of the picture; it is mainly through the effect upon her sensibility that the drama of the Bertrams is interpreted; she is very wide-awake, " Her eye was busy taking in everything within her reach "[1]; and the final events that convulse the placid existence at Mansfield Park serve to bring out her virtues more clearly. It is noticeable that Fanny's responsiveness to natural beauty is treated very differently from Marianne Dashwood's transports. But it must not be overlooked that in the passage where she gives way to her enthusiasm, looking out on " the brilliance of an unclouded night, and the contrast of the deep shade of the woods," the undercurrent of irony is of chief dramatic import. Fanny is standing at the window with Edmund, whom she has seen gazing after Mary Crawford " in an ecstasy of admiration "; the three have been discussing, not without heat, the reasons why he should or should not take orders; and Fanny dreads that the man she loves, who is visibly in love with Mary, may give way to that young lady's remonstrances and throw up his good intentions. In the drawing-room behind are gathered

---

[1] Chap. viii. She keeps a very close watch upon the behaviour of the Bertram sisters and Henry Crawford, and reports her apprehensions to Edmund : " Fanny was the only one of the party who found anything to dislike ; but since the day at Sotherton, she could never see Mr Crawford with either sister without observation, and seldom without wonder or censure ; and had her confidence in her own judgment been equal to her exercise of it in every other respect, had she been sure that she was seeing clearly, and judging candidly, she would probably have made some communications to her usual confidant. As it was, however, she only hazarded a hint, and the hint was lost " (chap. xii.).

the rest of the Mansfield company; tension is at its height between Maria, engaged to the intolerable Rushworth, and her sister Julia, both of them madly enamoured of Crawford. Sir Thomas Bertram is still away, and anything may happen with only the apathetic Lady Bertram and the mischievous Mrs Norris to exercise restraint. There is a bitter pang in Fanny's reflections.

Fanny spoke her feelings. " Here's harmony ! " said she; " here's repose ! Here's what may leave all painting and all music behind, and what poetry only can attempt to describe ! Here's what may tranquillize every care, and lift every heart to rapture ! When I look out on such a night as this, I feel as if there could be neither wickedness nor sorrow in the world; and there certainly would be less of both if the sublimity of nature were more attended to, and people were carried more out of themselves by contemplating such a scene." [1]

And then, after a few lukewarm words of sympathy, Edmund turns his back to the window, and moves forward by gentle degrees towards the pianoforte to listen to Mary Crawford's singing.

The lesson intended is the supreme importance of principles *The moral* in the education of children. Sir Thomas Bertram is a model of *in the* integrity and decorum, but lacking in vision; he stands too much *irony* aloof from his children; they do not appreciate his deep affection, he does not enjoy their confidence. Their mother is wrapped up in her ailments and her lapdog; their Aunt Norris indulges them for her own selfish ends. Brought up in luxury and idleness, with nothing to show for their education but a few empty accomplishments, the two daughters fight tooth and nail for the attentions of the debonair but shallow Henry Crawford. The older one, engaged to her rich booby and thoroughly tired of him, marries him out of pique, and then elopes with Crawford; the younger, to show that she too is a woman of spirit, runs off with a gay young spark whom her father disapproves. The comedy of intrigue is complicated with other entanglements. Crawford flirts with Fanny to pass the time, and falls seriously in love when he discovers that she is not an easy conquest but a woman who has to be won. Fanny all the while is silently in love with Edmund,

[1] Chap. xi.

the one sterling character among the Bertrams. But Edmund has been fascinated by Mary Crawford, and confides to his cousin Fanny all his hopes and fears; whilst Mary, on her part, candidly debates with Fanny whether she can possibly wean herself from the gaieties of life and become a clergyman's helpmate after Edmund's austere pattern. This is a more lacerating irony than the comic situations in the earlier novels, with the single exception of Elinor's ordeal when her lover is claimed by Lucy Steele. But this time irony becomes an instrument of edification. Its amplitude may be measured by a comparison of Sir Thomas Bertram's indignant lecture when his little niece, whom he had taken from a shabby home and brought up amid the splendours of Mansfield Park, has what he thinks the perversity to reject the rich Mr Crawford, with his complete change of mind at the end, when he is overjoyed to accept her for his own son.

Sick of ambitious and mercenary connexions, prizing more and more the sterling good of principle and temper, and chiefly anxious to bind by the strongest securities all that remained to him of domestic felicity, he had pondered with genuine satisfaction on the more than possibility of the two young friends finding their mutual consolation in each other for all that had occurred of disappointment to either; and the joyful consent which met Edmund's application, the high sense of having realized a great acquisition in the promise of Fanny for a daughter, formed just such a contrast with his early opinion on the subject, when the poor little girl's coming had been first agitated, as time is for ever producing between the plans and decisions of mortals, for their own instruction and their neighbours' entertainment.[1]

Such careful annotation of the whole drift of the story is a little heavy for Jane Austen; she did not so italicize the unconscious irony in that previous lecture when Sir Thomas could not speak too highly of Mr Crawford's merits, or when he reminded Fanny that his daughter Maria " is nobly married," the daughter whom he was a little later to cast out for having succumbed to Crawford's profligacy.[2]

The Crawfords, like Jane Fairfax and Frank Churchill in the next novel, may be described as supernumeraries, not leading

---

[1] Last chapter.   [2] Chap. xxxii.

characters nor yet minors; their rôle is to be an element of dis- *The rôle* turbance, the one pair creating discord in the family relations of *of the* the Bertrams, the others between them further misleading Emma, *Crawford* who is so ready to fall into delusions. Both pairs are interesting *pair* up to a point, and superficially very pleasing; but their characters are not deeply studied, hence the diverse effects which they make upon different readers. The Crawfords are types of the worldly, who take things as they find them; they are the antipodes of people like Fanny and Edmund whose characteristic is earnestness. They are fond of each other, and share each other's confidences; and their talk about their own affairs and those of the others illuminates the comedy and contributes a vivacity of its own. But they both put some strain on credibility, because they are one thing now and something a little different later. Henry Crawford, who has, almost deliberately, set the two Bertram sisters by the ears through his persistent flirtations with both, taxes credulity when he persuades himself and Mary that he is seriously in love with Fanny, and in love because of her principles. " Henry Crawford had too much sense not to feel the worth of good principles in a wife, though he was too little accustomed to serious reflection to know them by their proper name." He cannot persuade Fanny that he is genuinely in love; she has seen through him too well. And Jane Austen taxes credulity still more when she asserts in the last chapter that they would ultimately have made a match of it, if Mary had married Edmund, and Henry had persevered. Imagine what *Mansfield Park* would have been if she had declared for such a conclusion! To have made it credible, she would have had to recast Henry Crawford. As she has left him, he is not a totally coherent person; he has not been thoroughly thought out, and remains but a charming sketch. Admit that his falling in love with Fanny is true, what is there to be said for his elopement with Maria, shortly after he had been down to Portsmouth to see Fanny, while in fact Fanny was still there? Nor is Mary Crawford any more consistent; her character too is but perfunctorily analysed, and she says and does some incredible things. She is worldly, and far from dis-interested; but if she had been cynical enough to harbour the thought, she would never have written to one whom she knew to be so honest and warm-hearted as Fanny that she would not be sorry if Tom Bertram died and the property and title came to Edmund, whom she would then be willing to marry. But Mary, for the sake of the moral, had to be convicted of having a vitiated mind; she had to stagger and disillusion Edmund by seeing nothing worse than folly in the sad business of her brother's elopement with Mrs Rushworth. She had to be another illustration of the evil of no principles, and exhibit " a mind led astray and bewildered, and without any suspicion of being so; darkened, yet fancying itself light."[1] Jane Austen was rather hard upon two characters who by their technical services in the plot were invaluable; she accepted the services without paying in the regular coin of sound characterization. Edmund advising Fanny to marry Crawford! Crawford's proposal which opens the eyes not only of Sir Thomas but even of jealous and malevolent Aunt Norris to Fanny's real worth! Such comic effects could never have been secured without the help of the Crawfords. It is a pity that their artistic integrity should be open to question.

The play   The play, *Lovers' Vows*, the rehearsal of which produces scenes more dramatic than any designed by its author, has been the topic of much discussion. Why is there so much fuss about the propriety of acting it in a private house? The objection was partly to any sort of theatrical performance whilst the head of the house, Sir Thomas, was far away, and perchance ill or in peril; but a more peremptory objection was the nature of the play chosen for performance by a number of susceptible young people. *Lovers' Vows* was an adaptation by Mrs Inchbald of an ultra-sentimental German melodrama, " the eldest child of Kotzebue," as Cobbett termed it, which would have suited a troupe of Bohemian strollers but was very unfit for family consumption. Its gush and false morality put Fanny out of countenance when she only had to read Miss Crawford's part with Edmund, and she hates to have to watch these two acting in it together. Jane Austen's own opinion is evidently expressed in the reflections of Tom Bertram when he is recovering from his dangerous illness. He reproaches himself for what he had done or left undone to bring down upon them " the deplorable event in

[1] Chap. xlvii.

Wimpole Street," his sister's misconduct, and "felt himself accessary by all the dangerous intimacy of his unjustifiable theatre."[1] It was the dangerous intimacy fostered among a set of giddy young folk of both sexes by an emotional play of dubious morality that was the evil.[2]

Mansfield Park is a complicated story; at least six distinct lines of interest are interwoven without ever growing confused.[3] The constructive skill is first-rate, and is strictly based on a firm grasp of character and its far-reaching effects. In thorough craftsmanship none of the novels stands higher. The opening chapters show Jane Austen in full tide of accomplishment; and although the level of style, in both diction and narration, is not always kept to the same high mark, there is no conspicuous ebb. The subordinate characters are as adequately drawn in their degree as the foremost; and there is one comic figure that can be put beside Mr Collins himself, and has the advantage of being not in the least a caricature. Sir Thomas was too forbearing when he classed Mrs Norris as "one of those well-meaning people who are always doing mistaken and very disagreeable things"; she is naturally selfish and spiteful, though she may have persuaded herself that she was at least well-meaning. Having obstinately kept a blind eye to what was going on, Mrs Norris cannot be acquitted of a share in the disastrous sequel. But she has furnished never-failing amusement for the spectator; and Jane Austen dismisses her at the end as contemptuously as she had Mrs Ferrars and Lady Catherine. After all, true poetic justice has put her to shame and held her up to ridicule at every appearance.

Workmanship and style

[1] Chap. xlviii.

[2] A full account of the play is given by W. Reitzel (*Rev. of Eng. Studies*, ix., October 1933).

[3] Taking merely the love affairs and rivalries in the comedy of intrigue, we have : (1) Fanny in love from the first with Edmund Bertram, who is in love with Mary Crawford until her lack of principle disgusts him ; (2) Maria Bertram engaged and then married to Rushworth, then running off with Crawford, whom she always preferred ; (3) Julia Bertram, similarly disappointed of Crawford, eloping with Yates ; (4) Mary Crawford, setting her cap at Edmund, but unwilling to marry a clergyman ; (5) Henry Crawford, flirts with Maria and Julia, makes first insincere and then earnest love to Fanny, bolts with Maria, now Mrs Rushworth ; (6) Edmund Bertram, in love with Mary Crawford, makes Fanny his confidant, unaware that she is in love with him all the time. This is only a mechanical analysis of the relations between the characters on this particular side ; but there are other characters and other interests, and a very different analysis could be made from another point of view.

"Emma"   Jane Austen's next novel, *Emma* (1816), the last to appear in her lifetime, although it is comedy from end to end and never even skirts tragedy, is at bottom not less serious than *Mansfield Park*. A moral, nay, a whole sheaf of morals, may be drawn from the history of Emma's mistakes, as they may from any comedy that holds an undistorting mirror up to nature. But, as Meredith said of *The Misanthrope*, the moral is in the heart of the work, " throbbing with every pulsation of an organic structure," [1] much more than in Emma's painful reflections or in Knightley's lectures, in which it becomes explicit, without however trespassing against artistic propriety, falling so naturally as it does from the mouth of this anxious observer of her vagaries. In no other novel did Jane make a nearer approach to the thoughtful comedy of Molière, though it is the woman, not the man, who, as usual in her novels, convicts herself of folly and submits to the lash.[2] " Philosopher and Comic poet are of a cousinship in the eye they cast on life." [3] Here, as always in her work, the moral, or rather the philosophy, is not ethical in the stricter sense ; it has to do with manners more than with morals. It is the idea of a decorum above mere ethics, of values finer than any categorical precepts. It is Knightley's philosophy of life ; it is also Emma's. But she has to work out its implications, and by a course of trying experiences learn to apply them intelligently.

Simplex plot   *Mansfield Park* was a good deal more than the story of Fanny Price ; but here everything is subsidiary to the probation of Emma Woodhouse, and the course of the story is in comparison rectilinear. A young woman of great social talents, who " sets up for understanding," as heiress of Hartfield looked up to as leader in the society of Highbury, she thinks herself competent for the part of amateur Providence, charged with the destinies of her less far-seeing neighbours, whom she is prepared to couple off according to her views of matrimonial suitability. She falls into one delusion after another. But it is not a mere succession of scrapes from which she extricates herself in turn ; the embarrassments due to the first, and the second, and then the third blunder

---

[1] Meredith, *op. cit.*, 34.
[2] " The higher the Comedy, the more prominent the part they [women] enjoy in it " (*Ibid.*, 28).
[3] *Ibid.*, 30.

continue and complicate each other, till she finds herself in a position that threatens her own best chance of happiness. Out of sheer snobbishness, she separates Harriet Smith, the girl of questionable origin whom she has taken up, from the sweetheart who would have been an admirable match; and then she schemes to pair her off with this person, and then with that, all entirely above her station, until Harriet becomes a source of vexation, then of remorse for her disappointments, and finally of the liveliest apprehension to Emma herself. She persuades Harriet that the vicar, Mr Elton, is in love with her; and her manœuvres being misinterpreted lead not unnaturally to a most unwelcome proposal to herself from that presuming gentleman. Emma feels the deep humiliation of this, and Mr Elton's resentment causes further unpleasantness, constantly thrown together as they are in the small social circle of Highbury. Worse still, Mr Elton, furious at the rebuff, and burning to show that he is not an unacceptable person, rushes off to Bath, and soon comes back with a showy, underbred wife, who has the temerity to challenge Emma's precedence at Highbury and becomes another source of irritation. But now a fresh possibility for the wounded Harriet appears, in Frank Churchill, the stepson of Emma's old governess and dearest friend, Mrs Weston. This good-looking young fellow makes some impression even upon herself, and his father would be only too glad to encourage such a union. But Frank Churchill has other designs. He is secretly engaged to Jane Fairfax, who stays occasionally with friends in the village, a young lady whom the imaginative Emma, on the slenderest evidence, suspects of having been the unhappy object of a love affair with a married man. She is foolish enough to impart her suspicions to Frank Churchill, who flirts with her, as a blind to his engagement, and fools her to the top of her bent. But though Emma likes him, she magnanimously resolves to stand aside for the sake of Harriet, who shows signs of having transferred her affections from Mr Elton to Frank. And then, to her consternation, Harriet informs her that she is not in love with Frank Churchill at all, but with the incomparable Mr Knightley, and has reason to believe her sentiments returned. Irony upon irony, and now the unkindest cut of all! The truth is borne in upon her.

Why was it so much worse that Harriet should be in love with Mr Knightley than with Frank Churchill? Why was the evil so dreadfully increased by Harriet's having some hope of a return? It darted through her with the speed of an arrow, that Mr Knightley must marry no one but herself![1]

The scenes that follow are admirably dramatic and admirably terse, for Jane Austen could render the intensity of an avowal between such lovers as Darcy and Elizabeth Bennet or Emma and Knightley without any effusion of sentiment. Emma has been duly chastened; and the innate goodness and candour, and the consciousness of her imperfections which accepts rebuke so willingly from the one whom she has regarded almost as an elder brother, are enhanced when she awakens to the deceptions she has been practising on herself and to the fear that she has perhaps lost the man whom she now finds she loves far more than a brother.

With insufferable vanity had she believed herself in the secret of everybody's feelings; with unpardonable arrogance proposed to arrange everybody's destiny. She was proved to have been universally mistaken; and she had not quite done nothing—for she had done mischief. She had brought evil on Harriet, on herself, and, she too much feared, on Mr Knightley. Were this most unequal of all connexions to take place, on her must rest all the reproach of having given it a beginning; for his attachment she must believe to be produced only by a consciousness of Harriet's;—and even were this not the case, he would never have known Harriet at all but for her folly.[2]

Character-istic irony This short recapitulation has been sufficient to bring out the irony of the successive situations in which Emma's blindness has involved her, irony that does not relax to the very instant of the final explanation, for she still dreads to hear the name of Harriet pronounced by Knightley. He has just said that he envies Churchill, now openly the affianced of Jane Fairfax, and she fears to be told why he envies him. Emma tries to change the conversation, when Knightley startles her by saying:

"You will not ask me what is the point of envy. You are determined, I see, to have no curiosity. You are wise—but *I*

[1] Chap. xlvii.   [2] *Ibid.*

cannot be wise. Emma, I must tell what you will not ask, though I may wish it unsaid the next moment."

"Oh then, don't speak it, don't speak it," she eagerly cried. "Take a little time, consider, do not commit yourself." [1]

It is the old device of question and answer at cross-purposes; and Emma has, not indeed to assume the privilege of leap year, but to force herself to invite him to continue. She is still in the dark, still has no reason to suppose that his mind is not dwelling upon Harriet; and, sincerely, she desires not to give him pain. And so his next sentence is so startling that she is almost ready to sink with agitation; full enlightenment, blissful as it is, comes with the suddenness of a blow. How different the effect of the irony in the earlier episode of the picnic at Box Hill, in which everything seemed to come to a head, the dramatic tension and the comedy of mutual misunderstanding, for not a single member of the party knew exactly all that was going on under the surface; not Emma, full of her scheme for marrying Frank Churchill and Harriet Smith; not Frank Churchill, guarding the secret of his engagement to Jane Fairfax; not even the observant Knightley, suffering inly at Emma's levity and disregard of the feelings of kind Miss Bates, the only person who so far had not felt thoroughly uncomfortable. Emma and Churchill are flirting light-heartedly; Jane Fairfax, tortured with jealousy, no longer able to bear the strain of her false position, gives way at last to the exclamation which should have warned him that she would break off the engagement; Mrs Elton, bridling at the idea of Emma's being accorded the honours of presiding, and she and her husband muttering together and presently walking away—it is suppressed irritation and nerves on edge all round. Then follow Knightley's rebuke to Emma and her penitence, as they wait for the carriage to take them home—earnest of the poetic justice which was to come in the same shape but more painfully a little later, when she grew aware of the whole extent of her foolishness. For there is no other punishment for anyone, but to be shown up, to themselves or to the reader, under the steady glow of the irony. Apart from the contempt with which they are branded, the Eltons get off

[1] Chap. xlix.

scot-free; Emma's self-chastisement and penitence are all that are worth attention.

The only source whence anything like consolation or composure could be drawn was in the resolution of her own better conduct, and the hope that, however inferior in spirit and gaiety might be the following and every future winter of her life to the past, it would yet find her more rational, more acquainted with herself, and leave her less to regret when it were gone.[1]

Mr Knightley
It has been remarked already that Knightley is one of those characters of Jane Austen which are in the line of Sir Charles Grandison.[2] Knightley is a Grandison without the ancestral self-righteousness, without the least suspicion of a pose. Knightley and Grandison—the names are well-coined, and mark the essential difference between the two men. Knightley's liberality of mind and chivalrous temper are more beautiful than anything Richardson recorded of his mirror of virtue. It is because he is so devoid of any sense of superiority, so anxious that the woman he loves should be without a flaw, and so grieved to the heart by her lapses, that he can tell her unpleasant truths, and she can accept them with quiet submission. The fineness of both comes out equally in Emma's feelings after his gentle reproof of her witticism at the expense of Miss Bates. He had turned away and was gone before she could recover from the shock of anger against herself, before there was time to show that she was not sullen or resentful :

The truth of his representation there was no denying. She felt it at her heart. How could she have been so brutal, so cruel, to Miss Bates! How could she have exposed herself to such ill opinion in anyone she valued! And how suffer him to leave her without saying one word of gratitude, of concurrence, of common kindness![3]

There is more of Jane Austen, perhaps, in Knightley than even in Emma, though he is by no means one of the typical women's heroes.

Much comparison with the other lover, Frank Churchill, is scarcely worth while, although this easy-going person does serve to throw into higher relief Knightley's manliness and love of

[1] Chap. xlviii.   [2] See above, p. 63.   [3] Chap. xliii.

truth. But Churchill and Jane Fairfax are like the Crawfords in *The* the previous novel : they are not here of their own right but only *Churchill* as having a part in the events that agitate Emma. She is to be *and* deceived by their clandestine engagement, to suspect Jane Fairfax *Fairfax* of mystifications that do not exist, and fall back on Frank *sub-plot* Churchill as a second candidate for the hand of Miss Smith. Their part is expanded to the dimensions of a sub-plot, but this is not made either probable or very interesting. Jane Austen put them into a position which rendered it impossible for her to be sympathetic or even fair. She disliked secrecy so much that she treats them half the time as delinquents, wilfully deceiving their friends and calmly putting up with intolerable humiliations ; and then takes up their defence, as in the plausible but highly improbable letter to his stepmother, in which Frank Churchill endeavours to exonerate himself from the reproach of an unnecessary deception, of bitterly wounding Jane Fairfax, and of playing fast and loose with Emma Woodhouse.[1] Of the two characters, his is hollow and inconsistent, the lady's thin and vague, except when the pathos of the situation and a gush of feeling, when for instance she is stung by her lover's flirtation with Emma at the picnic, give her momentary life.

The other characters include some of Jane Austen's greatest *The comic* comic successes, two of them as amiable as they are ridiculous, *figures* and two belonging to the species that are inoffensive only on the printed page. That most winning and gentle absurdity Mr Woodhouse borders on caricature, of the kindliest sort. He could never have uttered all the preposterous sayings that are alleged. But comedy is allowed some licence, and may put into words, and even into epigrams, what such a quaint valetudinarian has but dimly thought. There is no caricature, however, about Miss Bates, the most lovable of all the bores drawn by Miss Austen or any other novelist. She tires Emma sometimes, who admits, however, that " there is not a better creature in the world," and can say nothing worse than that "what is good and what is ridiculous are most unfortunately blended in her."[2] This is far less than her due, as Emma knows, for there never was a kindlier, more unselfish being, more regardful of the well-being of others,

[1] Chap. l.   [2] Chap. xliii.

yet abashed and overwhelmed by their goodness to one so insignificant as herself.

The simplicity and cheerfulness of her nature, her contented and grateful spirit, were a recommendation to everybody, and a mine of felicity to herself. She was a great talker upon little matters, which exactly suited Mr Woodhouse, full of trivial communications and harmless gossip.[1]

But the clergyman is of the literary strain of Mr Collins, though of lesser stature and more within the bounds of realism. He is the man who apes gentility, and achieves a gross and presumptuous affability. Under the skin, he is a cad of the purest breed. Readiness to perceive an insult is combined with extraordinary obtuseness and brazen insistence. He and his wife are the kind of people who will never take " no " for an answer. In conceit and self-assurance they are a pair; but she is his superior in the vulgarity which becomes aggressive, and her bland patronage of Jane Fairfax grows almost insufferable, even to read.

The other characters Except Frank Churchill and Jane Fairfax, there is not a character in the book that does not hold together and stand distinct. Even that unoffending nullity Miss Smith and her yeoman sweetheart are solid enough to fit firmly into their niches. The Westons are a couple having much more individuality, but are not over-developed. And then there are the John Knightleys, minor characters, but by no means perfunctory sketches. Mr John Knightley is a chip of the same block as Captain Meadows or Mr Palmer.[2] His speech on the folly of quitting a comfortable fireside in order to " spend five dull hours in another man's house," gives the brutal common-sense view as compared with the Meadows-Palmer affectations.[3]

" Persuasion " *Persuasion*, which was written immediately after the publication of *Emma* in 1816, did not appear till 1818, when Jane Austen was

---

[1] Chap. iii.   [2] See above, p. 80.

[3] Mrs Goddard's school at Highbury, where Harriet Smith had been sent, appears to have been drawn from the Abbey School at Reading, run by Mrs Latournelle, which the Austen sisters attended. Mrs Sherwood, Mary Russell Mitford, Letitia E. Landon, Lady Caroline Lamb, and Fanny Kemble also went to this school. (See Sophia Kelly's *Life of Mrs Sherwood*, 1854; and " Jane Austen and Mrs Sherwood," by W. Roberts, in *Times Lit. Suppt.*, p. 780, 8th November 1934.)

in her grave. Being of moderate length, it was published by her brother Henry along with *Northanger Abbey*, which had so long been withheld, and he as her literary executor added the very appropriate titles to both. These were the first of her works to appear under her name, although her authorship of the rest was no longer a secret. *Persuasion* is the most intimate and for that reason the most moving of all her love stories. It describes another conflict with pride and prejudice. The depth of feeling in many of the passages relating how Anne Elliot regains after long years the man she had loved and lost seems as if it must be the reflex of some personal experience. Perhaps the story was the dream fulfilment of a hope or a vague aspiration which events had brought to naught. In chronology, as in the street topography of Bath, the book is very precise. The date is that year of destiny 1814. Eight and a half years ago, Captain Wentworth, a dashing young sailor already wearing laurels, and Anne Elliot, a girl of nineteen, had fallen headlong in love. But the Elliots had frowned on a union with a man having no connexions and nothing but an uncertain professional future to depend upon, and he had retired, hot with resentment and offended pride. And now they are thrown together again. Anne has never ceased to love Wentworth; often and often has she wondered if she would not have been wiser to resist Lady Russell's persuasion, and have boldly accepted the risks. To know that they will soon be in the same room again almost paralyses her senses. Captain Wentworth's wound, on the other hand, has never ceased to smart since Anne tamely dismissed him at the family bidding.

He had not forgiven Anne Elliot. She had used him ill; deserted and disappointed him; and worse, she had shown a feebleness of character in doing so, which his own decided, confident temper could not endure. She had given him up to oblige others. It had been the effect of over-persuasion. It had been weakness and timidity. He had been most warmly attached to her, and had never seen a woman since whom he thought her equal; but, except some natural sensation of curiosity, he had no desire of meeting her again. Her power with him was gone for ever.[1]

[1] Chap. vii.

So he reads his own mind; and, having won rank and wealth, he is looking round for a woman to marry. "He had a heart for either of the Miss Musgroves, if they could catch it; a heart, in short, for any pleasing young woman who came in his way, excepting Anne Elliot." He entangles himself with Louisa Musgrove, unaware that he does not care for her at all, that these are but "the attempts of angry pride," and that he has never really ceased to love the woman he thinks he despises. He might even have married Louisa, however much he afterwards protested "that he had for ever felt it to be impossible," had not the woman he had lost been there to remind him that he once had loftier ideas.[1]

The turning-point at Lyme Regis

There are formidable obstacles to be surmounted ere the parted lovers can be brought to an understanding again. Anne, as yet, is too well aware of his angry pride to cherish any hopes. She is puzzled and wounded by his flirtation with Louisa, and does not perceive that he is like the moth hovering round the candle, and that something more than simple curiosity has brought him into the danger zone. Such signs as transpire of the change going on within him are dramatic hints for the reader alone; Wentworth is hardly more aware of them than is Anne. But, when things are at a more critical pass than appears on the surface, occurs one of those spectacular incidents, recalling Pemberley and Box Hill, which are shocks that settle everything in a new equilibrium; it is the visit to Lyme Regis and Louisa Musgrove's accident on the Cobb, when she misses Wentworth's hand and falling on the stones is taken up apparently lifeless. Louisa is a long time being nursed back to health; and meanwhile Wentworth finds that he is regarded as a pledged man. He is startled and shocked, for his awakening has come at last; but, as he puts it later, "I was no longer at my own disposal. I was hers in honour if she wished it." Happily, Louisa did not wish it, or not for long; and to his relief he presently receives "the astonishing and felicitous intelligence of her engagement with Benwick," the bereaved lover who could not go more than six months without consolation. In this, the richest of all her stories in sentiment, Jane does not abstain from satire of sentimentalism.

Captain Wentworth is free; and Anne receives the news, first

[1] Chap. xxiii.

in the muddled postcript to a letter from her sister, and then in a chat, sparkling with humour, from that bluff old sailor Admiral Croft. The admiral has had a letter from the captain. " I hope," said Anne, " his letter does not breathe the spirit of an ill-used man."

" Not at all—not at all : there is not an oath or a murmur from beginning to end."
Anne looked down to hide her smile.[1]

A page or two later comes something unprecedented in Jane Austen, Anne's sensations at catching sight through the window of Captain Wentworth himself walking along Milsom Street. And then he enters, with a party of gentlemen and ladies, and " she felt that she was betraying the least sensibility of the two."

She had the advantage of him in the preparation of the last few moments. All the overpowering, blinding, bewildering, first effects of strong surprise were over with her. Still, however, she had enough to feel ! It was agitation, pain, pleasure,—a something between delight and misery.[2]

Anne's is a strong, tenacious spirit; she has suffered, and has bitterly repented her tame surrender; she is resolved not to let Fate outwit her again. There is still a chance of retrieving the error of her life. A better chance, in fact, than she realizes, for the barriers have actually gone down, and Wentworth is now the one to fear and hesitate. The end is still delayed. Jane Austen prolongs the suspense artificially, with the alleged possibility of a marriage between Anne and Mr Elliot, the improbable dandy who later runs off with the improbable intriguer, Mrs Clay, and so relieves the family of that lady's apprehended designs on Sir Walter. Wentworth is supposed to be deterred by jealousy of Mr Elliot from making it up earlier with Anne. At all events, the delay allows Anne to show her mettle, at the Upper Rooms, for instance, when she succeeds in bringing Captain Wentworth to her side, " in spite of the formidable father and sister in the background."
The scene in the hotel parlour where the state of their hearts

[1] Chap. xviii.   [2] Chap. xix.

The crucial scene

is mutually revealed, did not form the original solution. That she had thought too ordinary, too tame[1]; and after seeking counsel of her pillow Jane wrote this totally new version. Wentworth overhears what Anne thinks of woman's constancy, and the privilege she claims for her sex, " of loving longest, when existence or when hope is gone." He puts the letter, " I can listen no longer," under her eyes; and it only remains to find a speedy opportunity to unbosom to each other all their misconceptions and regrets. But for attentive readers of Jane Austen there rests a hard saying. Thinking it all over again later, Anne concludes that she had been right at the moment of crisis in obeying the advice of the friend who stood to her in the place of a mother. Possibly the advice was mistaken; she herself would never have given it.

But I mean that I was right in submitting to her, and that if I had done otherwise, I should have suffered more in continuing the engagement than I did even in giving it up, because I should have suffered in my conscience.[2]

There is Jane the moralist again, in the sphere beyond mere orthodox morals which was hers. And that she did think the advice mistaken is clear from her curt dismissal of the adviser's " correct opinions and well-regulated mind," well versed in propriety but somewhat ignorant of the heart:

There was nothing less for Lady Russell to do, than to admit that she had been pretty completely wrong, and to take up a new set of opinions and of hopes.

Good minor characters

The poignant drama of the parted lovers and their reconciliation is woven into the general social comedy with the mastery of ripe experience; and the rest of the characters, Musgroves, Elliots, Harvilles, the quality at the parties and concerts, and the middling people, such as Mrs Smith in Westgate Buildings, have the clear definition of the crowd of individuals in a steel engraving. As it is the year 1814, when the peace had come too soon for many,

[1] It can be read in the *Memoir*, xii.
[2] Chap. xxiii. It is a misinterpretation of Jane Austen to suppose that " Anne's error was want of judgment, of (*sic*) too meek a submission to the direction of an older friend " (*Personal Aspects of Jane Austen*, 71). What she meant was not quite so banal.

there are admirals and commanders and midshipmen enough in
the streets of Bath to give the book an extra charm. Jane knew
the quarter-deck from her sailor brothers. Admiral Croft makes
the raciest imaginable antithesis to Sir Walter Elliot; the vanity
of personal appearance is all the more preposterous, yet none the
less lifelike, by the contrast with its hale and hearty and weather-
beaten opposite. Mary Musgrove's blatant snobbery goes well
with such a father, and also with such a ready foil as these nautical
haters of flunkeyism. Characteristically, Jane Austen, though
she had a wholesome respect for social distinctions, bestows
her last word on poor Mrs Smith, as a complete illustration of
philosophic acceptance :

Her cheerfulness and mental alacrity did not fail her; and
while these prime supplies of good remained, she might have bid
defiance to greater accessions of worldly prosperity. She might
have been absolutely rich and perfectly healthy, and yet be happy.
Her spring of felicity was in the glow of her spirits, as her friend
Anne's was in the warmth of her heart.[1]

Persuasion was not intended to be her last work. During the
first three months of the year 1817, in the July of which she died,
Jane Austen was busy on a new story, known to the family as
Sanditon, of which the twelve chapters extant have now been "San-
published as they stand in the manuscript, with all the abbrevia- *diton*"
tions and alterations illustrating her mode of working.[2] *Sanditon*,
apparently, was to have been a mild satire on the fashionable rage
for seaside resorts. All that she left of it is a rough-shaped piece
from the workshop, which might have grown into something
interesting, although the characters as they stand do not promise
anything very definite. There is the optimistic projector, Mr
Parker, a landowner who has caught the infection, and thinks his
estate on the south coast and his bit of a seaside town ripe for
development; with his business partner Lady Denham, a self-
important woman of seventy, with various people hoping for the
reversion of her money. His sister, the self-coddling Diana, with
all the symptoms of hypochondria, including a hatred of physicians
and all their works; and her nephew, Sir Edward Denham, the

---

[1] Concluding paragraph.   [2] Oxford, 1925.

amateur Lovelace, who feels that he is called upon to seduce the lovely and unprotected Clara Brereton, are rather amusing.

> Her seduction was quite determined on. Her Situation in every way called for it. She was his rival in Lady D.'s favour, she was young, lovely & dependent.—He had very early seen the necessity of the case, & had now been long trying with cautious assiduity to make an impression on her heart, and to undermine her Principles.[1]

Anti-romantic to the end Anti-romantic to the last, Jane gets as much fun out of Sir Edward's pseudo-sentimental tirades as she had enjoyed twenty years or more before from the literature parodied in *Love and Freindship* or *Sense and Sensibility*. As to the "mere trash of the common Circulating Library," the method is the converse of that employed in *Northanger Abbey*. Sir Edward boasts that he is "no indiscriminate Novel-Reader."

> The Novels which I approve are such as display Human Nature with Grandeur—such as shew her in the Sublimities of intense Feeling—such as exhibit the progress of strong Passion from the first Germ of incipient Susceptibility to the utmost Energies of Reason half-dethroned,—where we see the strong spark of Woman's Captivations elicit such Fire in the Soul of Man as leads him—(though at the risk of some Aberration from the strict line of Primitive Obligations)—to hazard all, dare all, achieve all, to obtain her.[2]

He is an expert in the art of misquotation:

> "Do you remember, said he, Scott's beautiful Lines on the Sea?—Oh! what a description they convey!—They are never out of my Thoughts when I walk here.—That Man who can read them unmoved must have the nerves of an Assassin!—Heaven defend me from meeting such a Man un-armed." "What description do you mean?—said Charlotte. I remember none at this moment, of the Sea, in either of Scott's Poems."— "Do you not indeed?—Nor can I exactly recall the beginning at this moment—But—you cannot have forgotten his description of Woman."[3]

---

[1] *Sanditon*, 111.   [2] *Ibid.*, 106-107.   [3] *Ibid*, 89-90.

Sir Edward is pure farce, and it is difficult to see how this adumbration of a mock-romance, for Clara is formally accosted as the heroine, was to have developed.

Not quite a novelist, but the possessor of a charming though *Mary* limited talent, as fine in its modest way as Jane Austen's, was that *Russell* busy woman of letters, Mary Russell Mitford (1787-1855). She *Mitford* wrote poems and poetical tragedies, letters and reminiscences of high literary quality; and in *Our Village* (5 vols., 1824-1832), originally contributed to the *Lady's Magazine*, she invented a new and delightful literary form, the sketch, which is a pen-picture of life having a minimum of fictitious creation or even of story. Not the villagers only, but everything that makes the village, the houses and gardens, the trees and flowers, the environing fields and woods, come into the delineation as importantly as the human figures. What stories do occur are very slight, and are told, as a rule, simply to bring out character. Like Jane Austen, Miss Mitford believed that it is " trifling and everyday occurrences " that afford " the surest and safest indications of character "; but she approaches nearer to Maria Edgeworth in the well-meaning lesson often tucked into a story. Mary Mitford was a great reader, and she caught the very spirit of several other writers. Wordsworth she quotes and often echoes; she had his feeling for nature, but observed more like a Gilbert White. Then such a sketch as *Hay-carrying*, or *The Copse*, and many another, is just what one would expect from Charles Lamb, if he spent a week-end at Three Mile Cross. "The Beauty of the Village," in her *Country Stories* (1837), is Edgeworthian in its moral, but Maria Edgeworth could not have written it. And this, not only because Mary Mitford's style was probably the most limpid, vivacious, graceful, and pure written by any Englishwoman.

CHAPTER VI

SIR WALTER SCOTT—THE LAYS AND
WAVERLEY

JANE AUSTEN died at the age of forty-two. Scott, her senior, was forty-three years old when he published his first novel in 1814, three years after the appearance of *Sense and Sensibility*. In three more years she was dead, having only just had time to see the firstfruits of Scott's fiction, though she was acquainted with his poetry. These two were beyond challenge the greatest novelists between Fielding and Dickens, and their conjunction in time, brief as it actually was, has in it something paradoxical. They were both so great, and yet so fundamentally different. It was wonderful but not unprecedented, in this same period, to see a whole flight of poets in the sky at the same moment; poetry seems always to come with a rush, and literary history is characterized by whole generations of poets. But novelists of such parity and yet such disparity are rarer visitants. True, Fielding and Richardson had been contemporaries, and soon there were to be a Dickens and Thackeray, and later a Meredith and Hardy. But a more radical difference sundered the authors of *Mansfield Park* and of *Waverley*, the two novels that make the year 1814 a landmark, such a difference that they could only wonder at each other in mutual incomprehension. Scott was the fine flower of the romanticism which had been pushing out its tendrils underground during the last decades of the eighteenth century; Jane was the ultimate issue of the older age of reason. Scott was to renew the strength of fiction by harking back to the past, even to the Middle Ages. Jane, not less true to the principles laid down by Fielding, was to be thoroughly modern, so modern that she has won her most appreciative audience only to-day, when Scott's vogue is on the wane.

Everything in the antecedents and early circumstances of Scott

(1771-1832), even what seemed at the time unfortunate, conduced *Scott's*
to the making of the historical novelist. He was born in the right *beginnings*
country and the right place. The people of Scotland have always
been noted for perfervid patriotism; and Edinburgh, to this day
the most romantic city in Europe, was then in a double sense
the modern Athens, an acropolis of learning and culture, and an
ancient capital dethroned, but guarding heroic memories. The
very lineaments of the past survived in the stones of the Old
Town, not yet thrown into the shade by the New. Scott came of
an old Border family, descendants of that doughty moss-trooper
Auld Wat of Harden and his dame the Flower of Yarrow; and
his great-grandfather was Beardie, the famous unshaven Jacobite.
But his genius derived less from his father, the pious, hard-
working, conscientious Writer to the Signet, than from his mother,
Anne Rutherford, a woman of imagination and inexhaustible
memory, " a great genealogist," full of stories and local legends,
who was a resource to Scott even when he was in full career
as a romantic novelist.[1] He had the past in his blood; Scottish
history and tradition were his meat and drink. As a youngster he
devoured the ballads in Allan Ramsay's *Tea-table Miscellany*, and
used to shout " Hardyknute " till the friend of the house, the
parson of the parish, could not hear himself speak. His enthusiasm,
like that of most boys, " was chiefly awakened by the wonderful
and the terrible "[2]; and when, later on, the promulgators of
German sensationalism were stirring up Edinburgh, he became
one of their flag-bearers.

Scott went lame as the result of an infantile ailment, and was *His*
sent to live at Sandy Knowe, a farmhouse in Tweeddale, where *education*
with some breaks he stayed till he was eight and old enough for
school. The bracing air did not cure his infirmity, which was
incurable, but made him robust and active; and the still more
bracing tales of old Border life, the rough and hearty characters,
and the romantic scenery, left impressions never to be effaced.
At school, he was a late arrival, and he afterwards accused himself
of " indolence and inattention." [3] But he was really far from

---

[1] Mrs Scott " told them [their relatives of Harden] with great accuracy the
real story of the Bride of Lammermoor, and pointed out wherein it differed from
the novel " (Lockhart's *Life*, abridged, 179).
[2] *Ibid.*, 15.   [3] *Autobiography*.

indolent, and his natural ability and the energy with which he followed up everything that captured his interest put him speedily abreast of his schoolmates. He acquired a good reading knowledge of Latin, but neither at school nor at college could his odd dislike for Greek be overcome. He read French fluently and spoke it badly, and later on showed some competence in German. He spent some of his first earnings on Italian lessons, and read Dante, Boiardo, and Pulci with delight; and he was able to peruse Cervantes in the original. But at school as in later life it was English literature that he knew intimately and widely. In spite of a predilection for fairy-tales, Oriental fable, stories and ballads of chivalry, for everything, in short, that was marvellous and romantic, he quickly repudiated the spurious glamour of Ossian, and laid the foundations of as thorough and critical a knowledge as was possessed by only a handful of men in that age. He recounts his rapture on finding some odd volumes of Shakespeare, and sitting up to read them by the light of a fire. Spenser, he said, he " could read for ever." [1] One of the secrets of genius is that it knows from the first what is good for it. Hence the education of men of letters, with all its accidents and irregularities, often seems as if providentially arranged to fit them for their appointed work. It was certainly so with Scott's, even his spells of ill health being useful, since they promoted his omnivorous reading and sent him again and again to Kelso and the Borders, where he went on long rides, and when he was well enough on long tramps, in the country that was to be his richest source of inspiration. And he was already not only taking in but also giving out; he relates in his fragment of autobiography how he was the " inexhaustible narrator " of tales to the circle of schoolfellows who used to gather round Lucky Brown's fireside; and that happy faculty for improvisation never left him.

The young lawyer Scott's legal training itself was a part of this education. He never rose high in the profession, though its emoluments, especially those attached to the offices of sheriff and of clerk of session, enabled him to go on writing when literature was still an inadequate and precarious source of income. *Redgauntlet* gives a fairly literal account of these early experiences. Alan Fairford

[1] *Autobiography.*

is a bit of himself; Darsie Latimer is drawn from his stanch
yoke-fellow, William Clerk; and the canny old lawyer Saunders
Fairford, who tells the excellent yarn of the cow that drank the
ale as a stirrup cup without sitting down and could not be sued
for a standing drink, from Scott's father.[1] Other old cronies of
the Outer House figure elsewhere; in fact, Scott's legal worthies
and unworthies are among his triumphs of character-drawing. He
revelled in the intricacies of the law; many of his plots turn on
obscure legal points, and great trials furnish some of his most
impressive scenes. The law is a profession richly adapted to
equip the novelist, habituating him with the complications of
business, its shady and crooked byways in particular, giving views
of the hinder side of character, compelling a strict scrutiny of
motive.[2] Law, being so deeply rooted in the past, called out
Scott's antiquarian instincts, and confirmed his sense of the unity
of history, of the present as the continuation of the past, as only
the page that we are turning over now of what is ever with us.
Perhaps, also, his familiarity with the subtleties of forensic
argumentation encouraged the zest he was to show in *Old
Mortality, The Heart of Midlothian,* and other novels for the fine
distinctions of theological doctrine. Then the soldiering episode
of the years after the French Revolution, when young men joined
volunteer corps for national defence and sometimes saw service
in putting down a riot, left its traces on Scott the writer. The
warlike but lame young advocate had his opportunity when a
body of dragoons was formed in Edinburgh (1797). He was made
quartermaster, and took a strenuous part in drills and manœuvres,
heroic verse running in his head to the rhythm of galloping hoofs.
In poem or novel, Scott was always first-rate at battles, marches,
sieges, great military pageants; the martial spirit which would
have preferred, as he said and thought, a soldier's to a writer's
career, found vent once in an active rôle but very often in bouts
of imagination.

Percy's *Reliques* came into his schoolboy hands at the time

[1] Lockhart, i., see index.
[2] Scott, of course, was well aware of its likelihood to leave distorted views.
Redgauntlet, who in spite of his being maddened by a fixed idea, is a man of
profoundest wisdom and knowledge of the world, says to Alan Fairford : " You
are young and inexperienced, bred to a profession also which sharpens suspicion,
and gives false views of human nature " (*Redgauntlet*, xvi.).

*The
Border
Minstrelsy*

that he was rejoicing in the English translations of Tasso and Ariosto, and he found them still more exciting. There was no northern collection to rival Percy; on the Borders lay a field almost entirely unexplored, though some eyes were already upon it. Scott met one of these enthusiasts in 1792, Dr Elliot of Cleughhead, who had already collected a number of ballads, and encouraged the young man to look out for such booty on what Scott called his " raids " into the wilds of Liddesdale. He went on such raids for seven successive years, collecting not only ballads but also Dandie Dinmonts and the like, which his memory faithfully retained for use in the novels that were as yet not even thought of. Meanwhile, Scott had been stirred to poetical composition by the heady refrain of William Taylor's rendering of Bürger's *Lenore*, which he had heard read by Mrs Barbauld. He tried his hand at another verse translation of the same ballad, and allowed it to be printed (1796). He was more attracted at this age by the gloom and ghastliness of German romanticism, and even by the melodramatic horrors of Lewis's *Monk*, than by the milder sensations of the English Gothic school. He got hold of a skull and cross-bones, to decorate the top of his bookcase. Henry Mackenzie's lecture in 1788[1] had set him studying German, and now he came out with a translation of Goethe's historical drama, *Götz von Berlichingen* (1799), and, for the present at any rate, showed himself unable to discriminate between the finer work of that great poet and the crudest productions of the German school of terror.

*A pre-
paration
for the lays
and the
novels*

Scott outgrew this craze; nevertheless, he was never above using crude supernaturalism and violent sensation as a powerful condiment, in either poems or novels. There is plenty of it in the *Minstrelsy*, in the editorial expansions and reconstructions, in such ballads of his own contributing as " Cadyow Castle," " Glenfinlas," and " The Eve of St John," and, very conspicuously, in *The Lay of the Last Minstrel*, which was the direct outcome of his labours upon the *Minstrelsy* and was designed at first for inclusion in that work. But it goes well enough with ballads and legends descended from a barbarous and superstitious age; and Scott was learning, throughout the years devoted to

[1] See Volume V. 110 and note.

this great collection, to apply his historical knowledge in any given epoch almost with the insight and confidence of a contemporary. Those years of ardent and arduous research were to be fruitful for him in ways not yet conceived. For the matter in hand and for much that lay in the future, he was indebted to a distinguished body of collaborators, of whom two only need be mentioned here, John Leyden and Joseph Ritson. Leyden was a poet as well as an energetic collector of ballads; his collaboration was the most decisive in ensuring that the work should be on an adequate scale. But the services of that wild crank, but true scholar and bloodthirsty critic, Joseph Ritson, were almost equal. With their help and that of seven or eight others, not excepting the printer James Ballantyne, of Kelso, the *Minstrelsy of the Scottish Border* appeared (1802-1803) in three comely octavos.[1] The publication of *Götz* is memorable as having probably determined Scott to be a writer; the *Minstrelsy*, completed when he was thirty-two years old, established him as a man of letters of recognized erudition and eminence.

It was announced in the first edition of the *Minstrelsy* that two further works, *Sir Tristrem* and *The Lay of the Last Minstrel*, would shortly appear. *Sir Tristrem* (1804) was an unfinished metrical romance by Thomas of Ercildoune, edited by Scott; it had been crowded out from the *Minstrelsy*. The legend of the pranks of Gilpin Horner, which had been contributed by Lady Dalkeith, wife of the heir to the Duke of Buccleuch, head of his house, Scott had also found too pregnant to be handled with the concision of a ballad. He therefore evolved for it the form of the lay, a cross between ballad and epic, or, as he put it, an approximation to the mediæval metrical romance; and happily, for this gave the poem one of its chief beauties, he adjusted thereto another olden feature, the framework, in the part played so movingly by the minstrel. The aged harper, indeed, is the chief memory that most readers retain of the poem, unless it

"The Lay of the Last Minstrel"

---

[1] Lockhart gives the main facts of the growth of the *Minstrelsy* (i.-ii., consult index). An excellent summary of the work done by Scott's group and by other collectors will be found in *Currents and Eddies of the English Romantic Generation*, by F. E. Pierce, especially chap iii.—" The Scotch Group and the Antiquarian Movement in Poetry." For criticism, see Oliver Elton : *Survey of English Literature, 1780-1830*, i. 297-324.

be such a stirring episode as the midnight ride of William of Deloraine. For in the narrative Scott simply let his fancy loose on an adventurous improvisation, and the thread is as confused and confusing as any of the most entangled in the novels of later date. Precisely as in the novels, the main object announced is " to illustrate the customs and manners " of the time and place.[1] Scott's mind was charged with the wild and romantic details of ancient Border life and warfare, and the tale was a device for exhibiting all this in a connected and entertaining narrative. The connexions, however, were the weak point, as was always to be the case with Scott; the *Lay* is a sort of rhapsody, stirring episodes linked by description and pedestrian narrative, the descriptions of scenery and of stately bygone life being often more exciting than the deeds recounted.[2] The *Minstrelsy* had been a series of pictures of vanished times, with the high lights and tragic glooms in which they were seen by vanished bards. Those pictures had an authenticity which a modern poet could only simulate, though Scott and Leyden often did that marvellously well. A contemporary critic said of the *Minstrelsy* that it contained " the elements of a hundred historical romances "[3]; a year or so later he might have said, " such as *The Lay of the Last Minstrel*." For in the *Lay*, Scott combined historical erudition and romantic fancy in a close imitation of the ballad histories, and the result was a superior and in many ways a brilliant species of Gothic romance in verse, with the magical appurtenances dear to the tribe of Walpole and Radcliffe, unspoiled by any non-sensical explanation of the marvels. The success of the book was astounding; no poem had ever sold in such thousands. Scott at once became the most popular writer in the two countries, and was fairly launched on the career which ended only with the last of his novels.

[1] Preface to the first edition.

[2] Scott was well aware of his gift for picturing life and action, and thought that it failed him when natural scenery fell to be described, which was not quite true. He could not dissect a landscape with the eye of a painter, and had to give up his laborious attempts to sketch the places that interested him (*Autobiography*). The pictorial magic of the scene in which the old harper tries with hesitating hand to tune his instrument at the duchess's bidding made Pitt exclaim: " This is a sort of thing which I might have expected in painting, but could never have fancied capable of being given in poetry" (Lockhart, ii.).

[3] *Ibid.*, ii.

A volume of *Ballads and Lyrical Pieces* appeared next year "*Mar-* (1806); but Scott lost no time before starting work upon another *mion*" lay. *Marmion* (1808) was not meant to be epical; he disclaimed any such pretensions in the advertisement to the first edition, where again he apprised the reader of his intention " to paint the manners of the feudal times." What he offers is a " Romantic Tale," turning on private adventures, with Flodden Field as a chief episode. But in the canto dealing with the battle he came as near epic as he ever did in verse, and the splendid lines picturing Norham Castle surely dispose of his misgivings about any inability to describe the physical features of a landscape; they seem to have all the radiance of Turner's great mezzotint. But it is to be observed that it is one of those word-pictures in which the physical features embody history and the memory of great deeds; in such Scott was at his most inspired. *Marmion* is more carefully constructed than the *Lay*; but the knight involved in a base intrigue makes an indifferent kind of hero; it is a conventional Gothic novel thrown into a metrical form like the mediæval English versions of the *chansons de geste*, and the introductory epistles to its six cantos are a prosaic substitute for the bardic framework of the *Lay*. At the end, when the historical interest is spent and darkness falls on the battlefield, the poet returns to his plot and winds up the affairs of Wilton and Clare, the two whose devotion and constancy have been a foil to the perjured Marmion, with an allusion in the regular manner of a novelist to their approaching bridal.

The Lady of the Lake (1810) was begotten of the poet's "*The* enthusiasm for the beauties of mountain, glen, and forest in *Lady of* western Perthshire, as the short " Argument " declares. The *the* story is not historical, except that the details of Highland life are *Lake*" accurate; it is just such a one as the enchantments of the scenery might conjure up in a sympathetic imagination. It is romance as Stevenson was to define it: " the poetry of circumstance." " There is a fitness in events and places "; " something, we feel, should happen; we know not what." This is the poet's daydream, which has come to satisfy " the nameless longings " called out by the scene.[1] But the poem does not open with an elaborate

[1] " A Gossip on Romance " (*Memories and Portraits*, xv.).

description of the grandiose surroundings; Scott knew better, and plunges straight into the fiery rush of adventure, which he maintains to a spectacular climax terminating in a most unexpected disclosure, when Snowdoun's Knight stands forth as Scotland's King. As in the subsequent novels, the interest culminates in a series of highly wrought passages that stir the imagination: the great stag-hunt, the summoning of the clans, the combat of FitzJames and Roderick Dhu, and the grand finale. It is a tale of adventure, of mystery and suspense, and a well-kept surprise, things with which poetry has little to do, but familiar in the novel. And these are the characteristics of all Scott's narrative poems; for in his lays, a name that will do for them all, he had invented a new combination, the poem of exciting incident, the poem with a plot, complete with hero and heroine, villainy and intrigue, and a wedding to round everything off. There is a remote resemblance to the mediæval *roman d'aventure*; otherwise this was an innovation in poetry, whether justifiable by poetic canons is another matter. The point is that Scott was writing Waverley novels in verse for ten years before he began writing them in prose.[1]

"*Rokeby*"   *Rokeby* (1813), if its predecessor was pure romance, is more like the average novel of contending passions, with emphasis on the character-drawing. Scott wondered whether his public would be too much surprised at a poem in which " the interest turns upon *character*." [2] History, the state of confusion following the battle of Marston Moor, is subordinated to the domestic story. The best of *Rokeby*, however, is its setting in the Yorkshire dales. And yet the poem ought to have had a peculiar charm, if Lockhart was right in thinking that the Maid of Rokeby represents " the object of his own unfortunate first love." [3] Scott had in youth nursed an attachment to Margaret Stuart Belches, daughter of a wealthy baronet, whom his father, the canny Writer to the

---

[1] Some of the best criticism of the Waverley novels is to be found in the work of John L. Adolphus, *Letters to Richard Heber, containing critical remarks on the series of novels beginning with " Waverley," and an attempt to ascertain their author* (1822), which argued that the novels must be by the same author as the poems from the countless similarities of story, characters, treatment of scenery, poetic style even in the prose, historical erudition, etc., etc.

[2] Lockhart, i.

[3] *Ibid.*

Signet, considered too far above his station. She is the " false love " of one of Scott's most heart-felt lyrics, *The Violet*; the boy loved her, the man treasured this first affection to the end of his life. But Scott seems to have been as modest and as passive as the heroes of his own stories, and was not like them favoured beyond his due by fortune. After some years of hope and diffidence the young advocate learned that the lady was engaged to William Forbes, a prosperous banker, whom she soon married, and who afterwards proved himself one of Scott's stanchest friends in the financial troubles. It was as a gift to Margaret Belches that his *Lenore* had been printed. She is the Green Mantle of *Redgauntlet*,[1] she is Diana Vernon, and may have been in his mind's eye when he drew more than one of his other heroines, too good, or too ethereal and refined, for a lover of earthly mould. Within a year of his disappointment, Scott met and married Charlotte Carpenter (1797); she is said to have been the original of Julia Mannering.[2]

The sales of the earlier lays had been prodigious, and the first three thousand copies of *Rokeby* went off rapidly in January 1813, although the demand slackened much too soon. But there was a crisis in the business world that year which shook the Ballantynes; and Scott, who had a large stake in the firm, was anxious. His own expenses and these commitments made big sales a necessity, and there were signs that his particular vein could not be exploited for ever. *The Bridal of Triermain*, however, a fanciful variation of the romantic theme, duly came out and went into a second edition the same year, and he had planned another lay on the grand scale, *The Lord of the Isles*, and even written enough of the first canto to open negotiations with Constable. But the popularity of Byron's metrical tales, which were modelled on Scott's, but made a fierce, melodramatic appeal to emotions that Scott touched tamely when he touched them at all, already threatened his supremacy. Only the mild first two cantos of *Childe Harold* had

In competition with Byron

---

[1] The subject is fully treated, I believe, in Adam Scott's *Sir Walter Scott' First Love* (1896).

[2] Miss Carpenter's (or Mademoiselle Charpentier's) brother had a post in India, and Miss Mannering was the daughter of an Anglo-Indian officer. These Indian associations are supposed to clinch the vague general resemblance of traits between them (see *e.g.* Buchan, 55-56 and 139).

yet appeared, but they had gone into a fifth edition within the year (1812); and now the Oriental romances were capturing Scott's readers. *The Giaour* and *The Bride of Abydos* appeared in 1813, to be followed next year by *The Corsair* and *Lara*. Scott could not compete without changing his tune, and said of Byron later, " He *bet* me out of the field in the description of the strong passions, and in deep-seated knowledge of the human heart." [1] Byron possessed nothing like Scott's inexhaustible knowledge of human beings in all their diversity; but it is true that he had a profound insight into the heart, even if that heart was only his own. *The Lord of the Isles* was not completed and issued till 1815, the year after *Waverley*. It keeps closer to history and tradition than any of the other lays, in its picturesque account of the wanderings of the Bruce as they had been recorded by Barbour and Hailes. In the scenes in the West Highlands and in Skye, the poet is as lavish of pictorial description as in *The Lady of the Lake*, and the magniloquence sometimes reaches a sublimer note. Even the battle-piece of Flodden was almost outdone by the epical narrative of Bannockburn. Scott had wandered over the battle-field years before; he had recently been on a cruise in the Western Isles, visited Skye, and gone as far north as the Orkneys and Shetlands, gathering local colour both for the lay which he had in hand and *The Pirate*, which was still in the future. The character-drawing of barons and knights and Highland chieftains, in *The Lord of the Isles*, the dramatic strife of motive, and the deliberate complication of the plot, are in the style he had now made his own, and are features that reappear in the novels.

Origin of the Waverley novels   It was at this juncture that Scott bethought him of the fragment of a novel on the Forty-five which he had begun in 1805 and put away in a drawer, his friend Erskine thinking it dull. In 1810, looking for some fishing-tackle, he came across the manuscript, and showed it to Ballantyne, who was full of the great reception met with by *The Lady of the Lake*, and did not advise going on with a mere novel. But now in 1813 Scott found it again, read the seven chapters through, and determined to pin his faith on the success of a work doing in prose for a great episode of Highland

[1] Lockhart, x.

history what *The Lady of the Lake* had done in verse.[1] He wrote rapidly, and *Waverley* appeared the following July (1814), with no author's name on the title-page, Scott, now Clerk of Session, with hopes of the Bench, laird of Abbotsford, and a man of letters of such dignity that he had recently been offered the Poet Laureateship, not choosing to enlist himself among the purveyors of goods for the circulating libraries, or perhaps having shrewder ideas of the market value of anonymity. He kept up the mystification later out of a sportsman's delight in putting curiosity off the scent.

Scott was a born romancer. In the "General Preface to the Waverley Novels" afterwards prefixed to this first volume of the long series, he recalls his earliest impulses to story-telling. As a boy, he had been "a glutton of books," and had read "almost all the romances, old plays, and epic poetry" in a formidable collection in Edinburgh that included "the romances of chivalry and the ponderous folios of *Cyrus* and *Cassandra*," as well as the most approved works of later times. His prowess as a story-teller for his schoolfellows' behoof has already been mentioned; and he recounts how he and a favourite companion used to regale each other with tales of knight-errantry, battles, and enchantments, as they sauntered under Salisbury Crags and other haunts outside the city. He had the ambition to compose a tale of Border chivalry in the style of *The Castle of Otranto*, but gave it up after a few pages, which he prints in the appendix.[2] There follows the account of the beginning of *Waverley*, which was to have had the sub-title "'Tis Fifty Years since," the "Fifty" being afterwards altered to "Sixty." During 1807-1808 he had written a conclusion to an unfinished romance left by the antiquary Joseph Strutt, *Queenhoo Hall*; this also figures in the appendix. Strutt's novel, he said, was not unimaginative, though it had been left in the incoherent condition of a first draft; its fault was that the author displayed his antiquarian knowledge too liberally,

[marginal note: The historical novel *]*

---

[1] The account in Lockhart (take for convenience sake the abridged Life, pp. 85, 113, 130) is not quite the same as that in the General Preface to the Waverley Novels (*Waverley*, Dryburgh Edition, ix.-xxiv.).

[2] *Fragment of a romance which was to have been entitled Thomas the Rhymer.* Another fragment, *The Lord of Ennerdale*, a Radcliffian story of the Covenanters in the time of the Civil War (1645), is also preserved here.

even to the extent of rendering the language unintelligible to modern ears. Strutt had furnished Scott with a useful lesson; it was not he, however, but Miss Edgeworth whose work stirred the patriotic desire to write something that would present his countrymen as favourably and sympathetically as she had presented the Irish. Whilst he spoke in all modesty of the talents he might possess, he was confident of having that wide and intimate acquaintance with the country and the people which was an all-important qualification. With his vast historical knowledge and his instinctive tendency to look in days now elapsed for scenes, events, and characters suited to imaginative treatment, Scott naturally had historical fiction in view rather than that of contemporary life, such as most of Miss Edgeworth's. Yet, after all, in *Waverley* he did not go back so far as she had gone in tracing the successive generations in *Castle Rackrent*.

The historical novel in the eighteenth century

Historical novels of divers kinds and pretensions had been written already. There was an example before the public at that moment, in *The Scottish Chiefs* (1810) of Jane Porter, a long-winded patriotic story of Wallace and Bruce, fervid, sometimes eloquent, and conscientiously founded on the best authorities available, including legendary stories told by an old Border dame, Luckie Forbes, and the lady's own knowledge of the localities; having all the ingredients, in short, that could be prescribed for a good historical novel, except the life, the humour, and the genuine romance that Scott infused into the feeblest thing he ever wrote. But this was no worse in its lifelessness than previous attempts at historical fiction, by Leland and Clara Reeve, the Lees, Mrs Radcliffe, and the other romancers, than any, indeed, since Defoe, Count Hamilton, and Courtilz de Sandras, who were less writers of historical fiction than of history, or at least of facts, disguised as fiction.[1] The impotence of historical novelists before Scott was due to their entire lack of the historical imagination. It did not occur to them that to give any semblance of life to their revocation of bygone ages they must have a familiar knowledge of how people lived and carried on their private and personal concerns, and be able to think themselves back into a remote past, thrusting out of sight all that had happened, all that

[1] See Volume V. 176-177, 181-182, 186, 246-250.

had been learned and had changed man's very being, in the intervening centuries. Tell a story that accorded or did not clash with well-known facts anyone could do, though some did not learn enough history even for that. To present and interpret facts was the historian's business; to summon up a past epoch, to show men and women alive in it and behaving as they must have behaved in the circumstances, was the labour and joy of the genuine historical novelist.

The historical novel should be just such a novel of manners *The* as a contemporary might have written, though in language *historical* intelligible to-day. Being fiction, it should not consist of history *novel* or pretended history; hence well-known events and personages *a novel of* should be subordinated, exactly as they would be if the novelist *manners* were writing of his own day. To Scott the past was a living thing: the initial requirement came easy. He also saw that a new method of approach was wanted, if the past was to be seen in due perspective, as those living at the time, with private preoccupations of their own, would have seen it; and that Prince Charlies and Queen Elizabeths must be placed at a certain distance, if they were to be looked at; moreover, that battles of Bothwell Brig and other famous events are far more clearly and forcibly realized when they are part of the circumstance amid which a person with whom for the time being the reader can identify himself is risking life and all that he has.[1] By such means and with such an intimate knowledge and understanding, the historical novelist produces something that in its own way is history, an authentic picture of life as it was instead of mere romance draped in borrowed trappings.[2]

Even in the advertisements to his lays, Scott usually announced

---

[1] This seems to be virtually what Louis Maigron meant by " local colour," in *Le Roman historique à l'époque romantique ; essai sur l'influence de Walter Scott* (1898), where he points out the vagueness and unreality of the past as perfunctorily evoked by the seventeenth-century romancers. The eighteenth-century realists, led by Sandras and Count Hamilton, set the example of representing contemporary manners. Chateaubriand made an epoch in historical fiction by the masterly handling of local colour, especially in *Les Martyres*. But he was vastly outdone by Scott, with his exact knowledge and ability to depict the manners and sentiments of a past age.

[2] The reviewer (Scott or Erskine) in the article in the *Quarterly* (see *Famous Reviews*, ed. R. Brimley Johnson, 318) observes, " if sins against good taste are avoided and a true picture of the age is achieved, the novelist takes his seat on the bench of the historians of his time and country."

This is always Scott's first aim

that his primary object was to present the manners and customs of certain times and places[1]; he thought of them as definitely historical fictions. In *Waverley* and the novels and tales that followed, he makes it abundantly clear that this was his first and most important aim; it is the reason for his long prefaces, the historical surveys in the introductory chapters, his careful notes. *Waverley* is a " slight attempt at a sketch of ancient Scottish manners."[2] He had been a good deal in the Highlands when they were still little known, and had talked with old warriors of 1745; and it naturally occurred to him " that the ancient traditions and high spirit of a people who, living in a civilized age and country, retained so strong a tincture of manners belonging to an early period of society, must afford a subject favourable for romance."[3] He was so conscientious that he put at the end of the novel " A postscript which should have been a preface," not about the characters in the story, who have now been dismissed, but summarizing the effects of the Forty-five, in the destruction of the patriarchal system in the Highlands, reforms in the Lowlands, and advances in commerce and wealth that had made " the present people of Scotland a class of beings as different from their grandfathers as the existing English are from those of Queen Elizabeth."

Scott had made his decision between the irresponsibilities of romance and the seriousness of historical fiction. The Waverley novels are romantic novels, in the heroic and adventurous spirit that animates them, in the atmosphere of strangeness and remoteness with which even facts are invested, so that sixty years since seems more like a century or two away. But this came of the imagination which saw romance where it is not discernible to everyone, even in the commonest actualities.[4] It often looks as if literature

[1] In the preface to the first edition of *The Lay of the Last Minstrel* he wrote, for instance : " The Poem . . . is intended to illustrate the customs and manners which anciently prevailed on the Borders of England and Scotland."

[2] Preface to third edition.

[3] General Preface to Waverley Novels.

[4] There is something also in the contention that this romance of reality is a quality indigenous to Scottish literature. " Among the wild heights and eventful lives of the Scotch, romanticism and realism became identified as they could not [be] among tamer landscapes and a more sedentary people. In one sense of the word Scotch literature has been romantic down through the centuries " (F. E. Pierce : *Currents and Eddies*, 83).

His own differentiation between romance and novel should be borne in mind

was only a trade to Scott; he certainly had to make it pay. But he was never a mere mercenary. He was determined to entertain his readers, and he wanted them to buy his books. He sometimes changed his manner or his subject to comply with popular taste. But even so he chose his own way of entertaining, by interesting them in what interested him, by communicating his own zest for life, his love of the venerable, the gallant and heroic, all that most aroused his most generous nature. And so, with many lapses, oversights, and negligences, for which he was inadequately apologetic, he gave the world that splendid reconstruction of the past which is the main achievement of the Waverley novels.

He wrote *Waverley*, and it was the same with the subsequent *The three* novels, his mind overflowing with memories as fresh and vivid as *con-* if he had lived through the experience himself, and as sure as a *stituents of* *historical* contemporary of all the points of manners, social conditions, *fiction* sentiments and opinions distinguishing the period from any other. This was the first essential of historical fiction as he conceived it. The next was a sufficiency of human figures, the common herd and a sprinkling of the exceptional, the odd, the outlandish, suited for the comedy of humours, but all recognizably the offspring of that age and no other. Somewhere in his head there seemed to be an inexhaustible supply. They came trooping up at his summons, as if they already peopled the world which lived in his imagination. Third and last was the problem how to mobilize these ample resources; the plan of action, the story, the plot. Often a novelist is haunted by a story which cries out to be told. But Scott's starting-point was not an interesting tale; on the contrary, the story was devised last of all, as the machinery to set things going.[1] Hero and heroine came with the story; they were part of the mechanism, though in themselves of such minor importance

The former is " a fictitious narrative in prose or verse, the interest of which turns upon marvellous and uncommon incidents "; the novel, " a fictitious narrative, differing from the romance, because the events are accommodated to the ordinary train of human events, and the modern state of society." There is also the comic romance, a sort of parody of the serious romance—*e.g.* the *Tournament of Tottenham* (Percy) or the *Hunting of the Hare* (Weber). (See Scott's *Essay on Romance*.)

[1] Scott quotes Dryden, in the introductory epistle to *The Fortunes of Nigel*: " In short, sir, you are of opinion with Bayes—' What the devil does the plot signify, except to bring in fine things? ' "

that the lovers in one novel might have been interchanged with the set in another and no harm done to the dominating interest. The long and the short of it is that Scott took over the trite apparatus of the current sentimental novel, with its hero and heroine, who must be united at last in spite of the more or less interesting obstacles that threaten their eternal separation. This was the circulating-library tradition, the custom of the trade, which it did not occur to Scott or to many who followed him to repudiate.[1] And what has been said of his plots as a considered scheme for ordering and displaying his historical material must be discounted by his congenital carelessness. He was an improviser, in both the lays and the novels. He improvised his plots, and he did not stick to them when improvised. All the better, no doubt, for liveliness and truth to nature, that he often let the story take the lead, instead of forcing it to follow a predetermined plan. But it frequently led into swamps and thickets from which the story emerged in a dishevelled and nondescript condition. In *Waverley* he set out with only the roughest chart.

I cannot boast of having sketched any distinct plan of the work. The whole adventures of Waverley, in his movements up and down the country with the Highland cateran Bean Lean, are managed without much skill. It suited best, however, the road I wanted to travel, and permitted me to introduce some descriptions of scenery and manners, to which the reality gave an interest which the powers of the Author might have otherwise failed to attain for them.[2]

[1] Scott was well aware that he had failed worse than other novelists in the difficult task of making his central figures in the personal drama interesting, or even substantial. Everybody remembers the admission that Waverley, by no means the worst among them, is a "sneaking piece of imbecility." In the *Quarterly* review of *Tales of my Landlord*, partly by Erskine and in larger part by himself, and entirely written out by himself for the printer, it is no doubt Scott who says : "In addition to the loose and incoherent style of the narration, another leading fault in these novels is the total want of interest which the reader attaches to the character of the hero. Waverley, Brown or Bertram in *Guy Mannering*, and Lovel in the *Antiquary*, are all brethren of a family ; very amiable and very insipid sort of young men." He tells us why. They are " never actors, but always acted upon by the spur of circumstances." They are spectators, the author's medium ; they show the effects of what would else require detailed explanation. The author gains this advantage, but " by sacrificing the character of the hero " (the article is for the most part reprinted in Brimley Johnson's *Famous Reviews*, 309-328).

[2] General Preface, xv.

Though rough-shaped at first and not an exact fit, the frame- *The* work in this earliest, as in *Redgauntlet*, the last of Scott's greater *romantic* novels, is excellently adapted to the historical purpose. He was *plot and* about to show the pinched circumstances and continual alarms in *historical* which the disaffected gentry near the Highland line were living *situation* just before the rebellion; the semi-barbarism beyond that line, and the feuds and raids and blackmail that rendered Highlanders and Lowlanders uncomfortable neighbours. Then he was to describe the outbreak; disorder and panic in the villages, Edinburgh occupied by a Jacobite army, the Government troops defeated, England itself invaded, thousands of lives in peril. Nothing could have set all this in higher relief than the quiet and leisurely chapters written in 1805, describing Waverley's boyhood and youth at his uncle's stately English seat; the peace, the prosperity, the slumbering strength that were soon to be so rudely disturbed. Waverley, who is a stranger to the state of the country and whose curiosity is the most enterprising thing about him, finds himself on leave from his regiment in the home of his uncle's erstwhile comrade, the Baron of Bradwardine, who had been out in the Fifteen; and he has just time enough to make fast friends with that chivalrous old pedant before he has his chance of seeing a Highland chief in his lair. This trip of his on such a prosaic errand as the recovery of the baron's cows, like Frank Osbaldistone's journey into the Rob Roy country, is plainly a reminiscence of Scott's own mission, when he was an attorney's clerk, to the Braes of Balquhidder to collect certain debts.[1] Waverley visits the mansion of Fergus MacIvor, sees the chief in the midst of his retainers, fancies himself in love with the romantic Flora MacIvor, and witnesses a great stag-hunt, which, it gradually dawns upon him, is a gathering of the clans, for the standard has been raised for Prince Charlie. At this moment, he finds himself unaccountably embroiled with the military authorities, and so is left adrift between the two camps, half inclined to throw in his lot with the king's enemies.[2]

[1] See introduction to *Rob Roy*.
[2] A novel depicting domestic life in the Highlands : *Clan-Albin, a National Tale*, appeared in 1815, a year after *Waverley*; but the authoress, Mrs C. J. Johnstone, assures us that half of it " was not only written but *printed* " long before the publication of *Waverley*. It is a pretty, idyllic story of a babe of

Waver-
ley's
divided
sympathies
Scott was fond of having a pair of heroes, or a hero and an anti-hero, such as Ivanhoe and Bois-Guilbert, or Morton and Balfour of Burley, in *Old Mortality*, representing moral and political antagonisms. Here he has also two heroines, Flora MacIvor and Rose Bradwardine, figuring the call of romance and the claims of prudence, though it is the too-majestic Flora who rebukes his callow romanticism when he offers her his heart and sword:

> Consult your own good sense and reason rather than a pre-possession hastily adopted, probably only because you have met a young woman possessed of the usual accomplishments in a sequestered and romantic situation.[1]

It is a quadrilateral like that of Ivanhoe and the Templar, Rowena and Rebecca the Jewess, or Effie Deans and Staunton, with Jeanie and Butler. Waverley's indecision between a Government which has wronged him and a cause in which he cannot believe is complicated with his sentimental hesitation between Flora and Fergus and the homelier and safer Rose. This is romance, but the conflict of loyalties is very much to the historical purpose. Waverley is a cultivated gentleman from a more advanced civilization, representing in fact the enlightenment of Scott's own age, thrown into circumstances and invited to take part in acts that are odious to his principles. The past and the present are shown visibly at odds. Waverley has a thoughtful and critical mind, he is anxious to learn; hence Scott is able to insert divers historical lectures without unduly forcing the note, as in douce Mr Morton's pithy characterization of the ultra-Presbyterian, "Gifted Gilfillan," and of the intransigence of the Cameronians, which, like the name of Morton, is a foretaste of *Old Mortality*. It is rather prosy, but at any rate better historical fiction than the machiavellian plotting of that amusing stage villain, Donald Bean, the vamped-up mystery of the stolen letters that led to the cashiering of Waverley, and the explanation postponed so

unknown parentage saved by a village blacksmith; and great pains were obviously taken to present the hearty and kindly manners of the Highlanders. But the writer did not venture to give the dialect; the speech, uttered apparently in Gaelic, is the classic English of eighteenth-century domestic fiction.

[1] Chap. xxvii.

long after the events that all its dramatic force is frittered away.[1]

The characters that give the novel life are, not Waverley and The the two young ladies, but those who gave his inventive powers *characters* less trouble because they came, as it were of their own accórd, out of his teeming brain. The most memorable is that great humorist, that blend of enthusiasm and philosophy, of tenderness and hard fact, the baron, who only takes a longer pinch of snuff at a stroke that touches his heart. The Prince is drawn with the economy but the exquisite propriety of lines which is the distinction of all Scott's portraits of monarchs and great leaders. As to Fergus, the embodiment of Highland chivalry and self-immolating devotion to a cause, with his wit and urbanity, polished at the Court of Saint-Germain, his ambition and arrogance, and his irascible temper, a firebrand spurting flame at the least vexation, he is a synthesis of qualities rather than one of those beings who lived in the depths of Scott's imagination. The poor clansman, Evan Maccombich, is more authentic, and also more tragic, when he breaks the silence at the trial of his chief to offer himself with any six of the clan for the life of Vich Ian Vohr. Scott reached one of his great summits in Evan's reply to the laugh in court at this extraordinary proposal.

The Judge checked this indecency, and Evan, looking sternly around, when the murmur abated, " If the Saxon gentlemen are laughing," he said, " because a poor man, such as me, thinks my life, or the life of six of my degree, is worth that of Vich Ian Vohr, it's like enough they may be right; but if they laugh because they think I would not keep my word and come back to redeem him, I can tell them they ken neither the heart of a Hielandman nor the honour of a gentleman." [2]

Scott managed to put breath into the most casual and insignificant of those who flitted in and out of his stories. The baron's bailie

[1] How arbitrarily Scott selected what suited him and ignored what did not is obvious from the fact that there is no mention in *Waverley* of the real leader of the expedition. " Had Prince Charles slept during the whole of the expedition," says Chevalier Johnstone, " and allowed Lord George Murray to act for him according to his own judgment, there is every reason for supposing he would have found the crown of Great Britain on his head when he awoke " (quoted from *Memoirs of the Rebellion of 1745* in *Scott's Journal*, 115, note).

[2] Chap. lxviii.

and doer, Mr Duncan Macwheeble, of the clan Wheedle or the clan Quibble, with his legal pedantries and pusillanimous economics; and the half-wit David Gellatley, who so often hits the nail on the head, make many appearances and many comic interludes. But even those who are mere passing incidents are characters: the staid and discreet Major Melville, who commits Waverley to Stirling Castle, the pharisaical centurion Gilfillan who fails to lodge him there, inquisitive Mr Ebenezer Cruickshanks of the sign of the Seven-branched Golden Candlestick, Waverley's escort Callum, who proposes to kittle this gentleman's quarters " wi' her skene-occle " or dirk, and Mucklewrath the blacksmith and his virago of a wife. Gifted Gilfillan might have taken a place among the wild theologians at Drumclog; Scott makes it clear that he is a survival from a previous age, like the baron, " a character, Captain Waverley, which is fast disappearing." Some are not much more than mentioned: the lawyers, Messrs Clippurse & Hookem, Mrs Nosebag, and the laird of Killancureit, " who died of an atrophy." It is a pity that they could not be known more intimately; they are personages already. But take the handsome French cavalry officer, Monsieur le comte de Beaujeu, whom the Prince puts for a moment at the head of Fergus's regiment, when that young man has had one of his periodical outbreaks with Waverley. The count makes a page and a half of history and then is heard of no more, but what a figure he cuts!

" Ayez la bonté d'aligner ces montagnards-là, ainsi que la cavalerie, s'il vous plaît, et de les remettre en marche," says the prince. " Vous parlez si bien l'Anglois, cela ne vous donneroit pas beaucoup de peine." " Ah! pas de tout, Monseigneur," replied the Frenchman, and put himself at the head of the regiment. " Messieurs les sauvages Écossais—dat is, gentilmans savages, have the goodness d'arranger vous." . . . " Ah! ver well! dat is fort bien! . . . Qu'est ce que vous appellez visage, Monsieur? " (to a lounging trooper who stood by him). " Ah, oui! face. Je vous remercie, Monsieur. Gentilshommes, have de goodness to make de face to de right par file, dat is, by files. Marsh! Mais, très bien; encore, Messieurs; il faut vous mettre à la marche. . . . Marchez donc, au nom de Dieu, parce que j'ai oublié le mot anglais; mais vous êtes des braves gens, et me comprenez très bien." [1]

[1] Chap. lviii.

Waverley shows Scott fully developed; he did far better, but not in essentials differently. Here was the historical novel complete at all points; still hampered with plot and intrigue, and embarrassed by his hero and heroine of romance. These he was never to recognize as a clog or to abandon. Once or twice, as in *Rob Roy* and *The Heart of Midlothian*, one or both of them came to life, almost through his inadvertence. Otherwise, the best service they could render was to represent a point of view and act as the author's deputies, critics and interpreters of the past to the present.

CHAPTER VII

THE SCOTTISH NOVELS

SCOTT had found his vocation. Roused by the general enthusiasm that greeted *Waverley*, he wrote his next novel, *Guy Mannering* (1815), in six weeks, an unexampled speed which simply showed how packed was his imagination with reminiscences of character and incident bursting for release.[1] By 1819, the year of *The Bride of Lammermoor*, he had written nine of his Scottish novels, only two of less than full length, reaping the harvest of all that had grown and ripened from personal experience and vigilant conversation and inquiry from his earliest years. He was to break new ground with *Ivanhoe* (1819), quitting his native soil and the last hundred and fifty years for England and the Middle Ages; and the learning of a mighty reader with the training of an antiquary served him brilliantly. *Quentin Durward* (1823) extended his conquests to France, Burgundy, and Flanders. Then, after an aftermath of Scottish fiction in *Redgauntlet* and *St Ronan's Well* (1824), came the anxieties and depression of the financial failure, which bowed and crippled but did not break him. *Woodstock* was manfully finished in the stress of these calamities, after which the novels and tales of his declension sometimes approached but never quite recaptured the qualities of his prime. Twenty-three novels, besides stories of medium length, such as *A Legend of Montrose* and *Castle Dangerous*, and the short tales in *Chronicles of the Canongate*, were the output of fifteen years (1814-1829), apart from a mass of historical, biographical, editorial, and other work such as would have kept most men's hands abundantly full.

[1] The speed was so astounding that it has been suggested Scott had older material to work upon, as in *Waverley*. A letter of Una Pope-Hennessey to the *Times Literary Supplement* (28th April 1932) submits that *Guy Mannering, The Antiquary, Redgauntlet*, and *St Ronan's Well*, if not other of the Scottish novels, were based upon such earlier drafts. But Balzac bragged that he almost doubled Scott's rate of output.

Guy Mannering and his next novel, *The Antiquary*, were not written round any historical event; they are historical only in their rich and truthful picturing of manners and a state of society that could breed such characters as Meg Merrilies, Dandie Dinmont, and Counsellor Pleydell. Scott was not even well acquainted with Galloway; he had been there only once, on a professional visit in 1795 to collect evidence for his first important case, the defence of a minister charged with drunkenness and other irregularities.[1] He may perhaps then have picked up such a local character as the gaoler MacGuffog,[2] if not others, for use in the future. Here and again in *Redgauntlet* he was guilty of some trifling slips when he left ground with which he was familiar. But his knowledge of southern Scotland at the date in question was unrivalled, and he had recently furnished himself with local information, primarily for use in *The Lord of the Isles*, from an authority on the spot, Joseph Train, the supervisor of excise at Newton Stewart, a poet and collector of ballads who was preparing to collaborate with a friend in a history of Galloway. Along with other material, Train sent him a story current among the gipsies, about the astrologer who predicts fearful ordeals at the ages of five and of twenty-one for a babe just born. This brought back to Scott's mind the tale told him in boyhood by his father's old servant, John MacKinlay, and perhaps also a ballad of County Durham giving the story in ampler detail.[3] Such was Scott's starting-point; but, as he relates in the introduction, he speedily departed from this initial motive, and the theme of the tragic horoscope was discarded for the story of a missing heir.[4] The incident of the horoscope, however, not expunged but given a totally different bearing, must have suggested the gipsy's less scientific forecast and her invincible faith that Harry Bertram

---

[1] Lockhart, i., chap vii.　　　　　　　[2] *Ibid.*, abd., 44.
[3] *Ibid.*, v., chap. xxxiv.
[4] According to a magazine article of 1819, cited by R. Chambers (*Illustrations of the Author of Waverley*, 29-32), the "groundwork of the novel" was the history of the adventures and the eventual restoration to his estates of Sir Robert Maxwell of Orchardston, *d.* 1786. Thomas Seccombe (*Scott Centenary Articles*, 21) thought the idea of the missing heir was derived from the Annesley case, rehashed by Smollett in *Peregrine Pickle* (see Volume V. 50). Colonel John Buchan's surmise that "the celebrated Dormont case, decided in the Court of Session two years before, supplied the groundwork," sounds more plausible (*Life of Scott*, 138). See also W. S. Crockett: *The Scott Originals*, 45-48.

would eventually be restored to his inheritance. Thus Scott was enabled to link up the wild doings of his vagabonds and outlaws with the affairs of his tame people, the Mannerings, the Hazlewoods, and his nullity of a hero. But the plot reared upon this foundation is rambling, inconsequent, mystifying. It drops into the background; the reader loses and can safely ignore it, whilst he is held electrified by such crowded episodes, such spectacular scenes, as the fox-hunt and the salmon-spearing at Charlie's Hope, the grim adventure when Meg Merrilies hides Vanbeest Brown, *alias* Harry Bertram, from the murdering outlaws, the smugglers' attack on the gaol, or the grand recognition scene, when Dominie Sampson, Dandie Dinmont, and Counsellor Pleydell are on the stage together, along with those more closely concerned with the revelation. Scott was unsurpassable in such a concentrated piece as "Wandering Willie's Tale," or in those climaxes of dramatic tension which, with the extraordinary beings who stand above the conflict and yet dominate the stage, are the most haunting and indestructible memories left by his novels. But a complex plot with all its connexions organized into a perspicuous whole was a thing he was always attempting and always bungling. He was an improviser; but, on the other hand, he improvised with such a grip of all that mattered, that he could drop his intricate plan, like a superfluous map, and make a short cut straight to the summit ridges of wonder, terror, and suspense.

The great dramatic scenes   So the reader need not perplex himself with Harry Bertram's recent proceedings in India, or ask what had brought him into collision with his superior officer, but can fix a delighted eye on the stalwart young fellow making his way in the falling light across the Waste of Cumberland and suddenly coming upon Dandie Dinmont struggling with a pair of thieves. This is romance; and at the next turn come the idyllic scenes at Charlie's Hope. The terrible supervenes with Harry's night in the ruffians' lair; and the grotesque is at its highest pitch in Dominie Sampson's colloquy with Meg Merrilies at the Kaim of Derncleugh, when the terror-stricken witling tastes of the witch's brew and is handed the cryptic letter for Colonel Mannering, " the blood will be wiped out and the lost will be found "; to be quickly followed by the horrors of Dirk Hatteraick's cave and the appalling death of that miscreant and his wretched accomplice in the county gaol.   In between are such interludes of broad comedy as Pleydell at his high jinks, and comedy of the finer sort in the worshipful Sir Robert Hazlewood's examination of Brown for the assault on that great personage's son, when Brown, evidently a man of no pedigree, " considerably lacerated the clavicle of his right shoulder, and deposited, as the family surgeon declares, several large drops or slugs in the acromion process." This last is a touch of Scott's more elephantine humour, but it relieves the sinister irony of Glossin's byplay and the ghastlier under side of the comedy.

Scott's heroes are merely persons to whom a lot of things *Scott's* happen; and among the other nonentities must be numbered *outcasts* Harry's sister, Lucy Bertram, and the lady whom he loves, Julia *and* *Ishmaels* Mannering, the most insufferable of all Scott's patterns of propriety.   When, at the arrival of Harry who has escaped from the attack on the bridewell in which Glossin had meant him to perish, she retires from the room, murmuring, " Infatuated! a second time! " one can only ejaculate, " What a frump! "   The colonel may very well have been Scott's idealization of the military character that he would himself have liked to be, had not his physical infirmity denied it.   Colonel Mannering is a dignified gentleman, and that is all there is to say about him.   But, as usual, all the automatons are ousted from their factitious pride of place by those characters on whom Scott, often by a sort of unconscious art, lavished his imagination.   His delight in all kinds of humanity was the converse of his own companionableness.   He was just a man like anyone else, whose open demeanour, warm fellow-feeling, and instant comprehension, disarmed reserve and took him to the hearts of the strangest and most opposite.[1]   This same sympathy and affability, this natural brotherliness, gave him an

---

[1] Speaking of Lord Glenvarloch, in *The Fortunes of Nigel* (opening of chap. xxvii.), Scott has some pertinent remarks : " He was not, as the reader may have observed, very affable in his disposition, or apt to enter into conversation with those into whose company he was casually thrown.   This was, indeed, an error in his conduct, arising less from pride, though of that feeling we do not pretend to exculpate him, than from a sort of bashful reluctance to mix in the conversation of those with whom he was not familiar.   It is a fault only to be cured by experience and knowledge of the world, which soon teaches every sensible and acute person the important lesson, that amusement, and, what is of more consequence, that information and increase of knowledge, are to be derived

insight which was almost uncanny. Dandie and Pleydell and the dominie, like the baron in *Waverley* or Monkbarns and Edie in *The Antiquary*, are his bosom friends; he could respond to all their humours and rejoice in their absurdities as he could in his own. And this affectionate understanding extended to the whole disreputable race of beggars and vagabonds, pariahs and Ishmaels, fools and monomaniacs, the very dregs and putative foes of society. From among such outcasts he took many of his most savoury characters, and some of the most profound; and they are drawn by this stickler for law and order with a jovial friendliness and instinctive understanding that defies unbelief. He could sense the perverted heroism in a Dirk Hatteraick, and set it against the loathsome villainy of a Glossin; or bring out a similar contrast in *Redgauntlet* between Cristal Nixon and Nanty Ewart. There are honest scoundrels and dishonest; there is honour even among thieves; but it is Scott who almost alone shows the meaning of those ancient truths. Some of these abnormal beings appeal to his humour; the merry friar of Copmanhurst, for instance, or that gently caricatured oddity in the present work, Dominie Sampson, of whom more than one authenticated original has been pointed out, though he is of a type on which many novelists have tried their hands, from Goldsmith to Dickens. The appeal of something wilder, more elemental in human nature, in a word, more poetic, comes out in such creations as Meg Merrilies or Edie Ochiltree, the Children of the Mist, in *A Legend of Montrose*, or the Bohemian Hayraddin, in *Quentin Durward*, who dies game to the last. Madge Wildfire belongs to the strain, though some artifice, some self-imitation on Scott's part, mars her naturalness a little. Were such creatures of his making a sort of safety-valve for his high spirits, a mode of vicarious escape from overmuch propriety? Scott was himself a bit of an adven-

from the conversation of every individual whatsoever, with whom he is thrown into a natural train of communication. For ourselves, we can assure the reader—and, perhaps, if we have ever been able to afford him amusement, it is owing in a great degree to this cause—that we never found ourselves in company with the stupidest of all possible companions in a post-chaise, or with the most arrant cumber-corner that ever occupied a place in the mail-coach, without finding that, in the course of our conversation with him, we had some ideas suggested to us, either grave or gay, or some information communicated in the course of our journey, which we should have regretted not to have learned, and which we should be sorry to have immediately forgotten."

turer, a descendant of moss-troopers, with the ambitions of a
Quentin Durward, as his reckless financial adventures testify. Or
is all this simply romanticism at its utmost stretch? At all events,
such characters bear witness to the range of his vision, Shakespearian in its breadth though not Shakespearian in depth. There
are two sorts of character in Scott, his sham heroes and their like
being left out of the account: the characters who are all idiosyncrasy, and those who have something in them of the universal.
These beings from the wilds of human nature are for the most
part of the latter class.

Paulus Pleydell, Esq., "who with ostentatious obstinacy *The*
affected the manners of a former generation," is said to have been *inimitable*
drawn from Andrew Crosbie, at that time an ornament of the *four*
Scottish Bar.[1] Crosbie's clerk had a character and propensities
that "agreed singularly well with those of Mr Pleydell's de-
pendant, Driver,"[2] the gentleman who was found speechless with
drink, " but no sooner was his pen put between his fingers, his
paper stretched before him, and he heard a voice, than he began
to write like a scrivener; and, excepting that we were obliged
to have somebody to dip his pen in the ink, for he could not see
the standish, I never saw a thing scrolled more handsomely."
The dominie is credited with two originals, the Reverend George
Thomson, tutor at Abbotsford,[3] and a certain James Sanson whom
Scott knew in his youth.[4] Meg Merrilies is supposed to have been
drawn from two gipsy queens, of Kirk Yetholm in the Cheviots,
Jean Gordon, and her granddaughter Madge, the one being the
prototype of the character, the other of the person of Meg.[5] There
was great competition for the honour of being Dandie Dinmont's
indigenous ancestor; but it is probably true that " the whole
class of Liddesdale farmers is here represented."[6] Glossin, who
is most ably drawn, is a more extended study in the manner of Miss
Edgeworth's Thady Quirk, in *Castle Rackrent*. But, though it is
interesting to hunt for evidences of the way Scott's imagination
did its work, these identifications must not be taken too seriously.
He had been marking down odd people and interesting traits from

[1] Chambers, 32-41.   [2] *Ibid.*, 41-50.
[3] See Lockhart and Buchan.   [4] Chambers, 53-55.
[5] See Scott's Introduction and Chambers, 55-59.
[6] Chambers, 50-52.

boyhood onwards, in the capacious notebook of an unfailing memory, the contents of which had ripened and mellowed and undergone many permutations and transformations before they received their final shape as characters in the novels. Every one of the four most astonishing dramatis personæ in *Guy Mannering* has a trace, if not a whole portion, of that wild poetry which has just been discussed; even Pleydell, who no doubt thought himself, and was, an accomplished man of the world; even the simple dominie with his treasures of useless learning. Meg Merrilies is more poetical than anything in Scott's regular poems; and her laments for the pride and happiness that have flown, her imprecations and vaticinations and her terrible irony, are unsurpassed for eloquence in English prose, though to Scott it was only a "mixture of insanity and wild pathos." Dandie is the quintessence of that "romance of real life" diagnosed by Hazlitt. A butt, a simpleton, a dunderpate; a moss-trooper whose warlike propensities now find pasture in litigation or a bout at single-stick or broadswords with a neighbour of the same virile tastes; but what a paragon of manliness and native chivalry! Scott's triumph was to bring such a cast on the stage together; grotesque comedy could go no further.

"*The An-tiquary*" In his introduction to *The Antiquary*, Scott said that this and the two previous novels were "intended to illustrate the manners of Scotland at three different periods"; he was now coming to the end of the eighteenth century and his own lifetime. *The Antiquary* (1816) was his favourite among his novels, probably because the figurehead has lineaments drawn from himself. Jonathan Oldbuck, usually hailed by his territorial patronymic as Monkbarns, is from any reasonable point of view the hero, though Lovel performs in the conventional rôle, in an insipid love affair and another drama of a missing heir, which is the usual sop to the rage for stereotyped romance. In Oldbuck, Scott confessed to a disguised portrait of an antiquarian friend, the late George Constable. But he himself had many of the same foibles, and was by no means disinclined to poke fun at them. Connoisseurs have pointed out features from other worthies. More interesting, however, than this sort of pedigree-hunting is the obvious fact that Scott revived in the old antiquary tender remembrances of his own romance of twenty years since. "The Violet" was dead; the love of his youth had subsided to a quiet but inextinguishable sentiment; like Oldbuck, he yielded sometimes to this "melancholy feeling," and brooded wistfully over his "early and unfortunate attachment." The philosophy of old age which Oldbuck expounds to his young friend Lovel is that of Scott's own *Journal*, in which of all his writings he was to vouchsafe the most intimate glimpses into his own secret thoughts. For that affair had rankled, though he cherished its recollections. Perhaps it was this more than anything that accounts for his worshipful but remote and tenuous heroines, chilly embodiments of a chivalrous ideal. He put woman on such a lofty pedestal that he could hardly see her human features, much less the imperfections of our common clay.[1]

The plot-work is clumsy in the extreme. Lovel's apparently hopeless suit, the pecuniary troubles of the Wardours, and the snaring of the baronet by that preposterous trickster Dousterswivel, have to be linked up with the gloomy melodrama of twenty years ago, the earl's secret marriage, the old dowager's wicked pretence that he has married his own sister, the poor girl's suicide, and the disappearance of the child, now universally supposed to be dead. Scott had his scheme ready prepared; and, like a conjuror, he pulls it out of his sleeve at the last moment. There follows a terrific rush of incident. The baronet's debts are paid off by a son who seems to come into existence for that sole purpose. Lovel appears upon the scene as Major Neville, commandant of the troops at Fairport. And then there is a general disclosure. Lovel or Neville is the long-lost heir to the house of Glenallan, which everyone, including the present earl, had believed to be on the eve of extinction. He now marries Miss Wardour; the baronet's fortunes are restored, and Edie Ochiltree, Caxon the barber,

The plot and the finer super-structure

---

[1] Bagehot discusses at some length the inadequacy of Scott's heroines, which he puts down to the want of "the very peculiar instinctive imagination" in this respect which was possessed by Goethe (*Literary Studies*, "The Waverley Novels"). Dr T. F. Henderson's explanation of the thinness of Scott's heroines and the lukewarm tone of the love affairs is that he wrote the novels in middle age, and naturally took a fatherly sort of attitude towards the young people. But it was much the same in the poetical romances; and, further, the theory is inconsistent with the ways of a good many other middle-aged novelists (*Cambridge Hist. of Eng. Lit.*, xii. 23).

Captain Taffril, and other deserving friends, are made happy. An admirable conclusion, if it had been adequately prepared. But that is a matter of slight consequence; the plot is only a thread for stringing together a succession of crowded scenes in which Scott shows his powers, not as a mere sensational conjuror, but as the magician which he was now acclaimed. From the vivid informal opening when Oldbuck and Lovel find themselves in the same coach, incident follows incident with no slackening of interest. The storm in Knockwinnock Bay and the rescue of the baronet and his daughter by Edie Ochiltree and Lovel; the picnic in the ruins, the quarrel with peppery Captain M'Intyre, and the duel; the midnight burial of the Countess of Glenallan, and the earl's visit to the half-crazed Elspeth, who reveals the secret history of crime and imposture; the death and lyke-wake of Steenie Mucklebackit, and that wonderful idealized reminiscence of the old days of ballad-hunting when the antiquary overhears Elspeth chanting the ballad of Harlaw—these are the things that cleave to the memory when all the elaborate mystifications have been forgotten.

Some historical elements   There is one link with history. Scott recollected the French scare of 1805, when at a false alarm he and many other volunteers came spurring to Dalkeith, in his case a ride of a hundred miles done in the twenty-four hours. This suggested the Fairport incident, some time before which Lovel had been mistaken for a French spy. Even the aged bedesman is ready to carry a musket at the summons of his country, if there is a dyke to rest it upon.

"Me no muckle to fight for, sir? Isna there the country to fight for, and the burnsides that I gang dandering beside, and the hearths of the gudewives that gie me my bit bread, and the bits o' weans that come toddling to play wi' me when I come about a landward town? Deil!" he continued, grasping his pikestaff with great emphasis, "an I had as gude pith as I hae gude-will and a gude cause, I should gie some o' them a day's kemping."[1]

Edie and the baronet, still drinking to the king over the water though the Stuarts are extinct, are survivals of an older day. But Scott could remember the prototype of Edie, the Border gaber-

[1] Chap. xliv.

lunzie, Andrew Gemmells, mentioned in his introduction.[1] And was not Scott himself a survival, a dweller in the past as much as in the present? Monkbarns is Scott himself older by twenty years; a caricature of his own dry humour, his own learning, and his pedantry. He was on his favourite subject when he set Oldbuck lecturing the spendthrift nephew on the beauties of the law touching debtors, and demonstrating, more to his own satisfaction than the impatient captain's, " that in this happy country no man can be legally imprisoned for debt."

But the humorist is at his best in the passages giving what he *Peasant* promised in his introduction, the manners of the time, especially *humours* among the peasants. One of his most caustic bits of natural comedy is the gossip in the Fairport post-office between the butcher's wife, the baker's lady, and the rest of the scandal-ferreting tribe, on Jenny Caxon's love-letters. The utterances of old Elspeth brooding over the gloomy history of the Glenallans are in a strain as tragic as the eloquence of Meg Merrilies. " Eh, sirs! . . . it's awsome to hear your gudemither break out in that gait—it's like the dead speaking to the living." But to see who was the father of the Scots novel of lowly life that flourished later, take half a page that is neither romance nor comedy, but simply a view of workaday realities. Jenny Rintherout, the antiquary's maid, has slipped down to the Mucklebackits', " to see an there was ony cracks amang ye."

" Ay, ay," answered Luckie Mucklebackit, " I see ye hae gotten a' your braws on—ye're looking about for Steenie now— but he's no' at hame the night—and ye'll no' do for Steenie, lass —a feckless thing like you's no' fit to mainteen a man."

" Steenie will no' do for me," retorted Jenny, with a toss of her head that might have become a high-born damsel,—" I maun hae a man that can mainteen his wife."

" Ou ay, hinny—thae's your landward and burrows-town notions. My certie! fisher-wives ken better—they keep the man, and keep the house, and keep the siller too, lass."

" A wheen poor drudges ye are," answered the nymph of the land to the nymph of the sea.—" As sune as the keel o' the coble touches the sand, deil a bit mair will the lazy fisher loons work, but the wives maun kilt their coats, and wade into the surf to tak

[1] See also Chambers, 60-64.

the fish ashore. And then the man casts aff the wat and puts on
the dry, and sits down wi' his pipe and his gill-stoup ahint the
ingle, like ony auld houdie, and ne'er a turn will he do till the
coble's afloat again!—And the wife, she maun get the scull on
her back, and awa wi' the fish to the next burrows-town, and
scauld and ban wi' ilka wife that will scauld and ban wi' her till
it's sauld—and that's the gait fisher-wives live, puir slaving
bodies." [1]

It was in his natural dialogue, especially when spiced with broad
Saxon, that Scott had style.

**"Old
Mortality"**   During this same wonderful year he brought out two more
novels, *The Black Dwarf* and *Old Mortality* (1816), both under
a new serial title, *Tales of my Landlord*. *The Black Dwarf* was
a lamentable performance in crude Gothicism, enlivened but not
redeemed by a few passages in the vernacular style exemplified
above. But *Old Mortality*, in which he went back to the troublous
times of Charles II and the rising of the Covenanters in 1685,
is a masterpiece. It is more than a novel, it is an historical
monument, by far the finest of his representations of a past era,
its men, its manners, ideas, and events. Scott never built better.
The historical and the romantic stories are identified, apart from
some venial concessions to the latter at the close. The dominant
note is epical, as befits the national issues which are at stake and
the famous soldiers and statesmen who are in the forefront. The
harangues of the different types of preachers and the curter
speeches of the men of action are in the grand manner of the
classical historian, and both dignify the narrative and make it a
valid contribution to a disputed chapter of Scottish history. As
in *Waverley*, Scott puts a young man who by temperament,
mentality, and personal sympathies, is on the side of modern
enlightenment into the clash of parties, and shows him urged this
way and that by the fanaticism of extremists on both sides, his
appeals for moderation bringing down on him the odium of
disloyalty and treachery and exposing him to fearful risks. The
friendly rivalry between Morton, a moderate Presbyterian, and
the High Churchman, Lord Evandale, for the hand of Edith
Bellenden is skilfully interwoven with the vicissitudes of the

[1] Chap. xxvi.

rising, the victories and defeats, and the barbarous retribution meted out to the Covenanters. The sequel is less satisfactory. It follows the termination of the historical events, and is of the conventional kind, a young Lochinvar conclusion: Morton, supposed to be wrecked and drowned, comes back to his own, just in time to frustrate the union of Edith and his rival, Lord Evandale. These protagonists, like the rest in the other novels, are empty ciphers in comparison with the richness and solidity of the by-characters. Had Scott given us nothing better than these immaculate young men and their irreproachable young ladies he would have been as tedious as the obsolete romances of Cyrus and Cleopatra read by Edith Bellenden which he gently ridicules.

First on the line among the historical portraits hangs that of *Great* Claverhouse, with which Scott took infinite pains, fascinated by *character-* the contradictions of a chivalrous purity of principle and a reputa- *drawing* tion for insensate cruelty. He wrote *Old Mortality* with a painting of the scourge of the Covenanters gazing down from the wall of his study. He may have exalted some traits of that extraordinary man, but the strength and beauty of the drawing are undeniable. Intellect, military genius, sternness, and grace are conveyed with a minimum of strokes, for Claverhouse makes only two or three appearances, though it is at the most critical moments of the drama.[1] Much fewer lines went to some other historical characterizations; but the brutal Dalzell and Lauderdale, and the amiable, vacillating Monmouth, are adequately vignetted in a few phrases. Scott wielded a fuller brush in depicting the furious dissensions among the sectaries in the persons of the monomaniac Balfour of Burley, the insane Habbakuk Mucklewrath, and the wild zealot Macbriar, preaching his trumpet-tongued sermon after Drumclog and testifying to the faith by his heroism in the torture-chamber at Edinburgh. The worldlier Kettledrummle and Poundtext lend themselves to humorous treatment; but the tragic preponderates in the vengeful ravings of the rank and file. It is an unfriendly but not a hostile picture; Scott was scrupulous in weighing the evidence, though he admitted in a note that

---

[1] Professor Rait shows ("Scott and Thomas McCrie," in *Sir Walter Scott To-day*, ed. H. J. C. Grierson) that if Scott erred it was not on the side of over-friendliness to Claverhouse, as Dr McCrie complained in a violent attack on Scott's alleged caricature of the Cameronians in 1817.

" were he to write the tale anew, he would probably endeavour to give the character—of Poundtext the moderate Presbyterian— a higher turn."[1] His power of wedding opposites in one self-consistent character is evident in Macbriar, but not less in his testimony that these extremists, with all their frenzy and violence, could produce such saintliness as that of the widow Maclure, who shelters Lord Evandale from the insurgents. She had had her husband shot; one of her sons has died fighting for the Covenant, and a firing party slays the other before her eyes. She has gone blind with such agony; but rebukes Morton for cursing her oppressor, the scoundrel who persecuted her for saving Evandale.

" Dinna curse him, sir," said the old woman; " I have heard a good man say a curse was like a stone flung up to the heavens, and maist like to return on the head that sent it."

Other half-historical characters are Sergeant Bothwell and Major Bellenden, who take part in the comic as well as the tragic side of the story. But the best of such as these are the hind Cuddie Headrigg and his mother Mause, the latter " divided grievously between the safety of her son's soul and that of his body."

" Mind, my bonny bairn, ye hae battled for the faith, and dinna let the dread o' losing creature comforts withdraw ye frae the gude fight."
" Hout, tout, mither," replied Cuddie, " I hae fought e'en ower muckle already, and, to speak plain, I'm wearied o' the trade. . . ."
" But, my dear Cuddie," continued the persevering Mause, " your bridal garment! Oh, hinny, dinna sully the marriage garment! "
" Awa, awa, mither," replied Cuddie; " dinna ye see the folks waiting for me? Never fear me; I ken how to turn this far better than ye do; for ye're bleezing awa about marriage, and the job is how we are to win bye hanging."[2]

---

[1] It was not the preachers in the Covenanting camp who were rabid extremists, but the officers ; and there were no Indulged ministers, such as Poundtext, among the insurgents. Nevertheless, Scott's account of the intransigence and bloodthirstiness of the ultra-Presbyterians is not untrue on the whole (" Scott and Thomas McCrie," *passim*). The *Quarterly* review of the work already alluded to (see above, p. 138) was a reply to these charges of McCrie.
[2] Chap xxxv.

Both Morton and Evandale are anachronisms : two cultivated *The non-*
gentlemen, with humane ideas a century in advance of their time, *historical*
representing the spirit of toleration. This is what happens with *characters*
Scott. His historical characters, including those who stand for
the common man, nameless in history, are recognizably products
of the time; these others are his intermediaries, and belong
neither to this age nor to that. Scott was not a modern historian,
claiming to be scientific and to re-create the past as a contemporary would have seen it. He shows it through the eyes of these
spectators, who are in it yet hold themselves aloof. Morton and
Evandale, with their antecedents and their position amid the strife
of parties, are very carefully described; without such an introduction they would have been mere blanks, and even so they are
never much more in themselves. The strong personalities require
no such prelusive ceremony; they are too self-assertive, they are
themselves the epic, which rolls on from the merry spectacle of
the shooting at the popinjay, where most of them come forward
together, to the battles of Drumclog and Bothwell Brig, and the
final agony before the Privy Council. The visit of Claverhouse
to the Tower of Tillietudlem, the stern scene in which Morton
barely escapes being shot, his ordeal when Claverhouse saves him
from the fanatics waiting for the hour of midnight to strike his
doom, and the last act in Balfour of Burley's cave, have the same
intensity; they stand out with a terrific distinctness, though they
are simply culminating moments in the onward march of the epic.

Rob Roy (1818), on which Scott was working in broken health *" Rob*
for the best part of a year, is a novel of adventure, with more than *Roy "*
a dash of the novel of intrigue, and a beautiful love story almost
ruined by an inappropriate ending. He said he wrote it to supply
the curious with some account of the celebrated outlaw, and to
set forth the " strong contrast betwixt the civilized and cultivated
mode of life on the one side of the Highland line, and the wild and
lawless adventures " which were possible or actually going on
beyond " that ideal boundary." [1] That he was serious enough
about his historical purpose is confirmed by the extra length of
his introduction. Yet, strange to say, Rob Roy is not one of the
leading characters. So far as the plot is concerned, he is only an

[1] The language of Scott's introductions is often very slovenly.

understrapper. He lurks in the background, coming to the front when least expected; though when he does appear, it is always in the nick of time, and his services prove to be the one and only thing that could have saved the situation. And by the time that the Scottish cattle-dealer, Mr Campbell, encountered first in the wayside inn in Northumberland, has been identified as the laird of Craig Royston, and as the proscribed James MacGregor, *alias* Rob Roy, he has impressed himself as no man of buckram, but one having the strong features and the solidity of Scott's best. The tale begins in England, and does not enter the land of its titulary hero till it is more than half finished. Still more oddly, the hero on the romantic side, who must enjoy a certain formal precedence over the other, being indeed the autobiographer, is an Englishman.

A romantic story with an inconsequent sequel

The adventures of Frank Osbaldistone make a confused and improbable story, which would interest no serious reader but for the life put into it by two such originals as Andrew Fairservice and Bailie Nicol Jarvie, who play second fiddle to his insignificance, and further, by the most bewitching of all Scott's young ladies, the romantic Die Vernon. The pretext for sending Frank on his travels to fall in with Rob Roy and the bailie is incredibly shallow. His cousin, the villainous Rashleigh, who has taken Frank's place in the great merchant's counting-house and is being initiated into the mysteries of commerce, suddenly finds himself in sole charge of the firm's business, and the next news is that he has disappeared with a mass of securities and that the house is on the brink of ruin. The ensuing train of events and the proceedings by which his schemes are foiled remain a riddle, together with their connexion with the Fifteen. In the later chapters, which for good reason may be regarded as sheer anticlimax, the probabilities are still more violently set at naught. The Jacobite rebellion of 1715 is unnecessarily dragged in; Frank's uncle, the Northumberland baronet, dies in Newgate, and a family of stalwart sons are cut off in six months by various chances, leaving Frank to inherit the estates and marry Die Vernon. Is it possible that Scott did not see all that he missed by grafting on this conventional sequel? Good taste agrees that he should have stopped with the parting of Frank and Die Vernon in the Highland glen, when she rode off in the dark leaving him sobbing like a girl. After all, this is a sentimental romance, and the sentiment running through it from the moment of Die's first entry, the lonely girl among the boorish cousins in the Northumberland hall, separated from all of her own sex, and marked out by fate for a loveless marriage or the cloister, demanded a sad and irrevocable farewell. That would have been the poetic ending; and it would have coincided with Scott's own feeling, if this is but another reminiscence of his own loss.[1] But he was always at the mercy of his popularity. When conclusions are put to the vote, the happy-enders will always have it, and Scott had too much regard for his readers to play with their feelings. So he reverses all that the story had portended, and foists in a termination to please the vulgar.

Andrew Fairservice and the bailie are two of Scott's finest *Andrew* epitomes of his countrymen's idiosyncrasies, and their delightful *Fair-* talk is in the most pungent vernacular. The differences between *service* the pair, and the fine shades that scarcely amount to differences, *the bailie* are cunningly balanced. No one could wish for more delicate entertainment than Frank Osbaldistone ought to have enjoyed, if his sense of humour had been sufficiently acute, in the ride with two such companions from Glasgow to Aberfoyle. But Frank seems rather to have been irritated by Andrew's querulous explosions, his henchman's farewell speech, for instance, when he left England on Squire Thorncliff's mare. "You have stolen her, you rascal," he says.

" Na, na, sir—nae man can wyte me wi' theft. The thing stands this gate, ye see. Squire Thorncliff borrowed ten punds o' me to gang to York races—deil a boddle wad he pay me back

---

[1] Seccombe thought so, remarking that Scott was always " surreptitiously colouring both prose and poetry with the hapless love affair of his youth to an extent far beyond our present powers of tracery " (*Scott Centenary Articles*, 100). Professor George Gordon alludes later to " the lifelong constancy of Scott to the memory of a girl he had loved and not won " (*Ibid.*, 141). As already mentioned, Scott had gone like Frank Osbaldistone into the Rob Roy neighbourhood when he was a young man (introduction to *Rob Roy*) ; Frank has points of correspondence to Scott, especially in his relations to his father as a young man with poetic ambitions out of his element in the business. To call Frank a character drawn after Scott would be absurd ; he is void of character—that is, of any strong idiosyncrasy. But indirect autobiography is another matter, a question of disposition, sentiments, attitudes ; and there is in that sense a great deal of Scott in the heroes of his novels.

again, and spake o' raddling my banes, as he ca'd it, when I asked him for my ain back again;—now I think I will riddle him or he gets his horse ower the Border again—unless he pays me plack and bawbee, he sall never see a hair o' her tail. I ken a canny chield at Loughmaben, a bit writer lad, that will put me in the way to sort him. Steal the mear! na, na, far be the sin o' theft frae Andrew Fairservice—I have just arrested her jurisdictiones fandandy causey. Thae are bonny writer words—amaist like the language o' huz gardeners and other learned men—it's a pity they're sae dear;—thae three words were a' that Andrew got for a lang law-plea, and four ankers o' as gude brandy as was e'er coupit ower craig—Hech, sirs! but law's a dear thing."[1]

The mellifluous run of his animadversions on most things in this world is matched by the wit and wisdom and a similar gift of speech of the pawky Nicol Jarvie. Naturally, there is no love lost between such a pair. The bailie is hearty and generous and far-seeing, where the gardener never looks beyond the narrow plot of his crabbed and conceited and greedy self. Between them, somehow, all the foibles, and all the homely virtues, of which even Andrew is by no means devoid, of the lower and the middle-class Lowlander seem to be hit off; the bailie's wider vision embraces the Highland character too. He is a sociologist of no mean pretensions, as well as a humorist. These two and Diana Vernon save the book, which would have been poor indeed without them. She is the first live woman in Scott's fiction—at least, of Scott's own class, for he never failed to put life into those of the stamp of Cuddie's Jenny Dennison, in *Old Mortality*, "which," says Mr Poundtext, "is a girl of an ensnaring eye." Die Vernon is a woman with brains and the courage to use them, a rarity in his heroines. If she is her author's most lifelike portrait of "The Violet," then his regrets can be understood, though not his lack of emprise. Nor is it merely the glamour of her situation that makes the beauty of Diana, although this enhances it. It is always she who corrects Frank Osbaldistone's youthful ardour, with the good sense that saves Scott in his most imaginative flights. Her wit and shrewdness, her courage and self-command, are more like the sterling qualities of the bailie than the gifts of a mere heroine.

[1] Chap. xviii.

The Heart of Midlothian (1818), included among the *Tales of* "*The my Landlord*, is another historical epic, though the events take *Heart of* place chiefly on the domestic stage, losing thereby, however, not *lothian*" a particle of the epic grandeur and dignity. Scott evidently had a feeling that he must make some amends for the apparent harshness in his characterization of the oppressed Covenanters, in *Old Mortality*, though he refused to admit that he had been unfair.[1] If he had incurred any debt, he repaid it in generous measure by showing what that creed could beget in two such faithful peasant hearts as douce Davie Deans and his heroic daughter Jeanie. He stated in his preface to the *Chronicles of the Canongate* (1827) that the main story in *The Heart of Midlothian* was in essentials identical with that of a poor Dumfriesshire woman, Helen Walker, who had refused to swear a falsehood to save the life of her sister, on trial for child-murder, and travelled on foot to London, presented a petition to the Duke of Argyll, and obtained her sister's pardon.[2] The novel opens with a tremendous page of Edinburgh history, a full account of the Porteous riots. This episode is carefully dovetailed into the narrative; it deepens the interest, and swells the ground-tone of tragic dread. Effie is actually lodged in the Tolbooth at the awful moment when Captain Porteous is dragged out of his hiding-place and taken to be hanged in the Grassmarket; her lover is one of the ringleaders of the mob, and tries to rescue her at the same time; Butler, her sister's sweetheart, is the minister who was forced to wait upon Porteous in the short space before his execution. But these complications led Scott to bring in at the end of the novel several chapters in which the unfortunates are restored to worldly prosperity, but only to meet with other disasters, and " illustrate the great truth, that guilt, though it may attain temporal splendour, can never confer real happiness," and that past crimes " haunt the steps of the malefactor " and will be avenged in most unlikely

---

[1] This is hinted in the humorous introduction by Jedediah Cleishbotham, where *inter alia* Scott deprecates identification with " the author of *Waverley* " —the inscription on the title-page of *Guy Mannering*, etc.—and rebukes " the children of vanity " who have sought to identify him " with I know not what inditer of vain fables."

[2] See Chambers, 117-119, and W. S. Crockett : *The Scott Originals*, 231-242. It is not known that Helen Walker was actually cited as a witness at the trial of her sister.

ways.[1] But this romancing, of negligible interest in comparison with the great central drama, is not obtruded; the last chapters need not be read; and, without them, the book ranks with its immediate predecessor as one of the most truly dramatic, and richest in character, pathos, and humour, of all Scott's novels.

Scott's best heroine, Jeanie Deans

From the scanty material vouchsafed in the account of Helen Walker, Scott evolved the homely and modest but noblest of his heroines, the peasant, Jeanie Deans. In piety, resignation, and fortitude she is the equal of Bessie Maclure. Her unquestioning faith in the Cameronian doctrines of her progenitors has given her a heart proof against the subtlest temptations, and a serenity that nothing can ruffle or intimidate. There had been simple heroines in fiction before Jeanie. But she is not one of the half-miraculous patient Griseldas of mediæval romance, nor a pattern of good conduct and exemplary training like Pamela. She is an unassuming peasant girl, without the slightest consciousness that her heroism is anything out of the common. When her lover remonstrates, and explains that the king nowadays does not sit in the gate to administer justice, but does everything through his ministers.

" And if they be upright, God-fearing ministers," said Jeanie, " it's sae muckle the better chance for Effie and me."

" But you do not even understand the most ordinary words relating to a court," said Butler; " by the ministry is meant not clergymen, but the king's official servants."

" Nae doubt," returned Jeanie, " he maun hae a great number mair, I daur to say, than the duchess has at Dalkeith, and great folk's servants are aye mair saucy than themselves. But I'll be decently put on, and I'll offer them a trifle o' siller, as if I came to see the palace. Or, if they scruple that, I'll tell them I'm come on a business of life and death, and then they will surely bring me to speech of the king and queen." [2]

Jeanie and her father

In Helen Walker's refusal to tamper with the truth and in the journey that procured her sister's pardon, Scott had the main lines of his story laid down beforehand. But Helen was an orphan; whilst the only person ever pointed out as supplying a few traits for Jeanie's father was an almost legendary namesake, Patrick

---

[1] Note to reader, preceding the envoy.　　　　　[2] Chap. xxvii.

Walker, who suffered for the cause in his youth, and in later life was a pedlar and then a small shopkeeper in Edinburgh, with a reputation for polemical acuteness and for his fulminating denunciations of the ungodly.[1] Scott, however, must have full credit for the father of such a daughter as Jeanie, though there may be echoes of Patrick Walker in David's voice uplifted in spiritual arrogance against the backslidings of the present age.

"Out upon ye, Mr Saddletree!" exclaimed David, who, in an opportunity of giving his testimony on the offences and backslidings of the land, forgot for a moment his own domestic calamity—"out upon your General Assembly, and the back of my hand to your Court o' Session!—What is the tane but a waefu' branch o' cauldrife professors and ministers, that sate bien and warm when the persecuted remnant were warstling wi' hunger, and cauld, and fear of death, and danger of fire and sword, upon wet brae-sides, peat-haggs, and flow-mosses, and that now creep out of their holes, like blue-bottle flees in a blink of sunshine, to take the pu'pits and places of better folk—of them that witnessed, and testified, and fought, and endured pit, prison-house, and transportation beyond seas?—A bonny bike there's o' them!—And for your Court o' Session——"

Old Saddletree reminds him that to raise scandal anent the Court of Session was a crime *sui generis*—" *sui generis*, Mr Deans —ken ye what that amounts to?" " I ken little o' the language of Antichrist," rejoins David, and runs on in a furious tirade that brings him at last to "the soul and body killing Court o' Justiciary."

The habit of considering his life as dedicated to bear testimony in behalf of what he deemed the suffering and deserted cause of true religion, had swept honest David along with it thus far; but with the mention of the criminal court, the recollection of the disastrous condition of his daughter rushed at once on his mind: he stopped short in the midst of his triumphant declamation, pressed his hands against his forehead, and remained silent.[2]

The humour that waits on tragedy was never more poignantly displayed than in David and Jeanie's deliberations on the question

[1] Chambers, 119-124; Crockett, 230-231.   [2] Chap. xii.

of her evidence in the fatal trial, their anguish embittered by the pedantic literalness of the causidical Saddletree, who secures a half-day holiday for the children at Butler's school, " so that the bairns might gang and see the hanging, which canna but have a pleasing effect on their young minds, seeing there is no knowing what they may come to themselves." Yet Adolphus, one of Scott's best critics, is not alone in pronouncing a still more moving episode, the first interview of Jeanie Deans with her imprisoned sister in the presence of Ratcliffe, " a piece of writing which alone might entitle its author to sit down at the feet of Shakespeare."[1] The trial itself is seen through the eyes of these humble participants in the tragic ordeal; and in the grandeur of the subdued pathos appears again Scott's supreme gift, never to overstrain the terrible, the romantic, or the humorous. Who but he could have mixed with such perfect propriety the fooleries of Dumbiedykes and Saddletree, the gossip of Plumdamas, Miss Damahoy, and Mrs Balchristie, and the malevolent gibes of the rabble outside the court-house, with these solemn passions?

Characters of the broad highway   The incidents of the journey to London may have owed something to Fielding's comedy of the broad highway, though as much might have been said of like episodes in *Waverley* and *Rob Roy*. Jeanie's bare feet and tartan hood attract little attention in her own country, but in England she meets with many jests and gibes. Then her countrywoman, the good landlady of the Seven Stars at York, reminds her that there are highwaymen in England, " for ye are come into a more civilized, that is to say, a more roguish country than the north "; at which remark Jeanie's mind recurs to a bit of paper given her by Ratcliffe, the Edinburgh thief-taker, which she puts in the hand of Mrs Bickerton. Here there is a little touch betraying the antiquary.

The Lady of the Seven Stars did not, indeed, ring a bell, because such was not the fashion of the time, but she whistled on a silver call, which was hung by her side, and a tight serving-maiden entered the room.

" Tell Dick Ostler to come here," said Mrs Bickerton. Dick Ostler accordingly made his appearance;—a queer, knowing,

[1] Letters to Richard Heber, 96. Probably the reference is to *Measure for Measure*.

shambling animal, with a hatchet face, a squint, a game arm, and a limp.

"Dick Ostler," said Mrs Bickerton, in a tone of authority that shewed she was (at least by adoption) Yorkshire too, "thou knowest most people and most things o' the road."

"Eye, eye, God help me, mistress," said Dick, shrugging his shoulders betwixt a repentant and knowing expression.—"Eye! I ha' know'd a thing or twa i' ma day, mistress." He looked sharp and laughed—looked grave and sighed, as one who was prepared to take the matter either way.

"Kenst thou this wee bit paper amang the rest, man?" said Mrs Bickerton, handing him the protection which Ratcliffe had given Jeanie Deans.

When Dick had looked at the paper, he winked with one eye, extended his grotesque mouth from ear to ear, like a navigable canal, scratched his head powerfully, and then said, "Ken!— ay—maybe we ken summat, an it werena for harm to him, mistress!"

"None in the world," said Mrs Bickerton; "only a dram of Hollands to thyself, man, an thou wilt speak."

"Why, then," said Dick, giving the head-band of his breeches a knowing hoist with one hand, and kicking out one foot behind him to accommodate the adjustment of that important habiliment, "I dares to say the pass will be kend weel enough on the road, an that be all."

"But what sort of a lad was he?" said Mrs Bickerton, winking to Jeanie, as proud of her knowing ostler.

"Why, what ken I?—Jim the Rat—why he was Cock o' the North within this twelmonth—he and Scotch Wilson, Handie Dandie, as they called him—but he's been out o' this country a while, as I rackon; but ony gentleman, as keeps the road o' this side Stamford, will respect Jim's pass."

Without asking further questions, the landlady filled Dick Ostler a bumper of Hollands. He ducked with his head and shoulders, scraped with his more advanced hoof, bolted the alcohol, to use the learned phrase, and withdrew to his own domains.[1]

It is one of many rencontres with the strangest of humanity, each drawn with the same curious delight and stamped as an authentic individual. It is also one of the glimpses frequent in this novel into the murky underworld of criminals, double-dyed informers,

[1] Chap. xxviii.

and reckless defiers of the law, among whom Madge Wildfire dances like a corpse-light over the damned.

> " My banes are buried in yon kirkyard
> Sae far ayont the sea,
> And it is but my blithesome ghaist
> That's speaking now to thee."

The grim realism of Ratcliffe, Sharpitlaw the constable, and Meg Murdockson almost carries off the melodrama of Robertson, *alias* George Staunton, ally of the smugglers, and leader in the riot, who is Effie's secret lover. Of the interview with Argyll and the queen which was the goal of Jeanie's hard pilgrimage, all that need be said is that Scott here again showed that it was not from inability to draw an adequate portrait that he usually put his monarchs, great statesmen, and men of action in secondary places. Both are presented with the same address and the same simplicity as he was to show later in his Louis XI, Queen Elizabeth, and Mary of Scotland, the same, in short, as in his Jeanie, who comports herself in this situation with the modest assurance that would be expected of such a woman.

" The Bride of Lammermoor "

Scott dictated *The Bride of Lammermoor* and *A Legend of Montrose* (1819), the last of his *Tales of my Landlord*, whilst in a state of bodily anguish. " If I had not the strength of a team of horses," he said, " I could not have fought through it."[1] Adolphus wrote of the former that it was " a tale which no man but a poet could tell."[2] This was a good point in the argument that the author of the lays must be the man who wrote the novels. But, whilst there is something to be urged for reading *The Bride of Lammermoor* as a poem thrown into the outward shape of a novel, it would have to be as a romantic poem of the same hybrid class as the lays, good at rendering the circumstance and colour, the feats and adventures, and the evil dispensations of life, but showing men hurried along by events rather than shaping them. It is a tragic story indeed; the end is foreshadowed from the beginning; warnings and premonitions fill the mind with a sense of the predestinate—the prophecy of Thomas the Rhymer must

---

[1] Lockhart (xliv.) gives a pathetic account of this long fight against physical odds.

[2] *Letters to Heber*, 15.

be fulfilled, the last laird of Ravenswood shall woo a dead maiden to be his bride :

> " He shall stable his steed in the Kelpie's flow
> And his name shall be lost for evermoe."

But if tragedy, this is certainly not tragedy in which the pro- *Tragedy,* tagonist by his own folly or excess brings doom on his own head. *or the* The inevitability is external, much more so than in *Romeo and* *master-* *Juliet*, with which it is natural to compare it. The Master of *piece of* Ravenswood is another of Scott's passive heroes; he can show *romance ?* fight at need, but he is impotent in the hands of destiny. It is noteworthy that in *The Bride of Lammermoor* there is more of the element of what Scott called " gramarye," of gloom and portent, of the sheer supernatural, than in any of the preceding novels; it is similar to, though infinitely better than, the romantic novels of the Lee sisters and Mrs Radcliffe. Remember that Scott once thought of writing a novel in the Otranto style. In *Waverley*, he had brought in second sight and the apparition of the Bodach Glas; in *Guy Mannering*, astrology and an ancient prophecy fulfilled; Radcliffian mystery and the fateful bodings of the old witch Elspeth, in *The Antiquary*, the dreams and visions and prophetic invectives in *Old Mortality*, had deepened the prevailing atmosphere of dread; and there was much of the same sort in *The Heart of Midlothian* and *The Black Dwarf*. In *The Lay of the Last Minstrel*, in *Marmion*, and *The Bridal of Triermain*, he had used the Gothic paraphernalia with a prodigal hand; his lays had been Gothic romances in rhyme. And now he takes a family legend, of the same gloomy character as the ballad histories on which these were founded, and, with little of the rationalization expected in a novel, makes out of it a romance of plighted love trampled upon by a hard and ambitious mother, a marriage signalized by the death of the bride and bridegroom, and the long-predicted extinction of an ancient house, with all the accompaniments of omens, phantasms, and maledictions appropriate to the theme. Even Scott, when he rose from his bed and read the published book, of which " he did not recollect one single incident, character, or conversation," uneasy lest he " should be startled by meeting something altogether glaring and fantastic," said, though he hoped it would pass, " I felt it monstrous gross and grotesque," adding, " but still the worst of it made me laugh, and I trusted the good-natured public would not be less indulgent."[1] Obviously, Scott, in the torments of a cruel malady, had yielded himself to the spells of a romanticism which he usually repressed, or indulged with some discretion. On the other hand, it is not unfair to Scott or his romantic predecessors to see in *The Bride of Lammermoor* that masterpiece of Gothic fiction which so many had been trying to write and never succeeding. It has to perfection all they were aiming at; terror and suspense are refined into the semblance of tragedy, the ghastly and the grotesque become the ministers of dark foreboding. In this novel Scott shows himself more than in any other swayed by those motives which were of the essence of Radcliffian romancing, both sentimentalism and terror.

Gothic character-istics   Though much has been written on the sources of the tale, the germ of which was a tradition of the Dalrymples, Earls of Stair, accepted by Macaulay as a verified fact,[2] it has no historical foundation, and was probably only a bit of ancient gossip fossilized into legend.[3] Scott transplanted the scene from the west to the east coast of Scotland, and composed a story that accorded with what he assumed to be the facts. He was believed to have drawn Wolf's Crag, the melancholy retreat of the Master of Ravenswood, from Fast Castle, on the coast of Berwickshire, which he had seen only from the sea. This might well have suggested it; Wolf's Crag, nevertheless, is only the classic edifice of Gothic romance in a new setting.

A wilder or more disconsolate dwelling it was perhaps difficult to conceive. The sombrous and heavy sound of the billows, successively dashing against the rocky beach at a profound distance

---

[1] Lockhart, xliv.

[2] Speaking of Sir James Dalrymple, Macaulay says : " One of his daughters had poniarded her bridegroom on the wedding night." And later : " His wife, a woman of great ability, art, and spirit, was popularly nicknamed the Witch of Endor " (*History of England*, xiii.).

[3] Crockett is more than usually cautious about the story which was current in Wigtonshire. " It is unlikely that it followed, even approximately, the particular line taken in the novel . . . there is no contemporary corroboration for the facts as alleged " (*The Scott Originals*, 250-251). See also Chambers, 128-136. Chambers also puts forward a claimant to be the prototype of Caleb Balderston.

beneath, was to the ear what the landscape was to the eye—a symbol of unvaried and monotonous melancholy, not unmingled with horror. Although the night was not far advanced, there was no sign of living inhabitants about this forlorn abode, excepting that one, and only one, of the narrow and stanchelled windows which appeared at irregular heights and distances in the walls of the building, showed a small glimmer of light.

And Ravenswood Castle, now in the possession of the Master's ancestral enemy, the Lord Keeper, is likewise depicted with all the gloomy features appertaining to a chronicle of hatred, tyranny, and crime. How pleased Catherine Morland would have been had she found herself in such an abode in the wilds of Gloucester-shire; for *Northanger Abbey* had appeared only the previous year, and was after all not so very much out of date. Gothic fiction was far from defunct. Lucy Ashton is, indeed, one of those graceful, tearful young ladies that Scott had taken over from an outworn tradition, the Edith Bellendens, Isabella Wardours, and their kin. She has that haunting sense of being marked down by fate which had been the badge of romantic heroines from as long ago as Prévost. Scott himself seems to be aware of her literary pedigree when, after the pathetic speech when she likens herself to the wounded bird seeking a brake or whin-bush where it can die in quiet, he makes her scoffing brother cry out, " Ah! that's some speech out of your romances, and Sholto says they have turned your head." He scampers off, and Lucy pursues her reflections.

" It is decreed," she said, " that every living creature, even those who owe me most kindness, are to shun me, and leave me to those by whom I am beset. It is just it should be thus. Alone and uncounselled, I involved myself in these perils—alone and uncounselled, I must extricate myself or die."[1]

Scott could not reduce himself to the inanity of his predecessors. Lucy Ashton has life in his hands, and the beauty of a predestined victim; but it is the beauty of her pathetic situation. So too with his other protagonist. The Master of Ravenswood is drawn in sombre lines as the last heir of the ruined family; he acts his

[1] Chap. xxix.

part well, and, like the partner of his sorrows, he speaks in the natural accents which give lifelikeness to Scott's most romantic figures. In the talk of his young ladies and young gentlemen in love, he was often formal and stilted; but there is not much of this affected diction here. On the contrary, in many of the most moving passages the feeling finds spontaneous outlet in something like the overtones of poetry.

Tradi-
tional
characters

This was a case in which the story generated the characters, first the pair of lovers, and then the father and mother, arbiters of the event. Lucy Ashton is the innocent sacrifice to the demands of tragic romance, of the tale of woe as Scott had received it. He describes her first " as of a romantic disposition, delighting in tales of love and wonder, and readily identifying herself with those legendary heroines with whose adventures her memory had become stocked." So Mrs Lennox had described her Arabella, and Jane Austen her Catherine. But now, he said, the fairy wand had become the rod of a magician. Her lover was denounced as the enemy of her house. " She felt herself the object of suspicion, of scorn, of dislike at least, if not of hatred, to her own family, and it seemed to her that she was abandoned by the very person on whose account she was exposed to the enmity of all around her."[1] This was when Lady Ashton had forced a rupture with the Master of Ravenswood and was preparing her daughter's union with the affluent Bucklaw. Lucy weeps and laments, and then subsides into the passivity of sentimental heroines. Finally, in the madness of despair she stabs the bridegroom, and dies raving. All this is according to the grim old tale which Scott followed. His Master of Ravenswood is the ruined hidalgo with the faithful servitor, as old a figure of romance as the Spanish tales of chivalry in decay. The Master plays his part well enough; he is stately and impressive, but has no other distinction from the ordinary run of Scott's heroes.[2] It is the same with the other pair among the four chief personages : the pliable and intriguing Lord Keeper, well aware that from the worldly point of view it would

---

[1] Chap. xxx.

[2] Bagehot rightly dismisses the idea that Ravenswood is a character with any " inwardness," and says : " His proud poverty gives him a distinctness which otherwise his lineaments would not have. We think little of his love ; we think much of his narrow circumstances and compressed haughtiness " (*Literary Studies*, " The Waverley Novels ").

be no bad match to wed his daughter to the heir of the Ravenswoods, but without the spirit to stand up to his terrible wife when his friend the marquess is no longer at his elbow to keep her ferocity within bounds; and, lastly, that implacable woman herself, " the Witch of Endor," sworn enemy according to tradition of the rival house, who single-handed brings down the tragedy. All four are well drawn, with just enough personality to fulfil the needs of dramatic fitness.

The Gothic novels of the previous generation sometimes *Humorous* affected interludes of broad comedy, with lamentable results. *extrava-* Scott could never refrain from the incidental merriment that *ganza* lightens even the dark scenes of *Old Mortality* and *The Heart of Midlothian*. In this novel, which begins and ends in tragedy, for it opens with a funeral, he was a little too lavish with the low comedy that sets off the gloom and horror. The devoted servitor of tradition evidently got out of hand; and though Scott would never admit that Caleb was a caricature, he allowed that " he might have sprinkled rather too much parsley over his chicken." [1] The book was composed in agonies of pain. His friend Laidlaw who was taking it down used to beseech Scott " to stop dictating when his audible suffering filled every pause." " Nay, Willie," he answered, " only see that the doors are fast." And Laidlaw's exclamations of delight are on record at the more amusing bits : " Gude keep us a' !—the like o' that !—eh sirs ! eh sirs ! " [2] It was in a double sense a relief to the tragic tension. Caleb's raid on the Girders' kitchen, to furnish the empty table at Wolf's Crag, is uproarious extravaganza.[3] The dialogue here, and again in the later exploit, when Caleb pretends to burn down the ancient tower itself, threatened with another incursion of guests, shows Scott's style at its finest. Caleb's unconscious buffooneries may be overdone; but his are the absurdities that not merely furnish amusement but sharpen the pathos, as when he tries to make his master accept the gold which he has received as a tip from the Lord Keeper; or at the close, when the old man

[1] Lockhart, xliv.
[2] *Ibid.*
[3] Scott practically apologizes for its extravagance, in the note at the end of the book, citing a similar anecdote which, he says, was given him " with dates and names of the parties."

watching from the tower sees the Master ride straight for the fatal Kelpie's Flow, and then sees him no more.

A large sable feather had been detached from his hat, and the rippling waves of the rising tide wafted it to Caleb's feet. The old man took it up, dried it, and placed it in his bosom.

Gothic features as old as Shakespeare The tragic end is not merely foreshadowed at the outset, it is kept steadily before the eye by a succession of signs and forecasts. The dismal background weighs upon the spirit; the haunted fountain, the ancestral curse, the raven shot by her brother and staining Lucy's dress with its blood, and, more terribly, the wraith of old Alice appearing to the Master at the hour of her death, and the grim mirth of the witch-women laying out the body and anticipating with horrible glee the imminent downfall of those now rejoicing in youth, wealth, and power—all were the accessories of tenebrous romance from Prévost and Mrs Radcliffe to Poe and Hawthorne and the Brontës. But they are of older lineage too. Much of that which is called Gothic when found in a novel was the regular stage property of Elizabethan drama. The three hags streaking and winding the corpse in the churchyard, and gloating over the prospect of soon doing the same for himself, remind the Master of the three witches in *Macbeth*; but it is less a plagiarism from Shakespeare than a scene that can stand in competition.

" He is a frank man and a free-handed man, the Master," said Annie Winnie, " and a comely personage—broad in the shouthers and narrow around the lungies. He wad mak a bonnie corpse; I wad like to have the streaking and winding of him."

" It is written on his brow, Annie Winnie," replied the octagenarian, her companion, " that hand of woman, or of man either, will never straught him—dead deal will never be laid to his back, make your market of that, for I hae it frae a sure hand."

"Will it be his lot to die on the battle ground then, Ailsie Gourlay ? "

" Ask nae mair questions about it—he'll not be graced sae far," replied the sage.

Grimmer, if possible, is their chant as they look on at the bridal procession, and " girn and laugh " to themselves at the prospect of as braw a burial.

" D'ye see yon dandilly maiden," said Dame Gourlay, " a'
glistenin' wi' goud and jewels, that they are lifting up on the
white horse behind that hare-brained callant in scarlet, wi' the
lang sword at his side? "

" But that's the bride! " said her companion, her cold heart
touched with some sort of compassion; " that's the very bride
hersell! Eh, whow! sae young, sae braw, and sae bonny, and is
her time sae short? "

" I tell ye," said the sibyl, " her winding sheet is up as high as
her throat already, believe it wha list. Her sand has but few
grains to rin out, and nae wonder—they've been weel shaken.
The leaves are withering fast on the trees, but she'll never see
the Martinmas wind gar them dance in swirls like the fairy
rings." [1]

Once more, it is with poetry that *The Bride of Lammermoor*
must be compared.

A Legend of Montrose (1819) is another composite fabric of
romance and history, with the former predominating. It is a
thrilling tale for a boy, and the humours of Major Dalgetty
ensure its interest for those of a more discerning age. Scott wove
together by sheer narrative skill much incongruous material. He
had the doings of his Children of the Mist, a wandering tribe
of the proscribed MacGregors, with their fiendish revenge on
one of the Drummonds; and he had the strange story of the
murder of young Lord Kilpont after the battle of Tippermuir.
All this is loosely linked into a large episode in the campaigns of
Montrose, who was preparing his lightning-stroke against Argyll,
the winter march through the unguarded passes and the surprise

*" A
Legend
of
Montrose"*

---

[1] Chap. xxxiv. Rossetti must surely have got some ideas from this novel for
the bodings of the spaewife in his fatidical ballad, *The King's Tragedy—e.g.*

> " A year again, and on Inchkeith Isle
>   I saw thee pass in the breeze,
> With the cerecloth risen above thy feet
>   And wound about thy knees.

> And yet a year, in the Links of Forth,
>   As a wanderer without rest,
> Thou cam'st with both thine arms i' the shroud
>   That clung high up thy breast.

> And in this hour I find thee here,
>   And well mine eyes may note
> That the winding-sheet hath passed thy breast
>   And risen around thy throat."

of Inveraray. The facts were altered and rearranged. Lord Kilpont was turned into an Earl of Menteith, and coupled in unequal love with a mysterious Highland maiden, the captive harper who subsequently proves to be a lady and an heiress; he is wounded apparently to death, but recovers and receives his reward. But the Children of the Mist are the true heroes of the story; wild as the eagles and red deer of their mountains, they are romance pure and undiluted, and yet of Scott's own brand, the romance of reality, with but a pardonable touch of Ossianic hyperbole. Then to season his mixture of the ghastly, the sentimental, and the out-and-out poetic, Scott brings in the buffoonery and the bathos of his Scottish mercenary, Captain Dalgetty, the dauntless hero who will fight for any man that will pay him his wages; the military pedant, as absolute upon the point of honour, the etiquette of his profession, as upon the science of tactics or the art of fortification. He is one of Scott's most prized originals, without any mitigation, however, of his fundamental coarseness of fibre.

"There goes the hound," said Menteith, "breaking the face, and trampling on the body, of many a better man than himself; and as eager on his sordid spoil as a vulture that stoops upon carrion. Yet this man the world calls a soldier—and you, my lord, select him as worthy of the honours of chivalry, if such they can at this day be termed. You have made the collar of knighthood the decoration of a mere bloodhound."

"What could I do?" said Montrose. "I had no half-picked bones to give him, and bribed in some manner he must be,—I cannot follow the chase alone. Besides, the dog has good qualities."

"If nature has given him such," said Menteith, "habit has converted them into feelings of intense selfishness. He may be punctilious concerning his reputation, and brave in the execution of his duty, but it is only because without these qualities he cannot rise in the service;—nay, his very benevolence is selfish; he may defend his companion while he can keep his feet, but the instant he is down, Sir Dugald will be as ready to ease him of his purse, as he is to convert the skin of Gustavus into a buff jerkin." [1]

Montrose, who is only a minor character in the story that bears his name, speaks here with the voice of Scott, and Scott could

[1] Chap. xx.

always see the object from the two most opposite points of view. As long as he had this recipe for correcting his own extravagance, his own heroics, he was safe from criticism; and the only fault to be found with Dugald Dalgetty is that his creator lets him get out of hand, like Caleb in the previous novel, for the book might just as well have been called " A Legend of Captain Dalgetty."

CHAPTER VIII

IVANHOE AND OTHER ROMANCES

"Ivanhoe" sets the fashion in historical romance Ivanhoe (1819), most of which, like the two foregoing novels, was dictated from his sick-bed, marks a period in the history of Scott's work, and indeed of the novel all over Europe, for the change of ground, from his own country to England, and of period, from that which was within or not far beyond the remembrance of himself or of people he had talked with to the Middle Ages, had the effect of a new discovery. No one was likely in future to write historical romance in the puerile fashion of Horace Walpole, or with the ponderous dullness of *Queenhoo Hall*. The Scottish novels had made history, in so far as they had carried forward the art of fiction; but it was on lines already well established. This departure made history in a way of its own. Scott seemed to have torn down the curtains through which the man of to-day had had such uncertain glimpses of life in the past. No miracle could bring back all that had gone; but Scott showed in *Ivanhoe*, more decisively than in *Waverley* or *Old Mortality*, that by dint of study and research, aided by such imaginative understanding as enables poet, dramatist, or novelist to pierce beneath the outer integument of his fellow-men, else as inscrutable as the dead, a vivid and moving approximation to historical truth can be attained, far more like the past as it must have been than a dry-as-dust historian's reconstruction of the facts. The example was enough. French, and then Italian and German, as well as English novelists, turned from the present to the past, and historical novels, historical plays, and historical poems became the order of the day. It was as if bonds had been suddenly loosed, as if the world had grown larger. Byron had enchanted multitudes at home and abroad with his tales of strange lands and strange peoples. Scott opened out regions of wider extent: the historic past of his and other countries. Between tnem they did more than

any other two writers for the romantic movement in France, and ultimately for the romantic movement in Europe.[1] How and why will be discussed later. Scott would not have been surprised at the outbreak of historical romancing which speedily took place in all countries; what he would never have comprehended was the extraordinary social, moral, and even religious influence ascribed to the Waverley novels, a topic on which also something will have to be said later on.

Scott had crossed the Border in several previous novels; *Waverley* had begun in England, the first half of *Rob Roy* had been laid in Northumberland, where Scott had made several trips, and Jeanie's expedition from Edinburgh to London had led that wide-awake young woman across seven or eight English counties. *Fiction based on special research* But in this and most of the later English novels, he had but scanty local knowledge of his own, and tended to rely more and more on books and maps, and, if chance served, upon friends who had been on the spot. It was of course the same when he adventured on Continental themes, and the difficulties were probably no worse. Scott was never in Touraine, for instance; yet he did not go far astray in *Quentin Durward*, in which he eked out the knowledge gained by poring over Commines with his friend Skene's journal of a recent tour, and careful study of maps and similar material. In the present case he had not far to go for what he wanted; he simply took the accepted historians of his day, and relied for the rest on his wide familiarity with the ballads and chronicles. In the " dedicatory epistle " he made it clear that he painted with so broad a brush and with so much freedom and even licence in the detail that a little exact knowledge went a long way. He aimed at a general correctness of colouring, and was satisfied if in trying to put life into " the hard, dry delineations of an ancient manuscript," he introduced " nothing inconsistent with the manners of the age," and " the character and costume " remained inviolate. In the dialogue, again, he had to avoid the obsolete on the one hand and the obtrusively modern on the other. This was his tenth novel, and he knew the craft of historical romancer well enough to devise

---

[1] Louis Reynaud is very emphatic, and underlines the point : " En tout cas, c'est lui [Byron] qui, aidé de Walter Scott, *décidera de la révolution romantique en France* " (*Le Romantisme, ses origines anglo-germaniques*, 197).

a setting for a story as easily as he had devised stories for his settings. In *Ivanhoe*, however, criticism has been less severe on topographical inaccuracies than on the way Scott treated history with the strong hand, telescoping different generations and even centuries together, as Barbour had telescoped three Bruces into one, depicting survivals unknown to history from Saxon times, and making free with a Robin Hood from a later tradition. The excuse may be a lame one, but at least he put it forward, when he said in this preface, " it is extremely probable that I may have confused the manners of two or three centuries, and introduced during the reign of Richard the First, circumstances appropriated to a period either considerably earlier, or a good deal later than that era."

From realism to romance

Ivanhoe is romance, " a fictitious narrative," to quote his own definition, " the interest of which turns upon marvellous and uncommon incidents."[1] He had been moving in that direction in *The Black Dwarf, The Bride of Lammermoor,* and *A Legend of Montrose.* It is an exciting tale of adventure, with a background done in swift strokes by an expert scene-painter. It is a brilliant but very inaccurate costume novel. It has been described as a great historical masque; it would make an incomparable modern pageant. For it is the colour and glitter of the great spectacular scenes that have faded least, less even than the theatrical figures of Richard Cœur-de-Lion and Prince John, Front-de-Bœuf and the Templar, the merry friar of Copmanhurst and the Jewess. The feast in the Saxon hall of Cedric, the lists at Ashby-de-la-Zouche, the storming of Front-de-Bœuf's castle, described by Rebecca to the disabled Ivanhoe in an incomparable piece of oblique narrative, the stately trial by combat before the grand master of the Knights Templars, stand out for their visual splendour from among many scenes that make a different appeal, scenes of terror and humorous scenes, which are the best of all, such as that of the Black Knight and the holy clerk of Copmanhurst carousing in the latter's cell and singing jovial catches which the friar seeks to disguise with " a thundering *De profundis clamavi.*"

"What devil's matins are you after at this hour? " said a voice from without.

[1] See his *Essay on Romance.*

" Heaven forgive you, Sir Traveller ! " said the hermit, whose own noise, and perhaps his nocturnal potations, prevented from recognizing accents which were tolerably familiar to him— "Wend on your way, in the name of God and Saint Dunstan, and disturb not the devotions of me and my holy brother."

" Mad priest," answered the voice from without, " open to Locksley."[1]

The characters, great and small, are unusually numerous, and the vast majority are at the best semi-historical—that is, they are made up to fit into the imagined circumstances. Richard and John are almost the only two from written history, for, if there ever was a Robin Hood, he threw a very unimpressive shadow before him in Locksley. Scott's Richard is the gallant and jovial knight-errant of popular tradition; his John, the traditional coward and sycophant. The grisly form of Front-de-Bœuf was literally conjured up out of a name found in the Auchinleck manuscript. Cedric and Athelstane were flagrantly unhistorical, and the other two noble Saxons, Ivanhoe, whose mellifluous name came from an old rhyme, and the fair Rowena, are the indispensable lover and the high-born mistress of sentimental romance. This time Scott lets another female assert herself almost to the extent of being a rival heroine; and, not feeling called upon to make Rebecca perfect, he gave her a life and charm that were enhanced by the contrast with Rowena's insipidity.[2] To be branded as ineligible and a dangerous person, she had to be a Jewess; and she could hardly have come into the story at all without a partner in distress; hence her picturesque father, Isaac of York, and the grim scenes in which he is the pitiable emblem of the sufferings of his race in the Middle Ages. To balance the anti-heroine there is the anti-hero, the dark and dissolute Bois-Guilbert, a Lovelace in armour. The jolly friar is a matchless leader of the revels; but Gurth and Wamba play their smaller parts effectively, if they are second-rate in comparison with some of Scott's peasant humorists. Gurth's victory in bargaining with

---

[1] Chap. xx.
[2] What evidence exists for supposing Scott to have drawn his Rebecca and the love romance doomed to tragedy by her Jewish blood from Washington Irving's account of Rebecca Gratz is set out by Crockett (*Scott Originals*, 288-294).

the avaricious Jew is an excellent bit of the rustic comedy at which Scott was a practised hand.

The conclusion: Rebecca and Rowena

Ivanhoe would live by its episodes alone, and the suspense that links one incident to the next. But there is a plot, and a better one than in most of Scott's romances, linking Ivanhoe's fortunes with those of Richard and the disordered realm to which he returns. The hero had to be rewarded with the hand and wealth of Rowena; he was " too good a Catholic to retain the same class of feelings towards a Jewess." But Thackeray was not the first to object that it would have been happier for Ivanhoe and fairer to Rebecca had she become his wife. Scott defended himself by reminding his readers that such a union would have been impossible in those days. And at the same time he stated his views on the doctrine of poetic justice. A lofty character " is degraded rather than exalted by an attempt to reward virtue with temporal prosperity." It is not well to teach the young that " Verily, Virtue has its reward." " A glance on the great picture of life will show that the duties of self-denial, and the sacrifice of passion to principle, are seldom thus remunerated; and the internal consciousness of their high-minded discharge of duty produces on their own reflections a more adequate recompense, in the form of that peace which the world cannot give or take away."[1] Scott would have saved himself much ingenuity and kept closer to the tenor of real life had he always observed this doctrine, and not so often twisted history and probability to make prosperous conclusions for his romantic plots.

Novels of the sixteenth century

In the next two novels, *The Monastery* and *The Abbot* (1820), Scott came nearer home in both place and date. The former was written in large part before *Ivanhoe*, however, and so was a longer thrust into the dark backward of time than he had hitherto essayed. But if anyone knew all about the confusion and contention going on in the Border country when the Reformation was beginning, it was Scott. The ruins of Kennaquhair or Melrose Abbey lay hard by Abbotsford, and he was familiar with every valley and kink of the wild region where, at the age depicted, men still rode on forays, the hostility of Catholics and reformers was aggravated by the covetousness of lay barons and vassals of

[1] Introduction (1830).

the Church, and strife was at any moment ready to break out between the two kingdoms. The exact period seems to be the first years of Elizabeth; but the chronology is unpardonably confused; there are allusions to the Queen Mother, who was deposed from the regency in 1559; an English courtier appears talking the euphuism of twenty years later; and this gentleman quotes from the poems of Sidney, who could only have been at that time some five years old. Though he was dealing with the history of his own countryside, Scott's heart was not in the story, which drags along, enlivened by a few dramatic scenes in the Border peels or in the great religious house, till the intrigue, as he himself puts it, " is at length finally disentangled by the breaking out of hostilities between England and Scotland, and the sudden renewal of the truce." Still, the fighting on the Glasgow road, in the last chapters, shows the zest and also the military science of the old volunteer quartermaster, who would so gladly have been a professional soldier. Almost the only seducing figure in all these pages is the miller's daughter, Mysie Happer, Sir Piercie Shafton's lovely Molinara, though Scott was among his own folk. But the abbot Boniface must not be forgotten, destined to reappear in the sequel as the gardener Blinkhoolie, a charming and characteristic piece of extravagance. Scott unfortunately indulged his pedantry in two clumsier extravagances which became a byword: one, an antiquarian freak, the euphuistic Sir Piercie, the other, a folklorist freak, the White Lady of Avenel, deplorable result of his dabbling in Border superstitions and taking them only half seriously.[1] On the whole, *The Monastery* is best regarded as spade-work for the more shapely sequel, *The Abbot*.

Fiction here is as happily combined with history as it had been " *The* in *Old Mortality*. The love story of the page and the maid of *Abbot* " honour is not out of keeping, but adds the charm of romantic devotion to the tragedy of the queen's imprisonment in Lochleven Castle, where she is forced by the truculent envoys of the Council to sign her abdication. Catherine Seyton is a young lady with the wit and sprightliness which Scott usually kept for such buxom serving-maids as Jenny Dennison; and it is impossible not to be

[1] Lockhart attributed this " primary blot " to the persistence of " the German taste " and Scott's dwelling too much on what might have passed as a rapid sketch (chap. l.).

interested in the fortunes of her sworn liegeman, Roland Graeme, though he may be only one of the faultless young gallants of whom Scott had an endless stock in reserve. But Mary Stuart, though but the august mistress of the pair of hard-set lovers, holds the centre of the stage, and dominates the story, until the fatal day when, after Langside, she flees to England and the tender mercies of Elizabeth. Scott wisely left the question of her guilt or innocence in suspense. Romance is not concerned with the stern enigmas of tragic drama; and this is romance, the tale of a nameless boy and a maiden of high degree, a tale of the "marvellous and uncommon," in Scott's own phrase. Mary's helplessness and courage, her magnanimity and queenliness in the extremes of agony, make her the absolute impersonation of the strangeness and beauty which are the quintessence of romance. Scott does not analyse, as the historian or a modern historical novelist would have done; he lets her show her wit, her fortitude, and majesty, in action. Most impressively, perhaps, in the interviews with the fierce Ruthven, the harsh but generous Lord Lindesay, and the politic Melville. But the intellectual force which is one of the distinctions of all Scott's crowned heads comes out most in the irony, now courtly and urbane, now withering, of her duels with her gaoler, Lady Lochleven.

"Your Grace will drive this woman frantic," said Fleming, in a low tone. "On my knees I implore you to remember she is already dreadfully offended, and that we are in her power."

"I will not spare her, Fleming," answered the Queen; "it is against my nature. She returned my honest sympathy with insult and abuse, and I will gall her in return—if her words are too blunt for answer, let her use her poniard if she dare."

"The Lady Lochleven," said the Lady Fleming aloud, "would surely do well now to withdraw, and to leave her Grace to repose."

"Ay," replied the Lady, "or to leave her Grace, and her Grace's minions, to think what silly fly they may next wrap their meshes about. My eldest son is a widower—were he not more worthy the flattering hopes with which you have seduced his brother?—True, the yoke of marriage has been already thrice fitted on—but the church of Rome calls it a sacrament, and its votaries may deem it one in which they cannot too often participate."

"And the votaries of the church of Geneva," replied Mary, colouring with indignation, "as they deem marriage *no* sacrament, are said at times to dispense with the holy ceremony." Then, as if afraid of the consequences of this home allusion to the errors of Lady Lochleven's early life, the Queen added, "Come, my Fleming, we grace her too much by this altercation; we will go to our sleeping apartment. If she would disturb us again to-night, she must cause the door to be forced."[1]

Romance was in the ascendant also in the next three novels, "*Kenilworth, The Pirate*, and *The Fortunes of Nigel*, though in the last-named Scott's declared purpose was to depict "the state of society in the reign of James I," and bring out "the strong contrast produced by the opposition of ancient manners to those which are gradually subduing them," a purpose which he carried out with painstaking realism in the details of his picture. In all three he allowed himself a very free hand, and he admitted in his introductions that many of the incidents were "of a marvellous and improbable character." In *Kenilworth*, in which he proposed, at the suggestion of the booksellers, to do for the reign of Elizabeth what he had done so felicitously for the times of Mary Queen of Scots, he took flagrant liberties with chronology, in an endeavour to crowd into one diversified canvas all that popular fancy had imaged of the most exciting reign in English history. Constable had proposed "The Armada" as an alluring title, which would have pledged Scott to a full dramatic treatment of one of the most critical episodes in our national history. If he had undertaken the whole story of the threatened invasion and the defeat of the Armada, he would have had to show the nature of the forces and antipathies arrayed against each other, and then to exhibit his statesmen deliberating and making decisions, his leaders ordering and directing, and his soldiers and sailors carrying out their parts and winning victories, with the common people, in the background or the foreground according to his choice of a point of view, convulsed by the terrors and passions of war. He would have had to reveal the mainsprings of the drama, as well as that which every man could see. Even in *Old Mortality*, the ablest of his novels concerned with a complex historical event, that event

"Kenil-worth"

---

[1] Chap. xxx.

is not the main subject; Morton, whose experiences are of foremost interest, sees a great deal of the game, but having his own hand to attend to, he does not see all. Scott was always very sparing in his drafts upon actual history. Deliberately or involuntarily, he avoided the great episodes which are history in the making, or kept on the outskirts. He preferred to show his great personages as they walked and talked in the affairs of everyday life, rather than in the stress of momentous events, in the actual performance of the acts that certify greatness. This was not his province. The novel of adventure, at any rate in Scott's hands, was not the novel of action. His stories are packed with exciting incident. And yet his heroes are remarkable, not for what they do, but for the adventures which they go through before fortune crowns a career not carved out by themselves. They have no more will of their own, no more fixity of purpose or power of choice and decision, than the Gil Blas or Roderick Randoms of picaresque fiction. As a romancer, he dealt in adventure, not feats of audacity and will-power. As a creative novelist and humorist, he was more intent on the idiosyncrasies and picturesque vagaries of mankind than on the drama of human will at odds with circumstance. Hence, as so often noted, his plots are of trifling interest, merely contrivances for keeping things moving; and they were apparently the last item to be thought of when he had made his mind up about everything else.

Based on a fabulous tradition Scott rejected the title proposed by Constable, and with it all pretence at a novel of Elizabethan times which should be a piece of romanticized history. He was at first inclined to call the novel he did write " Cumnor Hall," after Mickle's doleful ballad of the death of Amy Robsart, which had caught his imagination and suggested an effective plot. He had read the popular version of the story in Ashmole's *Antiquities of Berkshire*, without making the further inquiries which would have proved it a distortion of the facts.[1] Kenilworth he had seen in 1815. Thus the spirit of place and a melancholy legend combined in the inception of a story of intrigue and crime which was also to embrace the petty politics, feuds, and jealousies of the Court, and the incidental

---

[1] A résumé of the facts is given by Seccombe (118-121). See also Buchan, 232-233. Scott printed Ashmole's account of the case and Mickle's ballad in the introduction added in 1831.

humours of tavern-keepers, serving-men, bumpkins, and pedants, which Scott, no more than Shakespeare, could leave out from a picture of manners. True or untrue, the story served. With the majesty of Elizabeth presiding in the background, the goal of contention and the dispenser of rewards and punishments, and with the wronged lady and the perjured Leicester in the fore-ground, Scott was amply provided. Sussex, Blount, Raleigh, and the rest of the courtiers, though they are occupied in rivalries of their own, come in rather as patches of colour in the sumptuous spectacle of Court life than as participants in the drama. The life and death of Amy Robsart, boldly expanded and reconstructed to fit into the comedy of the queen's dalliance with Leicester, takes the precedence, and the pathos and horror of the close bring *Kenilworth* into line with *The Bride of Lammermoor*, as a romantic story suffused with the hues of tragedy, but like its predecessor rising only in places above the level of good melodrama.

His Elizabeth is one of Scott's successes in portraying the great and conveying a sense of their greatness. There is nothing subtle or searching in his reading of her character; he frankly accepts the conception held by most patriotic Englishmen. But his Elizabeth both speaks like a living woman and bears herself like a queen. Scott did brilliantly in the chapter representing the " celebrated audience " in the palace at Greenwich, in which the mutinous Sussex and Leicester are brought to heel. Here, as he puts it, " Elizabeth united the occasional caprice of her sex, with that sense and sound policy in which neither man nor woman ever excelled her." [1] *Kenilworth* is a rich panorama of Elizabethan life, full of activity and splendour and of light and shade, with all those contrasts of nobility and baseness, beauty and squalor, which had made the fortune of hundreds of sensational plays. But the secret of the greatness of the age he was depicting, of its dynamic energy, Scott never reveals. *Kenilworth* is a great historical pageant with the history omitted, an historical play in which there is no real drama. And the same might be said of most of Scott's historical novels.

The portrait of Elizabeth

Austere landscapes and stormy seascapes, stored in memory or

[1] Chap. xvi.

"*The Pirate*" jotted down in the notebook of his northern tour in 1814, formed the setting and atmosphere of *The Pirate* (1821), and no doubt inspired the story.[1] The descriptions are among the best he ever penned, the story is not so good. He peopled his rugged Orcades with fisherfolk and peasants, the udallers or yeomen farmers, and the well-to-do burghers of Kirkwall, whose manners and customs he had glimpsed on his visit to the isles, and whose legendary lore he had picked up then and now embellished with lore from the Norse sagas.[2] The story of John Gow's piratical doings, which he had from an old woman who was the original for his Norna, gave him the idea, much the same as that of Wordsworth's *Ruth*, of the arrival of a lawless being from a far different world among the simple islanders. Cleveland, whose life has been spent roving the tropic seas, tries to dazzle the udaller's innocent daughter with his luscious descriptions of exotic scenery, wealth, and luxury in softer climes. The plot is far-fetched; the primitive maidens are distinguishable only in externals from the average of Scott's sentimental young women; and Norna of the Fitful Head is more stagy than the rest of his sibyls and witches, in spite of his having known her original, and of the Norse colouring with which he tried to vary the well-known features.

"*The Fortunes of Nigel*" The fewest historical facts and the raciest and best of his re-creations of an historical personage are the particular features of Scott's next novel, which forms a sort of sequel to *Kenilworth* in the bird's-eye view it gives of the following reign. Scott said that in *The Fortunes of Nigel* (1822) he wanted to set forth the violent clash between the " rough and wild manners of a barbarous age "

---

[1] A paragraph in Scott's *Journal* shows how a suggestive scene could set Scott's mind working : " Thomson described to me a fine dungeon in the old tower of Cassillis, in Ayrshire. There is an outer and inner vaulted [chamber], each secured with iron doors. At the upper end of the innermost are two great stones or blocks, to which the staples and chains used in securing the prisoners are still attached. Between these stone seats is an opening like the mouth of a still deeper dungeon. The entrance descends like the mouth of a draw-well or shaft of a mine, and deep below is heard the sullen roar of the River Doon, one branch of which, passing through the bottom of the shaft, has probably swept away the body of many a captive, whose body after death may have been thus summarily disposed of. I may find use for such a place " (*Journal*, ii. 207).

[2] Miss Edith Batho has traced many references to and borrowings from *Eyrbyggja* and *Eirikrssaga* in *The Pirate* (*Sir Walter Scott To-day*, ed. H. J. C. Grierson, " Scott as Mediævalist "). " Scott read Old Norse with difficulty, and probably used the Latin versions of Bartholinus." There is a paper of his on *Eyrbyggja* in his *Prose Miscellanies*.

and the restraints and seriousness, often pushed to the extremes
of fanaticism, which were the results of the new learning and
better education and of the rise of Puritanism. But, whilst he
described the licence and gross depravity of the profligate section
of society, in terms which he feared might seem over-coloured,
the comedy of the Scot in London bulks large on his canvas.
This was not one of the grave social evils named in the
introduction; but there can be no mistake about the snatch of
verse heading the first chapter:

> Now Scot and English are agreed,
> And Saunders hastes to cross the Tweed,
> Where, such the splendours that attend him,
> His very mother scarce had kend him.

The time is a year after the arrival of James I, and more than *The Scot*
a dozen, and they by far the more important half, of the dramatis *in London*
personæ are from the other kingdom. James is not the only
historic figure. Scott thought he would present a masculine
counterpart to that heroine who, having " no claim to high birth,
romantic sensibility, or any of the usual accomplishments " of
her order, had impressed by her simple worth, his Jeanie Deans;
and he found such a one ready made in the king's goldsmith,
George Heriot, founder of the famous hospital in Edinburgh.
" Jingling Geordie," as the facetious monarch loved to call him,
plays a more conspicuous part than is dramatically appropriate;
and another countryman, David Ramsay, the king's watchmaker,
has the distinction, though only a commoner, of furnishing a
daughter to be the blue-blooded hero's bride. This gallant damsel
falls in love with Nigel before the youth is aware of it, and
donning boy's clothes, and playing the guardian angel, she has
the privilege of rescuing him from some of his most dangerous
predicaments. Scottish too are the irrepressible servitor and
self-constituted censor of Nigel's morals, Richie Moniplies, who
begins life in a flesher's stall and ends as Sir Richard Moniplies
of Castle-Collop; and the soured, peevish, caustic, and often
tedious Sir Mungo Malagrowther, one of Scott's survivals from
a previous age. Nigel Olifant is, of course, a Caledonian. The
whole trouble arises from his being one of those impoverished

188 HISTORY OF THE ENGLISH NOVEL

Scotsmen who have come to London in James's wake alleging debts from the Crown, and have been warned that their claims will not be entertained. The anti-hero, Lord Dalgarno, who with the Duke of Buckingham has designs on Nigel's estates, is another Scot; but he does no credit to his native land and not much to his author. He is a theatrical villain of the deepest theatrical dye, a monster of vice and malignity, simply part of the melodramatic apparatus, and in his well-timed death an illustration of the adage that " our pleasant vices are made the whips to scourge us."

The plot and the portraiture   The story, which has to entangle the hero in perils to life and fortune, and at the same time afford a view at close quarters of the shadiest sides of life in the metropolis, is a tissue of complications. It goes like clockwork, but it is not always clear to the reader how it does go. Scott let his delight in the intricacies of the law, Scots law in particular, run away with him once more in *The Fortunes of Nigel*. The hero incurs as many risks from legal hazards as from the sword and dagger of Lord Dalgarno or from the thieves and desperadoes in Alsatia, the old malefactor's sanctuary of Whitefriars, where through Dalgarno's machinations he is forced to take refuge. All this is rampant melodrama—a violent sequence of alarms and escapes, plots and counterplots, disguises and startling revelations, the whole set in motion by the obscure business of the mortgage and the debt outstanding from the Exchequer.

James I   The pictures of street life in the more respectable quarters, the motley crowds of shopkeepers and apprentices, the dicing and drabbing and duelling of the young nobles and their bravoes, and the gloomy limbo of iniquity in Whitefriars, are done with the same sombre strength as Scott's painting of the criminal underworld in *The Heart of Midlothian*, a novel much in his mind whilst he was writing this. But the masterpiece is his James I, who lives in these pages as probably nowhere else, a strange and almost incredible mixture of the homely and the grotesque, mountebank and man of wisdom, the most pusillanimous of monarchs, yet not without an odd air of kingliness. His pungent Scots idiom and tags of northern Latin are inimitably comic.

"No, no, no—bread o' life, man, I am a free king—will do what I will' and what I should—I am *justus et tenax propositi*, man—nevertheless, keep by the door, Lord Huntinglen, in case Steenie should come in with his mad humour."

In *Peveril of the Peak* (1823) Scott lost what would seem to have been a great opportunity. The secret history of the alleged Popish Plot might have yielded situations as telling as any of those treated in the other novels. But *Peveril*, written in depression of spirits—he said, he feared it would "smell of the apoplexy"[1] —reads like a maladroit imitation of himself; and he came to grief, strange to say, even in one of the trial scenes which were ordinarily his great successes. Two or three of the characters could have been limned by no one but Scott, the unsavoury Chiffinch, the second Duke of Buckingham, the puritanical Major Bridgnorth, and some of the humbler folk; but even these are studies rather than creations, put together from his reading in Restoration plays and the like. Derbyshire, the Isle of Man, and even London, were a long way from home, and he did not this time have the impetus and gusto which a mere handful of Scottish characters gave him on alien soil. But Scott was soon to recover the lost ground. In the book that followed, with the backing of his Scottish archers and the ardour of new conquests, he was to plant his flag victoriously on the other side of the Channel.

In *Quentin Durward* (1823), a romance of adventure that laughs probability to scorn is bound up with a famous chapter in European history, the quarrel of Louis XI and Charles the Bold, and Louis' blunder in going to Péronne and nearly wrecking the whole fabric of his diplomacy. In the introduction, Scott states the more serious object of the novel: to illustrate the innovations in the body politic and the immense social changes that took place with the passing away of feudalism and of the spirit of chivalry. In this revolution he saw the overthrow of a code of principles, liable to faults and excesses, but at any rate "founded on generosity and self-denial," and their supersession by the sordid motives of gain and selfish ambition. Louis XI of France was one of the most active agents in subverting the old and

"Peveril of the Peak"

"Quentin Durward: the last of the Age of Chivalry"

[1] Lockhart, lvii.

instilling the new political doctrines. He was " a character so purely selfish—so guiltless of entertaining any purpose unconnected with his ambition, covetousness, and desire of selfish enjoyment, that he almost seems an incarnation of the Devil himself." Scott cannot find words too severe for Louis' total want of scruple or sense of moral obligation, though he admits him to have been a man of " great natural firmness and sagacity of character," a man of courage, and on the whole successful in a policy too refined for his opponents, although he sometimes overreached himself. In fact, he could not help feeling that Louis was a great man. The conventional Scott thought it his duty to hate such an inhuman being, and to denounce his sardonic irony as " detestable hypocrisy "; yet at the bottom of his soul Scott liked Louis, was seduced by his bonhomie, enjoyed his humour, and so much admired his presence of mind in the most unnerving straits that he lets him usurp the post of hero, whilst Quentin, like most of his compeers, sinks to the position of a minor personage. It is Scott himself who observes " that the little love intrigue of Quentin is only employed as the means of bringing out the story," not the romance, that is, but the real story, of the struggle between Louis and Charles which ended in the collapse of the old order. He was also perfectly aware that Quentin was far too like a child of the age of reason to be in his true element in that rude time. So he explains that the lad had been taught by an old monk " the duties of humanity towards others,"

and, considering the ignorance of the period, the general prejudices entertained in favour of a military life, and the manner in which he himself had been bred, the youth was disposed to feel more accurately the moral duties incumbent on his station than was usual at the time.[1]

So the world of the past is looked at through modern eyes; and, as in *Waverley* or in *Old Mortality*, the commentary becomes part and parcel of the narrative.

History and romance But the romance fits the history like a glove, although the stuff it is made of is rather flimsy and some of the anachronisms stretch it to breaking-point. Apart from the great adventure of

[1] Chap. vi.

Quentin Durward in escorting the two princely ladies from Louis' Court at Plessis-les-Tours to the Burgundian territory, the story is in the main a dramatization of Commines, and Scott makes it pivot on that extraordinary historic incident, the king's ill-advised visit to his rival at Péronne, when he found himself at the mercy of his unruly vassal, infuriated at that very moment by news of the rising at Liége. But to pile up the agony of the climax, Scott doubles the peril of Louis' situation by making this revolt of the Duke's subjects coincide with the murder of the Bishop of Liége by William de la Marck, boldly antedating that event by fourteen years. He calmly admits his peccadillo in the notes; and at the foot of a page recounting the marriage of one of his chief characters, the Lady Hameline de Croye, to the sanguinary de la Marck, he explains that, after all, she is only an apocryphal person. Mere improbabilities are trifles thin as air in a romance; it is easy to let oneself be carried away by the charming tale of the obscure archer who by prowess and devotion wins the hand of his princess. But who can feel any further interest in events which he has been told never took place, or in some person who he is informed never existed? These are the sort of errors into which Scott was led by his endeavour to be both romantic and historical at the same time. He might easily have avoided them, at the expense of some of the romanticism which he laughs at in the sage witticisms of the Count de Crèvecœur, or by the time-honoured device of still more romanticism.

Except for these stumbling-blocks, the story runs with ever-increasing momentum and with scene after scene of tense drama *Historical portraiture* and glowing pageantry from Quentin's strange encounter with the eccentric monarch, in his plebeian garb and cap trimmed with leaden images, outside the gins and pitfalls defending the castle of Plessis-les-Tours, right on to the theatrical finale at Péronne and Liége. It is high romance, with interchapters of grave historical drama; and, so long as the spell works, Scott compels belief in both the one and the other. He seems to know all there is to be known about the life of the time. He has all the minutiæ of arms and armour, costume, heraldry, sports and pastimes, and the habits and manners of all classes, at his finger-ends, like a man of the same day. Balafré, the Scots swordsman, and his chief,

Lord Crawford, head of the Scottish Archers, are his own kindred; the latter is drawn with a tenderness that loves even his foibles; the former, Quentin's hard-bitten uncle, almost comes up to that other blunt soldier of fortune, Major Dalgetty.

" A monk ! " exclaimed the uncle—" Holy Saint Andrew ! that is what never befell me. No one, from my childhood upwards, ever so much as dreamed of making me a monk—And yet I wonder when I think of it; for you will allow that, bating the reading and writing, which I could never learn, and the psalmody, which I could never endure, and the dress, which is that of a mad beggar—Our Lady forgive me !—[here he crossed himself]—and their fasts, which do not suit my appetite, I would have made every whit as good a monk as my little gossip at Saint Martin's yonder. But I know not why, none ever proposed the station to me.—Oh so, fair nephew, you were to be a monk, then—and wherefore, I pray you? " [1]

No one could make a more accurate allowance for race and nation, clan, social order, and all the accidents of history and situation that distinguish one member of the human family from the rest. Hence he could draw as good a likeness of Louis XI as of his own countryman James I, and put flesh on the bones of such half-legendary figures as Louis' sinister underlings, Oliver the barber and the provost-marshal, Tristan l'Hermite, with their myrmidons the hangmen, and the wretched Bohemians on whom they fleshed their daily appetite for slaughter. Granted something for light and shade, the historical picture is as impeccable as any novelist could make it; here Scott is a sound realist. It was only in forcing historical fact to conform to romantic fiction that he erred. Yet he could provide the drench of wholesome astringent to his own extravagances. There is worldly wisdom enough in Crawford and old Balafré, enough and to spare in Louis, who one after the other school Quentin's lofty enthusiasm. The same corrective is to be found somewhere in every one of Scott's romances. Here the repartee of common sense to the young knight-errant's heroics is put in the mouth of the shrewd Burgundian ambassador, Crèvecœur, who has been

[1] Chap. v.

listening to the lad's report of his safe conduct of the two fair ladies from Touraine to Flanders.

"Yet stay, young gallant—one word ere you go. You have had, I imagine, a happy journey through Fairy-land—all full of heroic adventure, and high hope, and wild minstrel-like delusion, like the gardens of Morgaine la Fée. Forget it all, young soldier," he added, tapping him on the shoulder; "remember yonder lady only as the honoured Countess of Croye—forget her as a wandering and adventurous damsel: And her friends—one of them I can answer for—will remember, on their part, only the services you have done her, and forget the unreasonable reward you have had the boldness to propose to yourself."

Enraged that he had been unable to conceal from the sharp-sighted Crèvecœur feelings which the Count seemed to consider as the object of ridicule, Quentin replied, indignantly, "My Lord Count, when I require advice of you, I will ask it; when I demand assistance of you, it will be time enough to grant or refuse it; when I set peculiar value on your opinion of me, it will not be too late to express it."

"Heyday!" said the Count; "I have come between Amadis and Oriana, and must expect a challenge to the lists!"

"You speak as if that were an impossibility," said Quentin. "When I broke a lance with the Duke of Orleans, it was against a breast in which flowed better blood than that of Crèvecœur —When I measured swords with Dunois, I engaged a better warrior."[1]

The satire hits the mark none the less truly in that Quentin's outbreak is not mere rodomontade; fortune had indeed been so indulgent that he could make good his vaunt; and so Scott, having delivered his admonition and shown that he was not too much in earnest, could now please himself and a million readers by giving the young paladin his lady love and spiting the Count de Crèvecœur.

St Ronan's Well (1824) stands rather anomalously beside the rest of the Waverley novels. Scott, who was always protesting that the kind of fiction of which Miss Edgeworth and Miss Austen held the patent lay outside his scope,[2] seems here to have

"*St Ronan's Well*"

---

[1] Chap. xxiv.

[2] "The women do this better : Edgeworth, Ferrier, Austen, have all given portraits of real society, far superior to anything man, vain man, has produced of the like nature" (Scott's *Diary*, 28th March 1826, quoted by Lockhart, lxx.).

endeavoured to transplant their comedy of manners to a miniature Harrogate or Tunbridge Wells on the banks of the Tweed. Into this he interweaves romantic tragedy in the manner of *The Bride of Lammermoor*. Tragedy does not coalesce easily with comedy, though in a novel presenting different types with all sorts of histories some latitude is permissible. But tragedy mixes still less congenially with the convolutions and enigmas of a surprise plot, which tantalize the reader with clues and false scents when his mind is preoccupied with the pity and terror of heart-rending events. The social comedy in *St Ronan's Well* was less akin to the Edgeworth and Austen strain than to Scott's own delineations of nondescript humours in *The Antiquary* or *The Heart of Midlothian*, with more than a dash of satirical pungency very like Smollett's. As to the tragedy, this seemed somehow to miscarry, and fell short palpably of the consistency and inevitability of *The Bride of Lammermoor*.

The story altered before publication   But it leaked out presently that the novel as it reached the public was not as Scott originally wrote it. This was the age that welcomed Bowdler's *Family Shakespeare*,[1] and Ballantyne and Constable were both evidently the sort of people who would have suppressed the indelicacies of *Hamlet* or *Othello* rather than offend their customers. The one appealed to Scott, supported by the other, to alter a story in which a young lady of birth and refinement was permitted to suffer the same wrong as they had taken no exception to, in a still more grievous shape, in the case of Effie Deans, who was only a peasant girl. Scott complied, very reluctantly; but warned them that the result of cancelling and rewriting some two dozen pages, presumably with no alterations elsewhere, would be " to perplex and weaken the course of his narrative, and the dark effect of its catastrophe."[2] To change the terms of the argument would logically have entailed recasting the story. So he compromised by altering the terms of an equation which is then supposed to work out to the same result as before. What might have been as fine a tragedy as *The Bride of Lammermoor*, or even finer, was turned into one of those pseudo-tragedies in which the blows of fate fall at haphazard or at the wayward will of the story-teller.

Even without the ambiguity due to his perfunctory emendation,

---

[1] This was published in ten volumes in 1818.   [2] Lockhart, lix.

the story as Scott plotted it out had none of the simplicity and *Scott's* obdurate logic of tragedy. It is a principle as old as the Greeks *mania for* that the preliminary data of tragic drama have to be accepted *over-elaboration* without challenge, however improbable; but this does not imply that the initial perplexities may be held in reserve, and sprung upon the reader at the very moment when his mind is full of the dire consequences of those antecedent events. Scott, with his habitual misapplied ingenuity, complicated his plot with a string of baffling conundrums the solutions of which are given when they have lost nearly all their dramatic force. What is it that has separated Clara Mowbray and Tyrrel; what shame and remorse have driven the girl half distracted; why is her lover forbidden even to approach her? Then, as the tale proceeds, what is behind her terror of Etherington, manifestly a feeling far more dreadful than would be aroused only by an unwelcome suitor or the fact that she has given her heart to another? The affair of the marriage into which he had entrapped her seven years ago by impersonating his brother is as yet undisclosed; and, even when this comes out, it is very far from accounting for all her fear and anguish. As to the sordid motive of his villainy, the will of the grand-uncle who leaves his estate on the fantastic condition that the inheritor must marry a Mowbray or lose it, and the question, still in abeyance, which of the two brothers is the legitimate heir, these are among the preliminary circumstances which should not have been clumsily interpolated at the very point where such interest as they have clashes with that of the tragic crisis.

But this was Scott's way; and, to give him his due, it was all *The* explained, though far too late, in the original version. In the *original* novel as it was partly recast, the wanton expansions of the plot *version* are elucidated, but the questions which involve the cardinal points of the tragedy remain unanswered. The reader is left without a compass; and, when the blow falls, it has the effect of a chapter of terrible accidents, as Scott foretold. Happily, the cancelled pages were not destroyed, and the authentic account, still extant, of Hannah Irwin's dying confession to Mr Cargill gives the necessary key.[1] Lockhart apparently never saw this,

[1] See the account by J. M. Collyer (*Athenæum*, 4th February 1893), setting the crucial passages side by side.

for his statement that in the original conception " Miss Mowbray's mock marriage had not halted at the profane ceremony of the church " is incorrect.[1] Hannah had been the confidant of Clara and Tyrell, and knew that " a secret marriage was necessary to Miss Mowbray's honour "; but, seduced and abandoned by Etherington, she revenged herself on this miscreant by helping him to impersonate Clara's lover.

" I was resolved he should wed her, and take with her infamy and misery to his bed."

Hence the indignation of Mr Cargill, when he knew how he had been doubly imposed upon :

"Wretch ! . . . and had you not then done enough?—Why did you expose the paramour of one brother to become the wife of another? " [2]

Antecedent circum-stances afterwards explained The state of Clara's mind can now be understood in the fearful meeting between the brother and sister, at midnight in the lonely old castle, when Mowbray barely stays his hand from killing the sister who had shamed their ancient house. Here, as they part, is a scene as gloomily suggestive as those which deepen the tragedy in *The Bride of Lammermoor*.

He held out his hand, and she placed, but not without reluctant terror, her trembling palm in his. In this manner, and with a sort of mournful solemnity, as if they had been in attendance upon a funeral, he handed his sister through a gallery hung with old family pictures, at the end of which was Clara's bed-chamber. The moon, which at this moment looked out through a huge volume of mustering clouds that had long been boding storm, fell on the two last descendants of that ancient family, as they glided hand in hand, more like the ghosts of the deceased than like living persons, through the hall and amongst the portraits of their fore-fathers. The same thoughts were in the breasts of both, but neither attempted to say, while they cast a flitting glance on the pallid and decayed representations, " How little did these antici-pate this catastrophe of their house ! " At the door of the bedroom

---

[1] Lockhart, lix.
[2] Chap. xxxviii. Scott altered " paramour " to " betrothed," and left it at that.

Mowbray quitted his sister's hand, and said, " Clara, you should to-night thank God, that saved you from a great danger, and me from a deadly sin." [1]

But these pages come before the revelation, not after, when it would have had its proper value. The book must be read over again, to be properly understood. So, too, the tragi-comedy of the old nabob Touchwood's visit, which relieves the tension for a while, and even holds out hopes of a happy issue. But his intervention was too late. Touchwood and Mowbray have scarcely parted when the stricken girl, who has wandered out into the night, listens from behind the curtains of the death-bed to Hannah Irwin's recital of the whole iniquity. Tyrrel arrives to find her dying. The villainous Etherington falls by the hand of Mowbray.

He and his sister are the protagonists of the drama; Tyrrel is *The* only another of Scott's passive heroes confronting the nefarious *characters* anti-hero, Etherington. *St Ronan's Well* on its darker side is simply the tragedy of Clara Mowbray, who has a certain pre-eminence among those who may be called Scott's regular heroines, not merely by the dignity and pathos of her situation but by something in herself. No sentimental miss like Lucy Ashton, tamely submitting to her fate, she has the wit and high spirit to hold her own among the wild animals at the Wells; and, having chosen her melancholy part, withstands the appeals of lover, brother, and the husband whose toils she in her ignorance thinks unbreakable, with the anguish and resolution of an Antigone. Scott did not err this time by foisting in a happy ending. Mowbray, the rough and even brutal sporting squire, moody and sullen, with fits of ungovernable fury, is drawn with realism and little poetry; yet even he, brooding over " the downfall of an ancient house," has his points of likeness to the Master of Ravenswood. Originals have been found for Meg Dodds, the termagant hostess of the Cleikum Inn, best of all Scott's low-comedy queans, and the absent-minded divine, Josiah Cargill [2]; but they only testify to Scott's truth when he is most original. Touchwood is one of those eccentrics who pride themselves on their eccentricities;

[1] Chap. xxxv.
[2] W. S. Crockett : *The Scott Originals*, 313-340.

the fire-eating Captain MacTurk is one of a commoner stamp, but never better drawn—

> " I thank Cot, I can bring good witness that I am as good a Christian as another, for a poor sinner, as the best of us are; and I am ready to justify my religion with my sword—Cot tamn ! "

As to the strange collection at the Wells, " the menagerie," as Clara terms them, they are less like a company of ladies and gentlemen than a pack of snarling and snapping tykes. It is not simply that the pencil of an Edgeworth or an Austen is conspicuously lacking; these creatures do not belong to the same world of manners. But Scott no doubt was faithful to what he had seen. There are evidences in the work of contemporary novelists with only enough skill to render literally what was before their eyes that such society existed. For instance, the fashionables in such a novel as Lady Morgan's *O'Donnel*, published only ten years before *St Ronan's Well*, jealous, spiteful, suspicious, passing agreeable moments in scoring off each other, are a crude but recognizable parallel to the wrangling and horseplay at the Wells.

" Red-gauntlet "

In *Redgauntlet* (1824) Scott poured out more of his own early reminiscences than anywhere else in the whole range of the Waverleys; in it he retraced old experiences in Edinburgh and along the Border, and lingered over the wild environs of Gilsland, where at the old spa he had first met his wife.[1] Alan Fairford and Darsie are himself and Will Clerk, their traits a little mixed through the fog of recollection, Darsie, Alan's second self, having in his composition as much as the other of the youthful Scott. And, naturally, his ancient, ill-starred love affair came back to mind in reviewing the past, and inspired the faint but winning features of Green Mantle. The Geddes household, again, are said to commemorate his own Quaker kinsfolk. And there are doubtless other originals, allowance being made for his transfiguring pen, known to Scott perhaps only from record or hearsay, such as the Pretender's mistress, Clementina Walkenshaw, caught sight of here rather than seen, and Sir Robert Grierson of Lag, savage persecutor of the Covenanters, of whom the Redgauntlet

---

[1] " It contains perhaps more of the author's personal experiences than any other of them, or even than all the rest of them put together " (Lockhart, lx.).

of Wandering Willie's tale is the awe-inspiring double.[1] The pretty scene in which the elder Fairford is congratulated on his son's maiden effort in court is not historical; but the legal life and lore, and above all the gigantic extravaganza of Peter Peebles's plea, may be regarded as the affectionate tribute of humour and imagination to the days when he and Will Clerk first "put on the gown."[2]

In construction, the book is as irregular, easy-going, almost haphazard, as any of Scott's novels; but this seems to befit the contents. Reminiscence goes well into the musing or gossipy but always leisurely form of the letters exchanged by Darsie and Alan. Then as life grows exciting, both of them take to narrative, which soon breaks into a run; and at last there is a violent race to the dramatic finish. But right in the middle of the formlessness comes that jewel of polished and repolished workmanship, Wandering Willie's tale. One thing, at any rate, in which he usually failed, Scott achieved, unity; for, though *Redgauntlet*, like most of its companion novels, combines romance with history, or pseudo-history, it is not two stories badly amalgamated, but one. The private and personal and the public matters blend completely. The supposed historical event never took place; yet it might have taken place, at a time when it was currently believed that the Pretender paid a secret visit to London, was detected, and reported to the authorities, but allowed to depart unmolested, George III being too firmly seated on the throne and too magnanimous to seek to avenge himself on his defeated and discredited foe.[3]

The tale goes darkly though not haltingly; but on this occasion *Strong* some obscurity is a gain. The mystery enveloping the person *pictorial* and designs of Mr Herries of Birrenswork, not entirely cleared *episodes* up even when Peter Peebles identifies that gentleman as the laird of Redgauntlet and a proscribed Jacobite, and the strangeness of Darsie's kidnapping, keep uncertainty and suspense on the stretch

---

[1] Crockett, 341-356.

[2] Scott dwelt with fondness even on the minutiæ of costume which were now antiquated or entirely vanished. Note, for instance, his long archæological description of the feminine gown and mask in which Darsie is rigged out as a disguise, when in the custody of Redgauntlet's warder, the truculent Nixon (chap. xvii.).

[3] See Scott's note, 37.

till the grand disclosure at the end. For it is not tragic passions that are the overmastering interest, as in the previous novel, but the results of a young man's encounter with the checks and complications of circumstances beyond his comprehension or control. That is the keynote struck at the outset, when Darsie, wandering at nightfall on the Solway sands, is suddenly snatched up by the strange horseman and carried out of the clutches of the advancing tide. This, so like the memorable episode of Knockwinnock Bay in *The Antiquary*, is one of a whole gallery of scenes, as strong pictorially as in fiery drama : Darsie's rescue, followed by the revels of the smugglers and fisher lassies at Brokenburn, where he plays the fiddle with Wandering Willie and receives from Green Mantle the first hint of an unknown danger hanging over his head; and that, by the raid on the fishing-station, when he is carried off by the same dark cavalier and his satellites. At this point the Edinburgh scenes come in : Alan's debut as counsel to Peter Peebles, the letter put into his hand whilst he is delivering his speech to the Bench, his instant departure, which is such a stupefying blow to the crazed litigant, and the trip in Nanty Ewart's brig, followed by the ride with a cavalcade of free-traders to the house where he finds himself under the same roof as Father Bonaventure, the disguised prince.

The final scene From Alan's adventures the tale now doubles back to those of Darsie, in close confinement, but why or wherefore he cannot guess. The little comedy of Justice Foxley and the warrant, and the bit of age-old romance, Wandering Willie playing his airs to show there are friends outside who will deliver the captive, both alike lead to nothing. But now comes the turning-point. Darsie in his woman's garb is brought as a prisoner to Father Crackenthorp's inn beside the Solway, and it speedily transpires that all the rest of the dramatis personæ who matter are there already. The Jacobite outbreak is to take place now, or take place never. The reason for all the plots and disguises is at length made clear, though so far as it is a scheme to involve Darsie in the rising it is flimsy indeed. But Scott, with no mean strategy, has brought everything to a point; and now appears his great twofold masterpiece in the art of setting a scene—a scene which is to play itself out as naturally and decisively as life, and touch all the extremes, from the loftiness of tragic drama to the most grotesque comedy. Here is Peter Peebles again, in flight from Nanty Ewart's avenging hanger, and dementedly clutching at Alan, his fugitive counsel. Green Mantle is there, and Darsie somewhere in the rambling old hostelry. Yonder stands the valiant Quaker, Joshua Geddes, not to be browbeaten even by Redgauntlet, who packs off the whole crowd of mismatched disputants in the safe custody of Nixon, to confound each other with their unintelligible squabbling. All this time, in an inner room, the leaders of the English, Welsh, and Scottish Jacobites are gathered in anxious conclave round their prince, their necks in a noose, debating the pros and cons of action which will put lives and fortunes to a final hazard. On the beach outside, Ewart and the treacherous Nixon are locked in a death-grapple. Suddenly the alarm is given: Nixon has betrayed them; the Government troops are at hand. The conspirators and their prince are caught in a trap. Nanty's brig, the *Jumping Jenny*, has put to sea; there is no possible escape. At this moment of despair, General Campbell appears upon the scene with the message of pardon. And so, the Pretender takes his last farewell, and Scott ends his last romance of the fallen Stuarts. It is a noble scene, this imaginary finale to the sad epic—high romance and generous enthusiasm sobered and corrected at last by the logic of facts; and it follows admirably on the heels of the other scene, of such very different extravagances brought to reason by other constraints.

Not one of Scott's novels is richer in heterogeneous character. *A gallery* Peter Peebles, " of the great plea of Poor Peter Peebles against *of pictur-* Plainstanes, *et per contra* ": *esque characters*

" If I am laird of naething else, I am aye a *dominus litis*,"

may be enrolled as fugleman of all Scott's monomaniacs. And among his children of the wild, who could offer a better poetic claim to pre-eminence than Wandering Willie's tale? Justice Foxley and Master Faggot his clerk, the laird of Summertrees, *alias* Pate-in-Peril, the Quaker and his sister, Provost Crosbie of Dumfries, with the grey mare his aristocratic lady, and, to mention no others, that great reconciler of shady transactions and strict piety, Tom Trumbull of Annan, known far and wide as old Turnpenny: minor characters all of them, but what a galaxy they are!

" I wish thou couldst remember, man, that I desire to know nothing of your roars and splores, your brooms and brushes. I dwell here among my own people; and I sell my commodity to him who comes in the way of business; and so wash my hands of all consequences, as becomes a quiet subject and an honest man. I never take payment, save in ready money."

It is a pity Alan cannot appreciate Thomas Trumbull, and is " disgusted with his company." [1] But Scott felt it necessary to apologize for this " hoary old reprobate," and even to expound the moral of Nanty Ewart's progress to ruin, and the villainy of Peter Peebles in his palmy days, when his extortion " reduced the aged to famine, and the young to infamy," and sent Nanty out on his hapless career.[2]

Later novels: "The Betrothed" and "The Talisman" Scott was fifty-five at the time of the financial crash that left him for the rest of his days tied hand and foot to the publishers, writing his hardest to pay off the enormous debt which he had undertaken to guarantee. He had done his best work, and nothing that appeared from 1825 onwards added in any appreciable measure to the greatness of his contribution to imaginative literature. The *Tales of the Crusaders*, accordingly, *Woodstock*, and his *Chronicles of the Canongate* may be dismissed with more brevity; though it must not be thought that if anyone else had produced such work, even after Scott had set the pattern, it would not have staggered belief. The disaster was impending and more or less foreseen all the time that Scott worked upon his *Tales of the Crusaders*. He felt so depressed by his inability to put into the first tale, *The Betrothed*, anything like the life and interest of *Ivanhoe*, his first story of mediæval times, that he actually proposed consigning it to the flames, fully printed as it was but for a chapter or two. But he and the publishers hoped that the genuine merits of *The Talisman* would bear the companion story to success, and so indeed it did when they appeared together, in June 1825. Scott was now toiling like a galley-slave on his useless. *Life of Buonaparte*, for which vast stores of information

[1] Chap. xiii.   [2] Chap. xx.

had to be ransacked. Loads of printed and other material poured in; " the first wagon delivered itself of about a hundred huge folios of the *Moniteur*; and London, Paris, Amsterdam, and Brussels, were all laid under contribution to meet the bold demands of his magnificent purveyor."[1] The blow actually fell in January 1826; but Scott, though racked with anxieties and business consultations, went on with *Woodstock*, which appeared in June, and brought in the sum of £8228 for the creditors. In May, he had lost Lady Scott, and he was tortured with the knowledge that his grandson, the " Hugh Littlejohn " of *Tales of a Grandfather*, could not live much longer. Without a pause, however, he began the *Chronicles of the Canongate*, of which the first two volumes appeared next year, containing " The Highland Widow," "The Two Drovers," and "The Surgeon's Daughter "; and the second series in three volumes, consisting of the novel originally called " St Valentine's Day, or the Fair Maid of Perth," a year later.

There was too much Gothic stage-craft and too little of Scott's genuine romance in *The Betrothed*. But in *The Talisman* he put together a good story of war and adventure, with some rousing scenes in the manner that had become second nature, helped perhaps by his hero being a Scottish prince, and the most substantial of his by-characters, the old baron of Gilsland, Sir Thomas de Vaux, a Cumberland borderer. Richard and Saladin are drawn competently in the heroic style, and not without humour. And Scott managed to depict the highland scenery and the mediæval life of Palestine with such a vivid pencil that he has had the warm approval of authorities on the land and its history. In *Woodstock*, the beauty of very different landscapes served no less effectively. Though task-work, it is a strikingly cheerful story, entirely apart from the farcical proceedings of the commissioners from the Parliament and the practical joking on which he relied for comic relief. His Presbyterian minister, the Reverend Nehemiah Holdenough, Trusty Tomkins, the roguish factotum of the plenipotentiaries, and the ribald, blasphemous, intrepid cavalier, Captain Roger Wildrake, compare with the best in such a parallel delineation of seventeenth-century

" Woodstock "

---

[1] Lockhart, lxii.

characters as *The Fortunes of Nigel*, and are well supported by the historical portraiture, Cromwell and the fugitive Charles, and the neatly differentiated Bletson and Desborough. Scott wrote *Woodstock* with care, and the style is not marred by his usual slovenliness. Further, it was a well-made plot that he started with; and, though he got into difficulties and risked daring anachronisms, he pulled through with credit.[1]

"Chron-icles of the Canon-gate" Some of Scott's prefatory lucubrations read as if he had made these a vent for mere garrulousness; but it is unsafe to skip them. The introductory epistles to *Old Mortality* and *The Fortunes of Nigel* are excellent; but the best of all hitherto is the delicate sketch of that humane old philosopher, Monsieur le marquis de Hautlieu, cloistered in the remains of his château on the Loire, which is the frontispiece to *Quentin Durward*. Did Skene unearth this relic of a more civilized, pre-revolutionary age; or was the marquis only a sport of Scott's learned fancy, another Monkbarns? His situation is that of a Ravenswood, without the tragedy, and he has his Gallic counterpart to Caleb.

" You will be entertained with my poor La Jeunesse," he said, " who, by the way, is ten years older than I am "—(the marquis is above sixty)—" he reminds me of the player in the *Roman comique*, who acted a whole play in his own proper person—he insists on being *maître d'hotel, maître de cuisine, valet-de-chambre*, a whole suite of attendants in his own poor individuality. He sometimes reminds me of a character in the *Bridle of Lammermoor*, which you must have read, as it is the work of one of your *gens de lettres, qu'on appelle, je crois, le Chevalier Scott.*"
" I presume you mean Sir Walter? "
" Yes—the same—the same," answered the marquis.[2]

The introductory causeries and playful attempts to beguile the reader as to the now not very puzzling question, who wrote the tales and the novels? are better stuff than the *Chronicles* themselves. There is no forcing the note in these quiet reminiscences, these bits of half-disguised self-portraiture, vignettes of some that he had known and held dear: Mr Fairscribe, another *alias* of his

---

[1] He is amusingly candid about his troubles with the plot as he laboured at *Woodstock*, in the *Journal* (i. 114 and 117). See also pp. 103-104 on the bogle.
[2] Introduction to *Quentin Durward*. It is explained that *la Bride* (the Bridle) is a mistaken translation of " the Bride " ; but the marquis remains sceptical.

own father; Mrs Bethune Baliol, circumstantial presentment of that gracious friend of his youth, Mrs Anne Murray Keith, in her stately home in the Canongate; and Mr Croftangry, himself as he would have been, without his fame, his Abbotsford, and the anxieties and killing slavery of his latter years. In the tale of Croftangry he lets out his confidences and his deeper thoughts on life, with a candour that he otherwise reserved for the entries in his *Journal*. Even such a poor, melodramatic novelette as *The Surgeon's Daughter* is half redeemed by the kindly portrayal of middle-class life in a Scots village and the sketch of his own medical man at Selkirk, Dr Ebenezer Clarkson, in the surgeon, Gideon Gray. The best of the tales ushered in by Chrystal Croftangry are the two little tragedies, " The Highland Widow " and " The Two Drovers," of the mother who fatally persuaded her son to outstay his furlough, and of the Highlander Robin Oig, urged irresistibly by all that he believed in to his savage revenge. The rest are in the Gothic mode : " The Tapestried Chamber," a conventional ghost story, " My Aunt Margaret's Mirror," a tale of crystal-gazing reminiscent of Nashe's Jack Wilton,[1] and a Border saga, " The Death of the Laird's Jock."

The *Fair Maid of Perth* (1828), last of the *Chronicles of the Canongate*, is a romantic novel of full length, dealing with the crime-stained period of Scottish history when the Duke of Rothesay, son and heir of the crippled Robert III, was made away, probably by agents of the regent, the Duke of Albany. The murder of the dissolute young prince is one prominent event, and a more showy historical scene is that of the great combat on the North Inch of Perth between the clan Chattan and the clan Quhele. Both are skilfully linked as cardinal incidents into the romance of the burgher's daughter and her wooer, the redoubtable fighting man, Hal o' the Wynd, and the jealousies, intrigues, brawls, and villainies of roistering nobles and double-dealing townsfolk which beset their path to happiness. What distinguishes this from Scott's other stories of the Middle Ages is the pathetic study of cowardice, in the young chief of the clan Quhele, who gives way to panic at the height of the battle and plunges into the Tay. Recently, in the tortured mind of Clara Mowbray, in

"The Fair Maid of Perth"

---

[1] See Volume II. 163.

that synthesis of opposites, the laird of Redgauntlet, in the love between Damian and the affianced of his uncle, in *The Betrothed*, and in the fierce struggle in the mind of Robin Oig, Scott had explored deeper than his wont into abnormal states. He said that in this tragic example of a man giving way in the hour of trial he was performing " a sort of expiation " to the manes of his brother Daniel, who had disgraced himself by a lack of spirit and conduct in service against insurgent negroes in Jamaica, and whose funeral he had refused to attend. As to Scott's last three novels, *Anne of Geierstein* (1829) and the two, *Count Robert of Paris* and *Castle Dangerous*, which completed his *Tales of my Landlord* (1832), the first carried on the history of Charles the Bold from where he had left off in *Quentin Durward*, had a good love story, and was not inferior to most sequels, the other two showed but smouldering gleams of his former strength.

CHAPTER IX

SCOTT AS A NOVELIST

SCOTT was a reviewer before he became a novelist. When *Scott's* he wrote his prefaces for Ballantyne's *Novelists' Library* (1821- *relations to* 1824), the Waverley novels were in full progress. But the *Fielding and other* familiarity displayed with the novels of the last sixty years proves *pre-* that Scott had long made a careful study of the theories and *decessors* practice of his predecessors. He did justice to Richardson, as the first to throw aside " the trappings of romance," though hampered by a didactic purpose. But he had more approval for Fielding, " father of the English Novel,"[1] with whom he coupled Smollett, whose genius he thought resembled that of Rubens.[2] When he himself turned to fiction, he improvised a method partly eclectic and partly original. As historian of manners and humorous delineator of character, he is of the Fielding school. He imitated Fielding in his faithful portrayal of the whole human scene, with all the multifarious characters that come into it, whether directly implicated or not in the drama which forms the main interest. But he had not the scrupulous artistic conscience of his master, falling far short of him in craftsmanship, and he could never devise and adhere to a methodical scheme. That groundwork of thought which revealed the wider bearings of individual acts, and exposed the inner fabric of human relations, lay outside his compass. Only at some chance moment of sudden insight, as when Claverhouse utters his noble sentiments on the brave man's disregard of death, when Redgauntlet lets fall one of his stern aphorisms, or Andrew Fairservice, or the bailie, or old Touch-wood, expound their worldly wisdom, does his mind reach below

---

[1] Preface dated 1820.

[2] " We readily grant to Smollett an equal rank with his great rival Fielding, while we place both far above any of their successors in the same line of fictitious composition." This was written in 1821, when he had read Miss Edgeworth and Miss Austen, to both of whom in their particular spheres he awarded superlative praise.

the surface. Such moments came to Scott in his later years when, harassed with illness, monetary anxieties, and the loss of his dearest, he confided the thoughts that come at those times to his *Journal*. But what Goethe said of Byron might well have been said of Scott: "The moment he reflects, he is a child." He was a practical man of the world, singularly well versed in affairs; but of a philosophy he had hardly the makings. His mind was neither speculative nor profound. He had his preferences and his prejudices, his conviction of the supreme value of sincerity, generosity, and a feeling heart. These were his principles of conduct, the foundations of his character. Though he could make this, that, or the other of his wiseacres talk like Polonius, he was no moral philosopher; the only proper description of Scott is the hackneyed " one of Nature's gentlemen."

Scott portrays characters rather than character   Thus Scott had neither the probing curiosity of the analyst nor the philosophic vision of such as Fielding. He contemplated the human spectacle with the eye of a lover, and the delight of a humorist amused even at his own foibles, not with the investigating zeal of the sociologist or any theoretical motive whatever. It was in the light of his fine ideals of character and conduct, his own generous nature, that he interpreted what he saw. And he saw the parts, the multitudinous individualities, more clearly than he saw the whole. He was more fascinated by the diversity in the unity than by the unity in diversity. It is among his principal literary virtues that the counterfeit world he presents is a living, moving, working machine. With his practical mind, his awareness of the elemental facts of life, the large and ripe experience of a man who knew his own business and that of an immense variety of other people, he could not fail to give this vivid sense of active being, this full verisimilitude. But his eye was rather for the diversities of his fellow-beings than for the essential homogeneousness of human nature, for the points in which men differ than for those in which all are alike.[1] He was so absorbed by the idiosyncrasies, the oddities and eccentricities, the aberrations that grow into manias, that those among his characters who are simply normal, such as his blameless heroes and heroines, interest neither

[1] " His imagination was singularly penetrated with the strange varieties and motley composition of human life " (Bagehot, *op. cit.*).

him nor anyone else. Fielding, with a grasp no less sure of the individual, paid due heed to the larger drama in which all are personæ. His comedy is therefore of a higher order. It is the eternal comedy of human weakness, folly, excess, the follies and excesses to which all are subject; and he makes their commonness, their universality, plain. He surprises not more by the vagaries of his eccentrics than by making them betray feelings common to the whole world, as when Parson Adams after his extravagant eulogy of resignation goes wild with grief at the supposed drowning of his little boy. Scott revelled in the humour of personal incongruities and the clash of heterogeneous temperaments; but of the higher, the universal comedy he was apparently impercipient. He enjoyed the playful irony of conversational give and take [1]; but the deeper and more tragic ironies left him abashed and confounded. Hence, when his Nanty Ewarts get out of hand, he takes refuge in the didacticism which, to his credit, he ordinarily avoids. The sardonic laughter of the old witches in *The Bride of Lammermoor*, gloating over the ruin of the great and the death of the young and beautiful, is the glee of hell; and the irony which he puts in the mouth of Ailsie Gourlay seems to him so diabolical, and he knew she would have said these things, that he thankfully observes, " It is some comfort to know that the old hag was tried, condemned, and burned on the top of North Berwick Law, by sentence of a commission from the Privy Council." [2]

One would think he wanted to exonerate himself from ever having entertained such sentiments, even at second hand, in the brain of one of his madwomen: imagine Shakespeare trying to evade responsibility for the three witches! But to think of Shakespeare is to realize the truth of Hazlitt's contention that " Sir Walter is an imitator of nature and nothing more." [3] In the strict sense, Scott was not the inventor of Ailsie Gourlay, *" An imitator of nature," not an inventor*

---

[1] Says Chrystal Croftangry : " One thing I have learned in life—never to speak sense when nonsense will answer the purpose as well " (*Chronicles of the Canongate*, v.).

[2] *Bride of Lammermoor*, xxxi.

[3] " Scott, Racine, and Shakespeare " (*The Plain Speaker*). Hazlitt pays every tribute to Scott's truth to nature. " But as to sheer invention, there appeared to be about as much [in *The Heart of Midlothian*] as there is in the getting up the melodramatic representation of the Maid and the Magpie."

Nanty Ewart, Meg Merrilies, Edie Ochiltree, Dominie Sampson, or any of those which seem his most characteristic figures, whether any trace has been found or not of an original being entirely irrelevant. Hence there is nothing paradoxical in there being a certain point at which he ceases to comprehend some of his more extraordinary individuals; they are transcripts, not his own creations. Sheer villainy he never could understand; it always landed him in the bog of melodrama. Without what Hazlitt calls "the creative principle,"[1] there can be no true comedy. Mere ready-made figures will not fit into that which must be an abstract of life in general. And, as true comedy lay outside his orbit, tragedy, at all events sustained tragedy, was for the same reasons inaccessible. It has been seen how far he came short in his two most serious attempts. He could show the way-side tragedies of life. Meg Merrilies, Elspeth of the Craigburn-foot of Glenallan, Nanty Ewart, Ronald MacEagh, the Child of the Mist, are tragic in all conscience; and they are exponents of that terrible irony which, apart from these half glimpses into a world that was not his, escaped him entirely. But, for good reason, he refrained from entering far into the history of such strange beings, and turned away gladly from these visions of hell to the solid earth and daylight.

Trite features retained by Scott

When he sat down in 1814 to finish *Waverley*, Scott had in him the stuff for a great series of historical novels : a teeming imagination, an inexhaustible knowledge of life and character, immense historical learning, and a passionate love of his native soil. These riches he poured out without stint and almost without method, beyond the general procedure derived from Fielding. The trick which it was his worst luck to have borrowed from other novelists was the conventional plot. Since Fielding's time—and it is almost a pity that *Tom Jones* was such a consummate example—this had become a mechanical thing, an arbitrary framework, hung together by the aid of coincidence, solution of a mystery, and like melodramatic devices. Jane Austen wisely did without this sort of plot; her scheme was essentially dramatic, prejudice, mis-understanding, or self-deception running its course and being at length combated and subdued. Scott built loosely on a plot of the

---

[1] "Scott, Racine, and Shakespeare" (*The Plain Speaker*).

commonplace, external type. But his story invariably breaks away very soon, and advances in the free and spirited manner of epic, concentrating from time to time in the great crowded scenes which have been reviewed. At the end, he usually remembers the plot, and drags it in again, altered by this time probably out of all recognition, to be hurriedly wound up. This clumsy handling of a contrivance which he might have better dispensed with is the most glaring evidence of his lack of artistic discretion or of proper mastery of his superb endowment. Along with the mechanical plot, he took over other well-known properties of his humbler fellow-workmen, the sentimental tale and much of the Gothic paraphernalia. From *Waverley, Guy Mannering,* and *The Antiquary,* to *Aunt Margaret's Mirror* and *Castle Dangerous,* there is not one, except *The Fortunes of Nigel* and *St Ronan's Well,* without some leaven or strong suggestion of the supernatural, some ghost or hallucination, legend, omen, or vision prophesying disaster; and even in these exceptions the sinister accompaniments make up for Scott's temporary abstention from full-blown Gothic accessories. In the dialogue between the author and Captain Clutterbuck introducing *The Fortunes of Nigel,* the former promises to abandon " the mystic, and the magical, and the whole system of signs, wonders, and omens," and assures his critic that " There are no dreams, or presages, or obscure allusions to future events." He kept his engagement to the letter; but by other expedients he made full amends to the most bloodthirsty appetite for horrors. The historical novel had its origin in the Gothic romance, and in giving it a new orientation Scott did not prune it of the ancestral attributes. He always had a taste for this kind of romanticism himself, and he believed his readers liked it; that was enough for Scott.[1]

---

[1] It is clear from his review of Hoffmann, entitled " On the Supernatural in Fictitious Composition " (*Essays on Chivalry, Romance, and the Drama*), that Scott's interest in the supernatural was romantic and sentimental, not scientific; that is, he enjoyed its sensationalism. " Supernatural appearances in fictitious narrative ought to be rare, brief, indistinct, and such as may become a being to us so incomprehensible, and so different from ourselves. . . . Even in *Hamlet,* the second entrance of the ghost is not nearly so impressive as the first; and in many romances to which we could refer, the supernatural being forfeits all claim both to our terror and veneration, by condescending to appear too often." " He who peruses a large collection of stories of ghosts, fiends, and prodigies, in hopes of exciting in his mind that degree of shuddering interest approaching to fear,

*Scott's
realism*

In spite of these concessions to the mode and to his own weaknesses, the historical novel as Scott remade it was as different from its forerunners as Fielding from Aphra Behn or Shakespeare from Nicholas Udall. This was because, with all his romantic predilections, he could not help being a realist. The practical sagacity and knowledge of mankind that made him prefer Fielding and Smollett to other novelists ensured that his reconstruction would be the image of a real world. Nothing less could satisfy him. He was best, of course, in those of his Scottish novels which did not go very far back. But even in his more romantic ventures into other lands and remoter times he still endeavoured, with something like the integrity of an historian, to present the whole framework and composition of society, higher and lower classes in their habits as they lived, public affairs and private occupations going on together, and clashing and intersecting in the chance medley of life, sports and pastimes and the like coming into the picture as inevitably as matters of graver moment. Where, as in his presentment of the eighteenth century, he can be compared with other novelists, Scott does not come off second best, for his eye took in far more. Fanny Burney's world, for instance, was but a segment of English life at that era. Richardson concentrated upon a group of persons implicated in a society scandal typical of his day, Scott worked upon a different scale; and, though he too had his limits, his range was far wider than Miss Edgeworth's, who had the most comprehensive outlook of any of his own contemporaries, and immensely wider than Miss Austen's, whose excellence was to have confined herself strictly to the narrow sphere which she knew at first hand. His limitations were in the depth of his penetration, not in the extent of his survey. He left out of view an enormous portion of that which constitutes our personal life, either because it did not come within his ken, for he was not introspective, or from a certain shyness, already touched upon, in his attitude to women and to the feelings of those of his characters who are supposed to be passionately in love.

which is the most valuable triumph of the supernatural, is likely to be disappointed. A whole collection of ghost stories inclines us as little to fear as a jest book moves to laughter." Later, he suggests that the feeling of superstitious awe in a certain tale could not have been " improved " by any further touches of horror. That word " improved " is eloquent.

From start to finish, Scott remained a romantic; and, to judge *Yet always* by the inability of those who have tried to be realistic to eschew *a romantic* romance, the historical novelist must needs be romantic.[1] Scott *novelist:* did not try to eschew romance. It is deeply infused even into *short-* those of his novels dealing with a time which was almost his *comings* own, *Guy Mannering*, *The Antiquary*, *St Ronan's Well*, and *Redgauntlet*. He could not do without the element of adventure; and this accounts for many of the shortcomings in his rendering of life and character, his dead-alive heroes, for instance, and a curious short measure in his otherwise lifelike portrayal of the great. The romantic novelist, with whom must be bracketed the sentimental novelist, deals in adventure, in that which befalls the individual rather than in what he or she does. Whether sentimental experiences or physical adventures, they come to the same; they are the things that happen, rather than what is meditated, schemed, and acted. It is a fallacy to suppose that the story of adventure is the same thing as the story of action.[2] On the contrary, its prime elements are the unexpected, the surprising, the marvellous, not that which is prepared, foreseen, and willed. Hence it is not unnatural that its heroes should be characterized by their lack of heroism, their feeble resolution, their failure to achieve. Scott's stories are not the record of events brought about by the imagination, will, and energy of his foremost characters. His plots are only so much dead machinery, arbitrary arrangements of circumstances and incidents to ensure a desired conclusion. The novelist whose characters are deeply and integrally conceived has no need of such mechanical scaffolding; events will be the result of personality exerting itself, striving, succeeding, or failing, to subdue circumstances or the inertia of others to its designs. There will be conflict, though it may be internal conflict, self-discipline being one form of action. Such fiction will be dramatic in essence, the direct opposite to romantic and sentimental fiction.

There was another reason, besides the artistic advantage of

---

[1] Bagehot argues that " a writer of the historical novel is bound by the popular conception of his subject; and commonly it will be found that this popular impression is to some extent a romantic one " (" The Waverley Novels ").

[2] See also above, pp. 183-184.

the external point of view, for making his great people secondary personages, and big historical crises, when they appear at all, only subordinate incidents. To have centred a story in one of the decisive events of history would have compelled Scott to do something that he sedulously avoided. He would have had to set forth the successive acts of will that brought about such events or the contention of wills and circumstances that culminated in the death-struggle. Scott never showed history in the making, as Shakespeare repeatedly did; he chose the exact opposite, to show characters as they were made by history. He preferred to be a romancer, to dwell on the fringes of history; but the result was that his men of action do not quite fill the part. Probably it was not in him to make them adequate dramatically. He could summon up a Bruce or a Cœur-de-Lion from the dead. He could show them thoroughly alive, and recount what happened to them, or what might have happened, when they were adventurers looking for their kingdoms. But he could not, or at any rate did not, tell how they evolved a policy, prepared the ground, made decisions, and eventually achieved their deep-laid purposes. He could give an almost epical account of a battle, the tactics and the derring-do; but not of the statesmanship and the far-sighted strategy and commanding will that brought the sum of things to a decision. It was like Scott to compose a full-length romance of the Forty-five and never mention the general responsible for such a feat of arms as the march to Derby and the retreat. He knew what Mary or Elizabeth would do or say in a parley with factious nobles; both bear themselves in his pages like women and like queens. But his Mary is better than his Elizabeth, for she was one of the passive characters that suited his imagination. It was easy for Scott to depict fortitude and non-resistance. His Mary is no heroine; she is the plaything of irresistible forces. He represents her as drifting with events; and, when the crisis arrives, it is at the bidding of a note from her friends outside the castle that she makes up her mind to resign the crown. Then, after the battle of Langside, she flees to England; and there is the end of her story in the novel of which she is the dominant figure. She merely disappears from its pages. Her own end is not yet.

Scott's great personages come up to expectations so far as *They loo* appearances go, but they are scarcely ever put to the test. When *great, but* that does happen, the result is disillusioning. Far from proving *do not act greatly* that they can achieve greatness, they are as lacking in initiative and the capacity to act with decision as the most ineffectual of his titular heroes. His Louis XI of France is an acute and unscrupulous politician, who sees through and despises his rivals and has the reputation of always outwitting them. Scott's picture could not be bettered of the strange monarch's petty superstitions, hypocritical piety, continual genuflexions to his guardian saints. But it is odd that he chose the very episode in which the intriguer overreached himself with the most perilous results as the cardinal incident in the history of Louis, and also the cardinal incident in the career of Quentin Durward. It was a curious way of making good the king's declared pre-eminence in statecraft. When Louis goes to Péronne, that stroke of policy which was to confound Charles of Burgundy, he walks into a trap, and finds himself at his enemy's mercy. The stroke fails; that is matter of history. But Scott, who has made Louis the principal agent in the drama and the arbiter of his hero's fortunes, does not show how it could ever have been successful, or how Louis fell into such a blunder. The plea that he had been misled by the charlatan Galeotti's horoscope is not to be reconciled with his alleged machiavellian subtlety. Finding himself in the humiliating position of a prisoner to his great vassal, Louis, his weapons gone, extricates himself by currying favour with Charles's ministers. The crafty statesman, famous for forestalling and mastering events, has turned into one of Scott's tame and ineffectual characters, the sport of circumstance. Even the manner of his ignominious escape from his false position does not carry conviction. In short, Scott's great ones look the part, but they lack the qualifications which avouch greatness. James I displays his mannerisms and absurdities, but not his political ability. Montrose and Claverhouse bear themselves as soldiers, but do not show at any decisive moment the mentality and vision of the man of great deeds. Their portraits are not in the style of those canvases of Rembrandt and Velasquez from which decision and command look forth as imperiously as from the page of the historian.

A reflex of Scott's own character No doubt, these shortcomings in his portrayal of the man of action are due to certain insufficiencies in Scott's own nature. It was not in him to paint them otherwise. If he himself had some spice of the adventurer, he was like those of his own creation, sanguine and courageous, but without the undeviating resolution that might have fulfilled his desires to be a great landed proprietor and the founder of a house. The story of his financial ventures, and of his reliance on the supposed cleverness, vigilance, and integrity of his partners, is the story that he was always recounting, of the young heroes who gain success only because they are favourites of fortune—the same story with another conclusion. It would be absurd to suggest that Scott was devoid of will-power; he was capable of a dogged pertinacity and untiring industry that staggered all who knew him. But of the will that forms and carries out great schemes he had little. As a young man, he failed to secure the girl he loved. In his material affairs, he was first the spoiled child and then the resigned victim of fortune. He had the fortitude to bear his misfortunes heroically, and the chivalry and endurance to perform miracles in clearing himself of the stigma of bankruptcy and leaving no debts unhonoured. But he was no more a master of events than were his Waverleys or Frank Osbaldistones. He could rise to the occasion; but he was not one of those who have the vision and the power to create occasions.[1] Hence it was only once in his long succession of novels that Scott achieved real drama, in the story of the great action performed by his humble peasant, Jeanie Deans. At the termination of the others, much has happened; but nothing has been accomplished, nothing done, save what external circumstances have brought to pass. Jane Austen's Darcy or Knightley is far more of the man of action, and a far truer protagonist of drama, for both of them did effect their purposes and make the impression which they intended upon the world they lived in. No wonder that Roland Graeme, in *The Abbot*, when he found himself

---

[1] Lockhart was so much impressed by Scott's ability in organizing the reception of George IV at Edinburgh that he credited his father-in-law with gifts that he never possessed : " I am mistaken if Scott could not have played in other days either the Cecil or the Gondomar." Scott was undoubtedly capable of " extraordinary exertion," " indefatigable energy," etc. ; but to talk about searching " the roll of great sovereigns or great captains " for his rival was absurd (Lockhart, lvi.).

in the presence of the regent, the " eminent soldier and statesman, the wielder of a nation's power, and the leader of her armies," experienced "a feeling of breathless awe, very different from the usual boldness and vivacity of his temper "[1]; or that Scott himself was abashed by the presence of the Duke of Wellington.[2] The mere man of letters, conscious of powers that he could hardly grasp even in imagination, naturally felt crushed by the man of decision and action.

Everybody remembers Carlyle's gibe at Scott's character-*Carlyle's* drawing: "Your Shakespeare fashions his characters from the *famous* heart outwards; your Scott fashions them from the skin inwards, *criticism* never getting near the heart of them."[3] If exaggerated, it is not untrue; though Carlyle might have given Scott credit for his rich diversity, and remembered that characters rather than character were the object in all the Waverley novels. It is tantamount to blaming the classifier for not giving a lecture on anatomy, though he may know enough anatomy for his purposes. Between Shakespeare and Scott there is indeed "a difference literally immense." Yet Scott's characters are not empty shows because their hearts are not laid bare. They have a misleading look of superficiality because Scott does not analyse. But he knew what was going on below the surface; he read the efficient motive of their behaviour with sureness and accuracy. The watch goes truly though only the dial is visible. Shakespeare could show the dial and also the works, as only the greatest can do. Hazlitt had put the truth better when he said that Scott drew his characters from nature instead of creating them out of his imagination. But one result of this reliance upon his incomparable powers of observation was that his characters are never overdrawn. No writer has been more justly praised for always preserving the modesty of nature. On the other hand, his reading of character had the limits which have from time to time been indicated. There was a point in his more complex and abnormal individuals, for instance, where his insight stopped, baffled. The originals of his Meg Merrilies

---

[1] *The Abbot*, xviii.
[2] " The only man in whose presence he ever felt awe and abashment " (Lockhart, xxxv.).
[3] *Miscellanies*, " Sir Walter Scott."

and Edie Ochiltree must have had something in them that eluded him; one seems to catch glimpses of a secret life only half revealed. Scott was fascinated by these denizens of another world than his, not merely because they were of "the class of society who are the last to feel the influence of that general polish which assimiliates to each other the manners of different nations,"[1] but for the very reason that he could not quite get to the bottom of them; they were too foreign to his own thoroughly respectable self; they had thoughts beyond the reaches of his soul.

A deter-minist

A foreign critic is no doubt right in maintaining that Scott's representation of the human world, in spite of its idealistic features, is radically determinist.[2] "His personages are not free. They are almost exclusively products of their heredity, their environment, and their profession; they are dominated by these influences." It is true of his characters, and true of Scott himself. He was by nature conservative, an upholder of the established order in church and state; he unreservedly accepted things as they were. His Jacobitism was only a freak of sentimental humour, which he played with because there was no harm in doing so at a date when no one took it seriously. So far as any philosophy can be drawn from the conclusions of his stories, where such indications may reasonably be sought, it is a philosophy of acceptance that he commends, cheerful submission to the creed, the political system, and the social order to which he and the characters drawn by him, whatever their rank and calling, had been born. Even principle with him was probably as much a matter of habit and upbringing as of moral or prudential reflection. He gratefully acquiesced in the inherited wisdom of his fore-

---

[1] Advertisement to *The Antiquary*; obviously referring to Meg Merrilies and Edie Ochiltree in particular.

[2] " Walter Scott, en dépit de son apparent idéalisme, part d'une conception de l'homme sourdement *déterministe* et *sensualiste*. Ses personnages ne sont pas libres. Ils sont presque exclusivement des produits de leur hérédité, de leur milieu, de leur profession, qui les dominent. Tous ont même quelque manie par laquelle s'affirme cette domination de l'inconscient en eux, et qui est une des sources de l' 'humour,' très savoureux d'ailleurs, de Walter Scott. C'est à peine s'il sont responsables. Au fond, l'art de Scott n'est pas seulement un peu matériel, il est matérialiste, et Carlyle avait raison de faire remarquer qu'il façonne ses personnages du dehors au dedans. De là, peut-être, leur nature assez terre à terre en général " (Reynaud, 184).

fathers, and the stability and security in which his lot was cast.

The good sense singled out by his critics as his leading characteristic, and the sure foundation of his other excellences,[1] was the common sense of the time and society to which he belonged, a time when the best people disliked fanaticism, affectation, or any extravagance whatever. M. Reynaud is right in detecting that one great source of his humour lies in the contrast and contradiction between the instinct of order and sobriety and the vagaries of the undisciplined mentalities which he so often drew. But he was always a romantic, and romance is continually finding itself at war with realism and perfect sanity. *Humour in* Scott was that anomaly, a romancer with a sense of humour.[2] *the clash of* Though such a spendthrift, he always had a balance in *romance* hand of hard facts and corrective wisdom. The best of *common* his humour proceeds from the friendly contention of his *sense* romanticism and sober sense. It is an immemorial device in story-telling to set inexperience and generous impulse on one side and maturity and discretion on the other. Quentin Durward is balanced, and periodically reproved, by Louis and Crèvecœur, Nigel by Moniplies and Jingling Geordie; the Master of Ravenswood has to put up with the cavilling of his testy old steward, the crafty Louis XI is matched against the headstrong Charles of Burgundy, Mause Headrigg's religious zeal with Cuddie's circumspection. But Scott also excels in putting the oppositions into one skin.

Poetry is combined with banal prose, romance with common sense, in such characters as the Baron of Bradwardine, Edie Ochiltree, Counsellor Pleydell and Dandie Dinmont, Wandering Willie and Jeanie Deans, to name but a few. A favourite plan was the deliberate anticlimax. Over and over again, after the romantic flight comes the swift descent, hitting the ground with a thud: after the wild idealism, the laugh on the other side, the good-natured mockery of the anti-romantic. Scott loved to take

---

[1] " Good sense, the sure foundation of excellence in all the arts, is another leading characteristic of these productions " (Adolphus, 68).

[2] With what glee he tells the story of Byron's rebuke to Tom Moore's rhapsody about a sunset in Venice !—" Oh ! come, d—n me, Tom, don't be poetical " (*Journal*, i. 112).

both points of view, to indulge both moods, the exaltation and then the bathos. The more romantic the trend of a story, the more need for the return to earth. This is what saves *Ivanhoe* from being only a brilliant masque, and *Quentin Durward* an airy romance of knight-errantry. Often the enthusiasm and dull matter-of-fact go in company. In his most high-flown adventure, when the quixotic Durward makes his way into the castle hall of Schonwalt and beards William de la Marck in the midst of his ruffianly lanzknechts, who have a moment before slaughtered the bishop on his own hearth, he has his Sancho with him in the stolid, peace-loving burgomaster, who comes out from the scene of fearful revelry still grumbling over the dues paid the dead prelate by him and his fellow-burghers, and the iron suit into which he has been constrained to insert his portly body.

" Peter, Peter," he said, resuming the complaint of the preceding evening, " if I had not had a bold heart, I would never have stood out against paying the burgher-twentieths, when every other living soul was willing to pay the same.—Ay, and then a less stout heart had not seduced me into that other battle of Saint Tron, where a Hainault man-at-arms thrust me into a muddy ditch with his lance, which neither heart or hand that I had, could help me out of, till the battle was over.—Ay, and then, Peter, this very night my courage seduced me, moreover, into too strait a corslet, which would have been the death of me, but for the aid of this gallant young gentleman, whose trade is fighting, whereof I wish him heartily joy. And then for my tenderness of heart, Peter, it has made a poor man of me, if I had not been tolerably well to pass in this wicked world;—and Heaven knows what trouble it is like to bring on me yet, with ladies, countesses, and keeping of secrets, which, for aught I know, may cost me half my fortune, and my neck into the bargain." [1]

All this is the comedy of humours. Throughout the story, the wily king and his cynical retinue of hangmen, Quentin's rough uncle, Balafré, the outspoken Crèvecœur, the bluff Dunois, and the canny burghers, contribute much more to the mirth than does the regular court jester, Le Glorieux. But Scott did not mean his version of a complicated page of history to be taken simply

---

[1] *Quentin Durward*, xxii.

as comic drama, any more than he meant it as pure romance; the one carries off the other. And the humour goes with the realism of his drawing of characters and manners to subserve the general verisimilitude.

Such balancing of romance and its opposite, of the poetic or *Scott and* tragic and the comic, is not uncommon in English literature, *Byron:* though rare at that particular date. Charles Lamb could do it in *their effect* his modest but exquisite way. But the parallel to Scott is Byron, *Continent* far removed as were *The Vision of Judgment* and *Don Juan* from *Marmion*, *Old Mortality*, or *Ivanhoe*. Whilst, however, it was Byron's fiery individualism and satire of an oppressive social system that roused Europe and made him a reinvigorating force in Continental literature, Scott exercised an influence no less extensive for reasons entirely different. These two alone among the English romantics were read and imitated abroad. Both were intelligible to the least learned; both had something to offer of universal interest. The deeper romanticism of Wordsworth and Coleridge, Keats and Shelley, meant nothing to the French; it was a long while yet before it had any effect even upon the higher classes of readers elsewhere. But Scott and Byron, who had next to nothing in common with Wordsworth and his school, gave to those who were emancipating themselves from the constraints of the classical tradition in French literature exactly what they vaguely desiderated. Scott released the imagination, revealed illimitable vistas, the incredible diversity of human nature and of human experience, the world of the past opening out from the world of the present. Byron's emotional romances of other lands and peoples, his stormy protests and scorching satire, challenged every creed, usage, and convention, and asserted the rights of the individual, giving the glory, not to reason, and certainly not to authority, but to the instincts and passions of the natural man. This is not the place to follow the track of Byron in the poetry and drama of Europe; but some brief notes are necessary on Scott and on the manner in which his influence was blended with that of the younger poet, for whom, it has been truly said, he prepared the way.[1]

[1] " Walter Scott n'avait fait que préparer l'avènement de son grand compatriote dans le Romantisme français " (Reynaud, 231).

Scott's novels were rapidly translated into French by various hands, and soon set new fashions in both fiction and drama.[1] Balzac attempted an historical play as early as 1819; but his *Cromwell* was stillborn, and he abandoned the theatre for the novel. His first two or three, romances or melodramas rather than novels, were only nominally historical; the time was supposed to be the sixteenth century or the Middle Ages, but the features of the period were only vaguely sketched. Not till he had studied Scott's method of reviving the past in all its minuteness and variety did he produce a novel fit to take its place in his projected *Comédie humaine*. *Les Chouans, ou la Bretagne en 1799* (1829), was constructed on the lines of a Waverley novel, Breton peasants and guerrillas taking the place of Highlanders. It was a realistic portrayal of characters and manners in a definite region at a moment of intense historical interest. Hardly any of his later work was historical in the same narrow sense. But it was from Scott, as Brunetière pointed out, that Balzac first learned the use of those petty details, which had hitherto been regarded as vulgar and beneath the dignity of fiction, to build up an imaginary world looking as solid as reality.[2] Alfred de Vigny had already followed Scott in *Cinq-Mars* (1826), keeping closer than his master to the facts, but failing to put any life into his borrowed figures. He was a disciple of Byron here as much as in his poetry; having, like others, deviated into prose romance in the same way as Scott. Byron led him to Shakespeare, and his *More de Venise* (1829) was a close rendering of *Othello*. His best historical play was *Chatterton* (1835), which owed little to Scott but a good deal to Byron. Similar influences are perceptible in Mérimée's *Chronique du règne de Charles IX* (1829), ostensibly a study in the manner of *Kenilworth* or *The Fortunes of Nigel*, but in its artistic detachment, irony, and occasional flippancy, very unlike Scott. Mérimée's earlier *Théâtre de Clara Gazul* (1825) and a Shakespearian play, *La Jacquerie* (1828), are but perfunctorily historical. Not much more can be said of the efforts

---

[1] For a list of the translations and the many editions, see *The English Novel in France, 1830-1870*, by Miss M. G. Devonshire (1929), pp. 141-147.
[2] See *Honoré de Balzac*, par Ferdinand Brunetière: "Le roman de Balzac a rendu a l'histoire ce qu'il avait lui-même reçu du roman historique" (p. 238).

at historical drama of Vitet, Mortonval, Barginet, and others, who at all events had the credit of exposing the empty pomposity of Casimir Delavigne and the older school of tragedy decked out in romantic plumes.

That eventful 1829 also saw the production of Dumas' *Henri III et sa cour*, first of many plays, by himself and others, which made a great show of local colour after the manner of Scott. Dumas' plays dramatizing history were to be followed a little later by his enormous series of romantic novels, exploiting French history from the end of the Middle Ages to the eve of the present. He acknowledged himself to be *un vulgarisateur*[1]; and as such he was competent, and even brilliant, in fudging up details from the masses of records and memoirs recently published, and converting them into semi-fiction, characterized by swift theatrical movement and striking scenes but slapdash and rather brutal figures, supposed to be drawn from history. Victor Hugo's *Han d'Islande* (1823), from the point of view of history or of local colour is an abortion. But the year of the decisive battle over *Hernani* (1830) is memorable also for his *Notre-Dame de Paris*. In the preface to his *Cromwell* (1827), he had set forth a programme for romantic drama evidently based on the practice of Scott—a familiar style, rising when required to the level of epic, and a mingling of the comic and tragic with the homespun of everyday life. *Notre-Dame* could hardly have been written without Scott's lead, unlike as it is to a Waverley novel; but a French critic is no doubt right in seeing in it the decadence of the genre.[2] Of sound history there is but a modicum, powerful as are the scenes in which the fifteenth century is summoned up again in all its gloom and squalor, splendour and violence. Claude Frollo and Esmeralda come out of Lewis's *Monk*.[3] The theatrical accessories are the apotheosis of Gothic romance; the grandiose symbolism and the half-lyrical, half-epical style is modelled partly on Byron and partly on Shakespeare. Similar constituents went to the making of Hugo's plays. The historical plots and the circumstance, costume, and colour make them a theatrical counterpart to the Waverley novels;

Dumas, Victor Hugo, etc.

---

[1] Quoted by Maigron (p. 375) from his *Causeries*.
[2] Maigron, 332.
[3] See Volume V. 211, note.

the spirit is Byronic or pseudo-Shakespearian.[1] The same influences are palpable in the historical painters, Géricault, Delacroix, and Delaroche. Flaubert, with his *Salammbô* (1862), and Gautier, with his *Capitaine Fracasse* (1863), derive from Scott, but belong to another era, the one applying new standards of archæological science and realism to the reconstruction of a more distant past, the other exploiting historical fiction in the interests of a new æsthetic.

Followers of Scott elsewhere It is unnecessary to follow the course of historical fiction any further in French literature. As to Scott's followers in other countries, it is enough to mention the names of Manzoni, Ebers, Hausrath, Dahn, Freytag, Galdós, Jokai, Tolstoy, Sienkiewicz, Merezhkovsky, Feuchtwanger, to be reminded that the historical novel was one of the greatest legacies of the romantic age. In England, Scott's commercial success as well as his literary example was an incentive to all kinds of novel-writing, though not more so than on the Continent. In the historical line, he was quickly followed by G. P. R. James, Captain Marryat, Harrison Ainsworth, Bulwer Lytton, and smaller men, and later by Kingsley, Charles Reade, Blackmore, Stevenson, and many who are almost or quite our contemporaries. Fenimore Cooper was saluted by some critics, not Englishmen, as at least Scott's equal. Since his day the historical novel has flourished nowhere more vigorously than in America. Scott was more responsible than even Maria Edgeworth for the great output of Irish peasant fiction by the Banims, Griffin, Carleton, and Lover, not to mention Lever. But all this will come into later chapters.

Scott and the Oxford Movement Most historians of religious movements in the nineteenth century agree in ascribing to the Waverley novels a considerable share in promoting that widespread reversion to ancient modes and ideals, that regard for old-established authority, and respect for the pomp and picturesqueness of the Middle Ages, which conspired with more purely spiritual motives in bringing about the Oxford revival. Newman admitted it gratefully. He recognized that it was Coleridge who provided the movement with a religious philosophy. But he said it had been the function of

---

[1] " Shakespeare était le maître qu'invoquaient les romantiques : en réalité Byron leur fournit plus que Shakespeare " (*Histoire de la Littérature française*, par G. Lanson, 1903, p. 964). Reynaud says roundly, Byron " a perdu en France le roman historique " (*Le Romantisme*, 238).

Scott, " by his works, in prose and verse, to prepare men for some closer and more practical approximation to Catholic truth." [1] His popularity was due in large part to his satisfying an inward need; and, " by means of his popularity he reacted on his readers, stimulating their mental thirst, feeding their hopes, setting before them visions, which, when once seen, are not easily forgotten, and silently indoctrinating them with nobler ideas, which might afterwards be appealed to as first principles." This Newman wrote in 1839, and he repeated it word for word in his *Apologia pro Vita sua* (1864). George Borrow laid the whole blame for the Oxford movement on Scott's shoulders, and the charge, however absurd as he framed it, corroborates Newman's opinion. Scott was a Protestant who accepted his religion as he accepted his politics and his moral and social principles, without question or criticism. As in duty bound, he takes the Protestant side, so far as a novelist may show his sympathies, in those of his novels which touch upon the Reformation and the strife between the Churches. In *Old Mortality*, his point of view is that of an Episcopalian, moderate and tolerant, but more in sympathy with the High Church doctrines of the persecutors than with those of the Covenanters, moderates or ultras. Scott had only contempt and dislike for bigotry of any kind, especially that which was rooted in formalism, which he knew to be peculiarly liable to the vices of spiritual pride and hypocrisy. But he rarely satirizes even the extravagances of a Roman Catholic; the religiosity of his Louis XI is simply one of that monarch's incongruous foibles. Bishops and archbishops, abbots and abbesses, monks and nuns, the whole hierarchy from patriarch to hermit, appear in his novels in impressive numbers and impressive rôles, from *Count Robert of Paris* to those dealing with the very last of the Middle Ages. Scott has been accused of being secretly anti-Catholic.[2] It would

---

[1] " Prospects of the Anglican Church " (*Essays Critical and Historical* (1890), i. 268). See also *Apologia* (1902), 96-97.

[2] Reynaud, 227 : " Son attitude secrètement anticatholique." *Le Romantisme, ses origines anglo-germaniques*, has been cited several times already, as a work of acknowledged learning. But it is the work of a special pleader, and its interpretation of the facts must be received with caution. It is one of the diatribes of the anti-romantics, the so-called " humanists," who denounce romanticism as anti-rational, materialistic, the slave of instinct, sensibility, imagination, and as one of the most dangerous phases of individualism. Scott would have been no less amused than astonished at the mischievous tendencies laid to his charge.

be hard to say where or how, unless his humorous presentment of the worldly prior and the jovial friar in *Ivanhoe* be regarded as a hostile attack. Had Scott been born of a Catholic family, he would have been as stanch a Catholic and as lacking in fervour as he actually was in his Protestantism. He venerated his religion, as he venerated what else was venerable. No doubt, if analysed, his sentiments were of the æsthetic rather than the strictly spiritual order. But that is not to say that they were anti-Catholic. Cardinal Newman was not speaking lightly when he repeatedly declared that Scott's influence lay behind the neo-Catholic movement in England.

CHAPTER X

OTHER SCOTTISH NOVELISTS

Scottish poetry had been flourishing ever since the advent of *Scottish* Burns; and not only the collections of ballads and songs, but also *poetry in* the original poems of Hogg, Tannahill, Tennant, and others, of *the ascendant* course including Scott, had easily found publishers. But a ban *relatively* seemed to rest upon Scottish prose fiction, especially if it indulged *to fiction* in the vernacular. *Waverley* had been twice laid aside, in 1805 and 1810, before Scott took it in hand again in 1813 and published it the following year. Miss Ferrier had begun her first novel, *Marriage*, about 1808-1809, and it was practically finished by 1810; it was not published, however, till 1818. Galt had long meditated the work that eventually became the *Annals of the Parish*, but did not apply himself to it seriously till 1813; and then, when it was nearly finished, his friend Constable told him that Scottish novels would not do, and he threw it aside until his success with *The Ayrshire Legatees* made it a feasible proposition. The only Scottish domestic fiction preceding *Waverley* was a didactic story, *The Cottagers of Glenburnie* (1808), by Mrs Elizabeth Hamilton, author of that odd book, *Memoirs of Modern Philosophers* (1800),[1] of the mock-Oriental *Translation of the Letters of a Hindoo Rajah* (1796), and of the well-known song, " My ain Fireside." In preaching cleanliness, industry, and method, to her village readers, she did not mince the grimiest details. Ignorant, uncouth, insanitary rustic life was depicted, and the local speech reproduced, with a fidelity more to the purpose than pages of argument; and this realism, of dialogue especially,[2] became a tradition in the Scottish peasant novel.[3]

---

[1] See Volume V. 253-254.

[2] " Towels ! " cried Mrs MacClarty; " na, na, we maunna pretend to towels; we just wipe up the things wi' what comes in the gait " (chap. vii.).

[3] Mary Brunton (see above, pp. 53-56) was Scottish; but her novels have so little in them of a distinctively Scottish nature that they need not be considered here.

Begin-
nings of the
Scottish
novel of
humble life

But Elizabeth Hamilton belonged to the past; she was an offshoot of the doctrinaire fiction of the end of the last century. It was Scott, and neither Miss Ferrier nor John Galt, who by the accident of prior publication became the founder of the modern school of vernacular novelists. There were glimpses of Lowland village life in *Waverley*, and much more than glimpses in *Guy Mannering*, *The Antiquary*, and *Old Mortality*. Scott knew the humbler classes of his compatriots as intimately as those contemporary writers who were more of their own kin; and they were never portrayed with more friendliness, humour, and pathos than by the author of *The Heart of Midlothian*, *Rob Roy*, *St Ronan's Well*, and the *Chronicles of the Canongate*. Gifted Gilfillan and David Gellatley, the Mucklebackits, Davie Deans and Dumbiedikes, Andrew Fairservice, Caleb Balderston, Meg Dods, and Old Turnpenny, are types that were never outdone, if they were ever equalled, by Galt or Miss Ferrier, or by any of the novelists who afterwards applied themselves to this genre, from George MacDonald and Mrs Oliphant to Stevenson, "Ian Maclaren," and Barrie. But that the novel and tale of Scottish peasant and lowly middle-class life did become such a distinct genre was no doubt owing to the work of Galt and Miss Ferrier, and of the occasional novelists, Hogg, Moir, and Lockhart, who tried their hands at the same style.

Susan
Ferrier

Susan Edmonstone Ferrier (1782-1854) was content to write three novels, the first two anonymous, and liked to be regarded as an amateur who amused herself by jotting down curiosities of character and manner, and not as a regular novelist. Born in Edinburgh, the daughter of an older colleague and friend of Scott, she knew Henry Mackenzie, and Jeffrey, Lord Cockburn, Mrs Grant of Laggan, Hogg, William Clerk, and others of the Scott circle; but she did not pretend to any intimacy with those below her own social level, and her drawing of English society is largely from second-hand knowledge. Many well-known people thought they recognized themselves or their friends among her characters; but she deprecated the charge of direct portraiture, and probably mixed and altered traits very much as Scott had done, with a great deal more caricature. Thus her father was said to be in part at least the original of Adam Ramsay, in *The Inheritance*;

but no doubt the eccentricities of the crusty but affectionate old miser are an addition, or much exaggerated. She corresponded for many years with Miss Charlotte Clavering, a connexion of the Argyll family; and her liveliness, her turn for broad jokes, and her extreme frankness, come out well in her letters to that lady, who proposed to collaborate with her in the first novel, *Marriage*, but actually wrote only the dullest part, "The Story of Mrs Douglas." Miss Ferrier's style was notably spirited, pungent, and graceful. But she lacked Jane Austen's irony, and also the reticence which was one of the subtlest gifts of the English novelist. It is an old mistake to compare the two. Her sparkling and more or less satirical cartooning of the superficies of character, the fops and prattlers, fools and eccentrics, is much more like Fanny Burney's; and she had the same proneness to repeat a situation, to show her oddities performing their tricks over again. The earnestness of her moralizing, also, a habit that grew upon her, is nearer to that of Dr Johnson's "character-monger" than to Miss Edgeworth's regular didacticism. The Ferriers were a serious-minded set; she was the aunt of the philosophic writer, J. F. Ferrier; and in spite of her high spirits and love of mockery she had a very grave sense of her responsibility as a commentator on the world.

She wrote to Miss Clavering: "I do not recollect to have seen *"Marri-* the sudden transition of a high-bred English beauty who thinks *age"* she can sacrifice all for love to an uncomfortable solitary Highland dwelling among tall red-haired sisters and grim-faced aunts." This is the point of departure in *Marriage* (1818), which tails off after the first volume into the very ordinary social and matrimonial adventures of Lady Juliana's two daughters, and of course spreads over a long period of years. But the opening is excellent; the author is on her own ground. The young lady, a spoiled child of English fashionable life, elopes with the son of a Highland laird, and has to live at his uncouth home, among a set of originals, overflowing with fussy kindness and with humours that delight the reader but exasperate the silly heroine.

"Welcome, a thousand times welcome, to Glenfern Castle," said Miss Jacky, who was esteemed by much the most sensible woman, as well as the greatest orator, in the whole parish;

"nothing shall be wanting, dearest Lady Juliana, to compensate for a parent's rigour, and make you happy and comfortable. Consider this as your future home! My sisters and myself will be as mothers to you; and see these charming young creatures," dragging forward two tall frightened girls, with sandy hair, and purple arms; "thank Providence for having blest you with such sisters!" "Don't speak too much, Jacky, to our dear niece at present," said Miss Grizzy; "I think one of Lady Maclaughlan's composing draughts would be the best thing for her." "Composing draughts at this time of day!" cried Miss Nicky; "I should think a little good broth a wiser thing. There are some excellent family broth making below, and I'll desire Tibby to bring a few."[1]

"Miss Jacky was all over sense. A skilful physiognomist would, at a single glance, have detected the sensible woman, in the erect head, the compressed lips, square elbows, and firm, judicious step." Miss Grizzy was "merely distinguishable from nothing by her simple good nature, the inextricable entanglement of her thoughts, her love of letter writing, and her friendship with Lady Maclaughlan." That lady is a composing draught in herself, and with "her ridiculous dress and eccentric manners," imperiousness and complete indifference to the feelings of those she terrorizes, soon reduces Lady Juliana to a state of fluttering exhaustion. It is with regret that the reader bids adieu to Glenfern and Lochmarlie castles for the banalities of English polite society.

"*The Inheritance*" *Marriage* may be said to correspond to Fanny Burney's *Evelina*, and *The Inheritance* (1824) to the more elaborate *Cecilia*. This appeared anonymously, like the first novel; but instead of a modest £150, Miss Ferrier, as a result of the boom in Scottish fiction, received £1000. For her next, *Destiny* (1831), she obtained £1700, surely an excessive remuneration. *The Inheritance* contains her best characters; but for their proper exhibition she thought it necessary to rehash the stale old plot of the changeling who is heir-presumptive to a great estate. Gertrude actually becomes Countess of Rossville. But from time to time a mysterious stranger makes his appearance, prostrating her mother with fright. At length, Lewiston, who is an American, lets the cat out of the bag: he claims to be her father. Her supposed mother had been childless, and passed the daughter of

[1] Chap. iii.

an unfortunate friend off as her own. Though Lewiston is shown
up as an impostor, the deception cannot be refuted, and Gertrude
forfeits her coronet. But the loss of her wealth and peerage is
the test that relieves her of her false lover, the arrogant English
aristocrat, Colonel Delmour; and ultimately she marries the
faithful Lyndsay, who afterwards inherits the title. Miss Ferrier
might have remembered where such a story came from when she
described the empty-headed Lady Betty, reading

all the novels and romances which it is presumed are published
for the exclusive benefit of superannuated old women, and silly
young ones; such as *The Enchanted Head*—*The Invisible Hand*
—*The Miraculous Nuptials*, etc., etc. She was now in the midst
of *Bewildered Affections, or All is not Lost*, which she was reading
unconsciously, for the third time, with unbroached delight.[1]

There are two first-rate characters in *The Inheritance*, Miss *Her best*
Pratt and Uncle Adam, and half-a-dozen or more who are *characters*
capitally drawn but not of such rare mintage. Miss Pratt is not
another Miss Bates, though the comparison is inevitable; she is
neither simple nor tender-hearted and unselfish. She bores her
company more than Miss Bates bored Emma Woodhouse; and
occasionally, owing to her creator's lack of artistic reticence, she
bores the reader too. But her virtues are many; and the reader
triumphs with her, when, in the midst of an appalling blizzard,
no other conveyance being available, the highly practical lady,
cousin to half the noble families of Scotland, arrives at the
residence of Lord Rossville in a hearse.

"Miss Pratt," began the Earl, mustering all his energies—
"Miss Pratt, it is altogether inconceivable and inexplicable to
me how you, or anyone else, could possibly so far forget what
was due to themselves and me as to come to my house in a manner
so wholly unprecedented, so altogether unwarrantable, so—s—
so perfectly unjustifiable—I say, how any person or persons
could thus presume——"
A burst of laughter from Miss Pratt here broke in upon the
Earl's harangue.
"My dear Lord Rossville, I beg your pardon; but really the
notion of my *presuming* to come in a hearse is too good—'pon my
word, it's a piece of presumption few people would be guilty of,

[1] Chap. iii.

if they could help it. I assure you I felt humble enough when I was glad to creep into it." [1]

Miss Pratt must be understood as including the nephew, Anthony Whyte, whose perfections she is always quoting. Anthony Whyte never appears, and like another celebrated character leaves the reader firmly convinced that there is no such person.

Mr Adam Ramsay, almost ashamed of his warmth of heart towards his niece Gertrude, and vainly trying to dissimulate his tender memories of the long-lost Lizzie Lundie, and the weakness that led him to dip into a mere nonsensical novel, Guy Mannering, is equally good.

" Interest—ugh !—Folk may hae other things to interest them, I think, in this world. I wonder if there's ony o't true? I canna think how ae man could sit down to contrive a' that. I didna misdoot that scoondrel Glossin at a'. I would gie a thoosand pound out o' my pocket to see that rascal hanged, if hanging wasna ower gude for him ! "

"Well, you may be at ease on that head, as even worse befalls him," said Lady Rossville.

"Weel, I rejoice at that; for if that scoundrel had gotten leave to keep that property, by my troth, I believe, I would have burnt the book; "—then, ashamed of his ardour in such a cause, he added, in a peevish tone—" But it's a' nonsense thegither, and I'm no gaun to fash my head ony mair about it." [2]

It was kind of Miss Ferrier to pay such a tribute to the Waverley novels, for which she herself had but tepid admiration. But she almost spoiled her portrait of Uncle Adam by a solemn explanation of his eccentricities, as only the result of misguided efforts to be himself and defy the world.

Uncle Adam flattered himself that he was one of the happy few who had escaped from its thraldom—but, alas ! poor man, its yoke was still upon him, and, unconscious of its chains, he hugged himself in his freedom. . . . Man is not born to be free; and when all restraint is laid aside, the wickedness of the human heart displays itself in the most hideous forms. [3]

Lord Rossville, doing " the honours in his most elaborate and massive style," is always entertaining, though he is not a character

[1] Chap. lv.   [2] Chap. lxxi.   [3] Chap. xviii.

of such rarity. His lecture to Gertrude, at any rate, when that *Minor* young lady is so daring and so modern as to climb out of the *character-* window and go for a walk before breakfast, makes an admirable *drawing* scene.

" A young female is seen issuing from the window of my study at a nameless hour in the morning—the tale circulates—and where, I ask,—where am I ? "

"Where was you ? " inquired Lady Betty.

Which fatuous question entirely unhinges the nobleman's oration. Miss Bell, who marries and fidgets over Major Waddell, would be commonplace but for one proud remark :

" It's very well for people to write poetry who can't afford to buy it," said Miss Bell, with a disdainful toss; " the Major has bought a most beautiful copy of Lord Byron's works, bound in red morocco—rather too fine for reading, I think; but he said he meant it to lie upon my sofa-table, so I couldn't find fault." [1]

Miss Ferrier's last novel, *Destiny* (1831), was not so light-hearted; she was still sorrowing for her dearly-loved father, and she allowed seriousness and didacticism to run away with her. But her Highland chieftain, Glenroy, her blethering, time-serving minister, M'Dow, and the leal and lowly Mrs Macaulay, are drawn with her wonted power, although they are anything but creatures of comedy.

A more important place in the ancestry of the Scottish novel *John Galt* must be ceded to the author of *Annals of the Parish*, which had been on the stocks as long as Miss Ferrier's first novel, and came out three years later. The life of John Galt (1779-1839) has many points of likeness to that of Smollett, with whose work, further, his has perhaps more in common than with Scott's. Son of a captain in the mercantile marine, he was born at Irvine, in Ayrshire, and worked as a clerk in the custom-house and then with a business firm at Greenock till 1803, nursing all the while literary ambitions, writing verses, a tragedy, and articles for the press. Then he came to London, went into partnership in a business that failed, and started reading law, but was never called to the Bar. He went touring in Europe and Asia Minor, wrote and

[1] Chap. xxv.

edited travels, had no success as a playwright, was editor of a short-lived *Political Review* and later of *The Courier,* wrote biographies and the like, edited *The New British Theatre* (1814-1815), and contributed to various prints, including *Blackwood's Magazine,* where *The Ayrshire Legatees* appearing in 1820 gave him a new start as a novelist. For several years now his annual output included at least two novels, along with other work, such as a *Life of Byron* (1830), which went at once into a second edition. The most disastrous episode in Galt's life was his secretaryship to the Canada Company. He was in that country for three years (1826-1829), and had the honour of being founder of the town of Guelph, in Ontario. On his return to England he was imprisoned for debt. He had been as miscellaneous and as industrious as Smollett, and suffered as many mortifications. Exhausted at last with overwork, he came back to spend his last five years at Greenock, and died there at the age of sixty.

"Annals of the Parish"

His *Annals of the Parish* (1821) were not at first conceived as a novel. Galt says in his *Autobiography* that he long toyed with the idea of a Scottish *Vicar of Wakefield,* but did not know a minister who could have sat for the character. When later on he was thinking over a scheme for relating the vicissitudes of life in an Ayrshire township during the half-century since the accession of George III, it occurred to him to make his pastor the historian, instead of putting the tale in the mouth of the schoolmaster, as he first proposed. The Rev. Micah Balwhidder, minister of Dalmailing, is an unassuming and rather commonplace individual, who was put into the living against the will of his parishioners, but does his duty by them faithfully; and, though he knows himself to have no exceptional talents, makes the most of such as he has, is proud of the sermons that have moved his flock, and when at last the elders persuade him to resign, still has as good a conceit of his eloquence as Gil Blas' archbishop, without, however, being irritated when this is not appreciated.

" I felt no falling off in my powers of preaching; on the contrary, I found myself growing better at it, as I was enabled to hold forth, in an easy manner, often a whole half-hour longer than I could do a dozen years before."

Mr Balwhidder is entirely unconscious of the humour in that extra half-hour of his. Soon after his induction, the spirit had descended upon him and he resolved to write a book. After considering an orthodox poem, like *Paradise Lost*, or a treatise on the efficacy of Grace, he decided at last upon the journal, for he was all his days " a close observer of the signs of the times " ; and, if not quite so shrewd as he thought, was aware that what some looked upon as " prophecy and prediction " was simply the foresight taught by experience. He was honest with himself, and wrote down what seemed to him the literal truth. But Galt was justified of his choice of a narrator by the manner in which the truth is enriched and clarified in its passage through such a mind. Public and private affairs are charmingly mixed, and are on the same scale of magnitudes. An outbreak of smallpox and the departure of Charles Malcolm as a cabin boy, the first admission of tea at the manse, the death of the first Mrs Balwhidder and then of the second, a murder, the American War of Independence and the recruiting therefor, the daring operations of smugglers, the Gordon riots, the repercussions of the French war and the French Revolution, the industrial revolution in the form of the establishment, prosperity, and bankruptcy of a cotton mill and the growth of a miniature cottonopolis, with a thousand domestic details, are jumbled together as they would be in a local news-sheet, with the local gossip, but also with reflections that would not discredit a sociologist having more than average insight into human nature. For everyone concerned in the transactions is a human being, in whom the pastor takes considerably more than a professional interest. He has no sense of humour himself, but he is the occasion of humour, both in himself and in others.

Galt showed himself elsewhere a master of the harsh, terse, *Galt's* graphic portraiture, often etched in with a bit of visual malice, *coarse,* that was a gift of his countrymen, Dunbar and Burns, Smollett *incisive* and Carlyle. There is no malice in the old pastor, but causticity *portraiture* is not lacking, even if it be unconscious. How vividly we see the Lady Skim-milk chasing the two lassies, " pursuing them like desperation, or a griffon, down the avenue " ; or old Nanse Banks, the sempstress, " a patient creature, well cut out for her calling, with bleer eyn, a pale face, and a long neck, but meek and contented withal, tholing the dule of this world with a Christian submission of the spirit "; or the conceited dancing master:

The very bairns on the loan, instead of their wonted play, gaed linking and louping in the steps of Mr Macskipnish, who was, to be sure, a great curiosity, with long spindle legs, his breast shot out like a duck's, and his head powdered and frizzled up like a tappit-hen.

Mrs Argent, "a lady of considerable personal magnitude, of an open and affable disposition," is from the next book; but obviously comes from the same drawing-board as "that old light-headed woman, the Lady Macadam," who died, but was succeeded by her "full equivalent" in "the hot and fiery Mr Cayenne." The pretty incident of the unexpected return of Charlie Malcolm to his home and his adorable mother—the heroine of the book, if there is one—brings to mind Smollett's tenderness in his account of the long-absent son's return to his aged parents, in *Humphry Clinker*.[1]

It was between the day and dark, when the shuttle stands still till the lamp is lighted. But such a shout of joy and thankfulness as rose from that hearth when Charlie went in! The very parrot, ye would have thought, was a participator, for the beast gied a skraik that made my whole head dirl; and the neighbours came flying and flocking to see what was the matter, for it was the first parrot ever seen within the bounds of the parish, and some thought it was but a foreign hawk, with a yellow head and green feathers.[2]

A character after Smollett

Comparison with Smollett is more to the purpose, however, in the case of the blasphemous Mr Cayenne, who introduced progress to Dalmailing in the form not only of cotton but also of ideas. When two democratic weavers were brought before him he called them traitors and reformers.

They denied they were traitors, but confessed they were reformers, and said they knew not how that should be imputed to them as a fault, for that the greatest men of all times had been reformers,—"Was not," they said, "our Lord Jesus Christ a reformer?" "And what the devil did He make of it?" cried Mr Cayenne, bursting with passion; "was He not crucified?"
I thought, when I heard these words, that the pillars of the

earth sunk beneath me, and that the roof of the house was carried away in a whirlwind. The drums of my ears crackit, blue starns danced before my sight, and I was fain to leave the house and hie me home to the manse, where I sat down in my study, like a stupefied creature awaiting what would betide.[1]

But later the minister and Mr Cayenne drew a little more cordially together, " although he had still a very imperfect sense of religion, which I attributed to his being born in America, where even as yet, I am told, they have but a scanty sprinkling of grace." The Kailyard novelists who descended from Galt were famous for a sentimental enjoyment of death-beds. None of them, however, except the author of *The House with the Green Shutters*, who restored the masculinity of Galt, ever did anything comparable to the last moments of Mr Cayenne.

" How do you find yourself, sir? " I replied in a sympathizing manner.
" Damned bad," said he, as if I had been the cause of his suffering. I was daunted to the very heart to hear him in such an unregenerate state; but after a short pause I addressed myself to him again, saying that " I hoped he would soon be more at ease, and he should bear in mind that the Lord chasteneth whom He loveth."
" The devil take such love," was his awful answer, which was to me as a blow on the forehead with a mell. However, I was resolved to do my duty to the miserable sinner, let him say what he would. Accordingly, I stooped towards him with my hands on my knees, and said in a compassionate voice, " It's very true, sir, that you are in great agony, but the goodness of God is without bound."
" Curse me if I think so, doctor," replied the dying uncircumcized Philistine. But he added at whiles, his breathlessness being grievous, and often broken by a sore hiccup, " I am, however, no saint, as you know, doctor; so I wish you to put in a word for me, doctor; for you know that in these times, doctor, it is the duty of every good subject to die a Christian." [2]

The three Mrs Balwhidders, whom it is the old man's fervent hope to meet again hereafter—nay, a whole population—are all distinctly drawn, with a sense of fellowship and of the pathos of

[1] Chap. xxxiv.   [2] Chap. xlvi.

life equal to the unconscious humour. In his first novel, Galt was as gentle and kindly as Smollett in his last and mellowest.

"The Ayrshire Legatees"   *Humphry Clinker* was undisguisedly the model for *The Ayrshire Legatees* (1821), which had appeared the year before in *Blackwood*. This is written in letters, not in the Richardsonian manner, nor altogether in that of *Evelina*; but like those in Smollett's last novel, by correspondents of incongruous dispositions and contrary points of view. Dr Pringle, another Ayrshire divine with a superficial resemblance to Goldsmith's Dr Primrose, comes up to London with his wife, and his son and daughter, to see about a legacy. It is the year of the death of George III, and of the proceedings against Queen Caroline; and Galt gives their ingenuous impressions of things he himself was witnessing. Dr Pringle, who when he has a row with a hackney coachman proceeds to take the number and finds it fastened on, is a very rustic Matthew Bramble. His thrifty better-half does well enough for Aunt Tabitha: and the sentimental Rachel and her brother Andrew, who is "infected with the blue and yellow calamity of the *Edinburgh Review*,"[1] make a passable Lydia and Jerry Melford.

Parody of contemporary schools   This young gentleman's sumptuous style is an excellent parody of the contemporary "highbrow." He writes from Windsor a high-falutin account of the dead king's lying in state.

> "A change came o'er the spirit of my dream," and I beheld the scene suddenly illuminated, and the blaze of torches, the glimmering of arms, and warriors and horses, while a mosaic of human faces covered like a pavement the courts. A deep low under sound pealed from a distance; in the same moment, a trumpet answered with a single mournful note from the stateliest and darkest portion of the fabric, and it was whispered in every ear, "It is coming." Then an awful cadence of solemn music, that affected the ear like silence, was heard at intervals, and a numerous retinue of grave and venerable men,

> > "The fathers of their time,
> > Those mighty master spirits, that withstood
> > The fall of monarchies, and high upheld
> > Their country's standard, glorious in the storm,"

> passed slowly before me, bearing the emblems and trophies of a king.[2]

---

[1] Established 1802.   [2] Letter xii.

The romantic Rachel has great respect for her accomplished brother, but represents a slightly different school.

What my brother thinks of her majesty's case is not easy to divine; but Sabre is convinced of the queen's guilt, upon some private and authentic information which a friend of his, who has returned from Italy, heard when travelling in that country. This information he has not, however, repeated to me, so that it must be very bad. We shall know all when the trial comes on. In the meantime, his majesty, who has lived in dignified retirement since he came to the throne, has taken up his abode, with rural felicity, in a cottage in Windsor Forest; where he now, contemning all the pomp and follies of his youth, and this metropolis, passes his days amidst his cabbages, with innocence and tranquillity, far from the intrigues of courtiers, and insensible to the murmuring waves of the fluctuating populace, that set in with so strong a current towards " the mob-led queen," as the divine Shakespeare has so beautifully expressed it.[1]

Mrs Pringle's homely remarks on George the Fourth's determined rustication are a refreshing contrast.

Is it not a hard thing to come to London and no to see the king? I am not pleesed with him, I assure you, becose he does not set himself out to public view, like ony other curiosity, but stays in his palis, they say, like one of the anshent wooden images of idolatry, the which is a great peety, he beeing, as I am told, a beautiful man, and more the gentleman than all the coortiers of his court.[2]

The irony which is so obvious in this satirical sketch, for *The The Ayrshire Legatees* is very brief, comes more subtly into Galt's *Provost* next work, *The Provost* (1822), in which a self-made man tells his own story, having left this record of his municipal achievements in the hands of his widow. Almost as soon as Mr Pawkie opened his shop " at the Cross, facing the Tolbooth," in Gudetown, he began to meditate upon the advantages that would accrue to himself and the borough if he became a member of the town council. His ambitions soared to the proudest heights: he saw himself a bailie, and even a provost; and, with the fine tact which was always to characterize him, he managed to inspire others with the same prophetic views and get himself suggested for the

[1] Letter xxviii.   [2] Letter xxx.

first vacancy. And so, by unremitting attention to his own business and the town's, which he always identified, for he liked to feel that if he made any modest profit out of a contract the public benefited in an even larger measure, he sat upon the egg which he got with his wife and "clocked it to some purpose." The time overlaps that of the *Annals*, extending from the close of the American war, all through the revolutionary period, to the years after Waterloo. It was a time when it behoved the leaders in a royal burgh to restrain "the inordinate liberty of the multitude," "to bridle popularity, which was becoming rampant and ill to ride, kicking at all established order." Accordingly, he "resolved to discountenance all tumultuous meetings, and to place every reasonable impediment in the way of multitudes assembling together,"[1] and incidentally to abolish the town fairs, which promoted disturbance and were a thorn in the side of regular tradesmen, cutting prices and underselling, "so that both private interest and public incited me on to do all in my power to bring our fair-days into disrepute."

Galt's irony

Then, in the affair of the church, which wanted reseating, though its walls were coming down and it ought to have been rebuilt, he was able to discomfit Bailie M'Lucre, who had a secret interest in a whinstone quarry, and oblige William Place, the joiner. "A most reasonable man in all things he was," and "the kirk was in a manner made as good as new." Thus did Mr Pawkie succeed in furthering his interests in both worlds, being satisfied with very moderate advantages to himself from transactions that were for the infinite benefit of the town. He prided himself on having set his face against the time-honoured policy of those in public life, the pilfering and swindling and jobbery; and, as he says in his valediction, "Although, in the outset of my public life, some of my dealings may have been leavened with the leaven of antiquity, yet upon the whole, it will not be found, I think, that, one thing weighed with another, I have been an unprofitable servant to the community. Magistrates and rulers must rule according to the maxims and affections of the world; at least, whenever I tried any other way, strange obstacles started up in the opinions of men against me, and my

[1] Chap. xviii.

purest intents were often more criticized than some which were less disinterested." Mr Pawkie is as frank a recorder of his own doings and motives as Samuel Pepys, and is perfectly unaware of anything radically wrong in his combination of self-righteousness and a watchful eye for his own interest.

There is pathos in many incidents, much more than the Provost is aware of; for example, in the execution of Jean Gaisling who "had murdered her bastard bairn," and in the affair of the press-gang, when the mob smashed his windows, for having signed the warrant. But the town clerk advised him that " this calamity, if properly handled to the government, may make your fortune "; and he took the hint. He was, in fact, thanked for his zeal in the public service, and indemnified for his loss "in a manner which showed the blessings we enjoy under our most benevolent constitution; for I was not only thereby enabled to repair the windows, but to build up a vacant steading; the same which I settled last year on my dochtor, Marion, when she was married to Mr Geery, of the Gatherton Holme."[1] The most tragic chapter is "The Windy Yule," describing the Christmastide when the whole town throngs the kirkyard hill to watch the terrible plight of five of their own ships in the bay. Two founder with the loss of all on board, and the other three are swept by mountainous seas in full view of the wives and children, powerless to help. But the most humorous chapter is the last, telling how the Provost, about to lay down his honours, with his inimitable tact and self-restraint, contrives to prompt two junior members of the council to bring up a proposal for a piece of plate and an address, which are duly presented on his resignation. The burgesses and the ragtag and bobtail of Gudetown are drawn as incisively as the people of Dalmailing; Bailie M'Lucre, the Rev. Dr Swapkirk, Mr Galore the great Indian Nabob, Mr Sharpset, Mr Peevie, and Dr Whackdeil of Kirkbogle, are as good as their names. But this is essentially a monograph, a study of unconscious propensities. Coleridge said of it, " In the unconscious, perfectly natural, Irony of Self-delusion, in all parts intelligible to the intelligent Reader, without the slightest suspicion on the part of the Autobiographer, I know of no

Pathos and unconscious humour

[1] Chap. xxi.

equal in our Literature "; and added: "This and *The Entail* would alone suffice to place Galt in the first rank of contemporary Novelists—and second only to Sir W. Scot (*sic*) in technique."[1]

"*The Entail*"   The long-winded *Sir Andrew Wylie of that Ilk*, which appeared this same year, is a work of broader and coarser humour, and notable only for the witty Sir Andrew himself, another example of the Scot who rises by his own efforts from the bottom to the top. That incredible piece of social affectation Lord Sandyford is supposed to be an attempt to draw Galt's friend, the Earl of Blessington. It was followed by Galt's masterpiece, *The Entail* (1823), which both Scott and Byron are said to have read through three times, and on which the high praise of a better critic, Coleridge, has just been quoted. It is the history of three generations, and one of the few novels that embrace so much of human life that there is room for tragedy, bitter and profound, and also for the truest comedy. The tragedy is the work of the first generation, and overshadows the second, after which sunshine returns. There is also a sort of epilogue, in certain final chapters, of a more jubilant and romantic note, into which Galt was betrayed by his easy-going tolerance of the artifices of commercial fiction.

The tragedy of Claud Walkinshaw   His protagonist is another dour, plodding, indomitable Scot, who starts from beggary to build a fortune; and succeeds, but only to ruin his own and his children's happiness. Claud Walkinshaw is the sole surviving heir of the lairds of Kittlestonheugh, who lost their estates in the Darien adventure. The boy was reared by an old family servant, in a garret in a Glasgow close, and goes out to earn his living as a pedlar. For many years he endures the extremes of poverty and hardship, carrying his pack through the Lowlands and the Border. But he had sworn to himself that he will win back the lands of his ancestors, and refound the family of Kittlestonheugh. Bit by bit he scrapes together enough to set up a shop in Glasgow; and presently he buys a corner of the old property, the farm of Grippy. He is now in the forties; it is time to marry, since the next thing is to beget

---

[1] Written on the dedication page of a copy owned by Coleridge (see letter from A. J. Ashley, in *Times Lit. Suppt*, 25th September 1930).

children to carry on the name. He marries the plain but level-headed daughter of a small laird, Grizzy Hypel, who, long after tragedy has overwhelmed Claud, is to develop into one of the finest originals in Scottish fiction, a great figure of comedy. Children are born and grow up; and he proposes to old Hypel to entail his estate of Plealands on the eldest, so that a substantial portion of the Kittlestonheugh lands may be kept together. But Hypel insists that the inheritor shall take his own name, and settles Plealands upon Claud's second son, though after his death it is found that the lawyer, Mr Omit, had forgotten the vital clause about the change of name. But the mischief is done. Claud Walkinshaw, now one of the wealthiest men in Glasgow, resolves to disinherit his eldest boy, Charles, who has married a portionless lass, so that the second son, Wattie, who had obeyed orders and married the well-to-do Betty Bodle, may be laird of Kittleston-heugh, or of as much of the ancient patrimony as Claud can get hold of. And Wattie, on whom all is to be entailed, is a born natural. Useless for the honest old legal adviser to remonstrate!

"The property is my own conquesting, Mr Keelevin, and surely I may mak a kirk and a mill o't an I like."

"Nobody, it's true, Mr Walkinshaw, has ony right to meddle wi' how ye dispone of your own; but I was thinking ye maybe didna reflect that sic an entail as ye speak o' would be rank injustice to poor Charlie, that I hae aye thought a most excellent lad."

"Excellent here, or excellent there, it wasna my fault that he drew up wi' a tocherless tawpy, when he might hae had Miss Betty Bodle."

"I am very sorry to hear he has displeased you; but the Fatherlans family, into whilk he has married, has aye been in great repute and estimation."

"Ay, afore the Ayr Bank; but the silly bodie the father was clean broken by that venture."

"That should be the greater reason, Mr Walkinshaw, wi' you to let your estate go in the natural way to Charlie."

"A' that may be very true, Mr Keelevin; I didna come here, however, to confer with you anent the like of that, but only of the law. I want you to draw the settlement, as I was saying; first, ye'll entail it on Walter and his heirs-male, syne on Geordie

and his heirs-male, and failing them, ye may gang back, to
please yoursel', to the heirs-male o' Charlie, and failing them,
to Meg's heirs-general "[1]

Such is the intricate legal arrangement, which once entered
into remained unalterable, and was to be the source of tragic
complications for the best of two lifetimes. For Claud finds
himself checkmated. Wattie's Betty Bodle dies in childbed,
leaving him with only a little girl, who also does not live long.
The ill-used Charlie leaves his wife a widow, with children
unprovided for. And Geordie has no male children. When
Mr Keelevin brings the old man the news of Charlie's death
there is an "earthquake-struggle." Then he recovers his
speech:

"I had a fear o't, but I wasna prepar't, Mr Keelevin, for
this," said the miserable father; "and noo I'll kick against the
pricks nae langer. Wonderful God! I bend my aged grey head
at Thy footstool. O, lay not Thy hand heavier upon me than I
am able to bear! Mr Keelevin, ye ance said the entail could be
broken if I were to die insolvent—mak' me sae in the name of
the God I have dared so long to fight against. An' Charlie's
dead—murdered by my devices! Weel do I mind when he was
a playing bairn, that I first kent the blessing of what it is to hae
something to be kind to; aften and after did his glad and bright
young face thaw the frost that had bound up my heart, but aye
something new o' the world's pride and trash cam' in between,
and harden't it mair and mair. But a's done noo, Mr Keelevin
—the fight's done and the battle won, and the avenging God of
righteousness and judgment is victorious."

Mr Keelevin sat in silent astonishment at this violence of
sorrow. He had no previous conception of that vast abyss of
sensibility which lay hidden and unknown within the impenetrable
granite of the old man's pride and avarice; and he was amazed
and overawed when he beheld it burst forth, as when the fountains
of the great deep were broken up, and the deluge swept away the
earliest and the oldest iniquities of man.[2]

But before he can make any provision for Mrs Charles and
her orphans, Claud Walkinshaw is no more; and the half-wit who
succeeds him has but one clear idea, that he must never put his

[1] Chap. xviii.   [2] Chap. xliii.

signature to a piece of paper, or rob the child of his dead Betty
Bodle of a single bawbee.

" If my father," said he, " did sic a wicked thing to Charlie as
ye a' say, what for would ye hae me to do as ill a wrang to my
bairn?   Isna wee Betty Bodle my first-born, and, by course o'
nature and law, she has a right to a' I hae; what for then would
ye hae me to mak away wi' ony thing that pertains to her?   I'll
no be guilty o' ony sic sin."

Wee Betty Bodle dies, and the idiot seizes his brother's little
girl, and protests that it is still his own Betty Bodle.   But George
Walkinshaw, as hard as his father and more sordid, has his eye
upon the property, and gets his brother cognost by a jury, and
pronounced mentally incapable.   The examination is one of
Galt's richest scenes.   Wattie, who has been coached by his
friends, disconcerts the hostile advocate.

" You do not think you are a daft man? " said the advocate.
"Nobody thinks himsel' daft.   I daresay ye think ye're just as
wise as me."

But his pathetic delusion about Betty Bodle settles his fate, and
George installs himself at Grippy.

The leading figure in the drama from this point, however, is *Leddy*
George's mother, the relict of Claud Walkinshaw.   She has been *Grippy,*
ejected from the old mansion, and left on a small allowance in a *a great*
Glasgow lodging.   First, she manages to get George's daughter *comedy*
married to an ineligible young man; and then, when George has *figure*
had to be reconciled to the situation and she discovers a flaw in
his title to the estate, she sues him for the cost of their board and
lodging, and he is glad to compromise for a thousand pounds.
But Leddy Grippy boasts: "They would need long spoons that
sup parridge wi' the de'il, or the like o' me, ye maun ken."   When
the son-in-law, in right of his wife, succeeds to the estate, and
though that right is at variance with the terms of the entail, the
chicanery of a Writer to the Signet is on the point of making
his possession safe and absolute, she beats the lawyers at their own
game.   Only those on the other side have seen the actual document.
But Leddy Grippy extracts from the enemy enough to give her
a good inkling, and browbeats them into the conviction that she

knows the rest. " I dinna need Mr Whitteret, nor ony siclike, to instruct me in terms of law."

The lawyer began to quake for his client as the leddy proceeded:
" For ye ken that the deed of entail was first on Walter, the second son; and, failing his heirs-male, then on George and his heirs-male; and, failing them, then it went back to Charles the eldest son, and to his heirs-male. If there's law in the land, his only son ought to be an heir-male, afore Milrookit's wife, that's but an only dochter."

She throws scorn at amicable arrangements, gives them a dose of her " jawing tacks "; and, not only dispossesses the usurping laird and restores the property to her grandson, but also sticks to her ill-gotten thousand pounds, and sends the lawyers packing with the threat of an action for conspiracy.

"What's the use of an amicable arrangement? Isna the law the law? Surely I didna come to a lawyer for sic dowf and dowie proceedings as amicable arrangements; no, Mr Pitwinnoch, ye see yoursel' that I hae decernt on the rights o' the case, and therefore (for I maun be short wi' you, for talking to me o' amicable arrangements) ye may save your breath to cool your porridge. My will and pleasure is, that Walkinshaw Milrookit shall do to-morrow morning, in manner of law, then and there, dispone and surrender unto the heir-male of the late Claud Walkinshaw of Kittlestonheugh, in the shire o' Lanark, and synod of Glasgow and Ayr, all and sundry the houses and lands afore-said, according to the provisions of an act made and passed in the reign of our sovereign lord the king. Ye see, Mr Pitwinnoch, that I'm no daw in barrow't feathers, to be picket and pooket in the way I was by sic trash as the Milrookits."

And at her final word the lawyer, fearing for his reputation more than for the threatened action, hastily retires.

" I can see as far through a millstane as ye can do through a fir deal, and maybe I may tak' it in my head to raise a plea wi' you in an action of damages for plotting and libelling in the way that it's vera visible ye hae done, jointly and severally, in a plea of the crown; and aiblins I'll no tak' less than a thousand pounds; so, Mr Pitwinnoch, keep your neck out o' the woody o' a law-plea wi' me, if ye can; for, in the way of business, I hae done wi' you; and, as soon as Mr Whitteret comes hame, I'll see whether I ought not to instruct in a case against you for the art and part conspiracy of the thousand pounds." [1]

In *Ringan Gilhaize* (1823), a novel of the Covenanters and the battle of Killiecrankie (1823), Galt entered into competition with Scott's *Old Mortality*, with indifferent success. *The Spaewife* (1823) and *The Omen* (1825) followed the delusive lure of historical romance seasoned with the supernatural. He came back to his own ground in *The Last of the Lairds* (1826), the principal character and the talkative and meddlesome leddy being of the same strain as some of those in *The Entail*. But his monetary embarrassments made Galt latterly a regular bookmaker, and he repeated himself and used second-hand stuff from other writers in the novels and magazine stories that followed. Some of these have been collected only in recent years. The title-story in *A Rich Man and other stories* (1925) is *The Provost* over again. It is the autobiography of Archibald Plack, Esq., late Lord Mayor of London, who began life as an errand boy in Glasgow, and by stinting and saving rose through the degrees of porter, money-lender, and banker, to wealth, married his daughter to an impecunious lord, and now addresses these letters full of worldly advice to his grandson at college. He cannot conceal a sneaking admiration for the young spark, though he chides him for " keeping devouring horses " at the university, when " it would be more to your advantage, maybe, if you read the Scriptures." There is often such a taste here of Galt's old irony. In one of the other two tales, *Tribulations of the Rev. Cowal Kilmun*, the simple and pious but over-cautious pastor is almost as good as the minister of Dalmailing; but his searchings of heart over the man he married to a beautiful girl, whom he left at the kirk door and returns from America to find dead, are dull compared with any score of pages in the *Annals*.

Galt was something more than the dedicatee of a long popular example of Scottish petty fiction, *The Life of Mansie Wauch*, "*Mansie Wauch*"

---

[1] Chap. xcvii. Galt's intimacy with the works of rival novelists comes out in several incidents—*e.g.* that in chap. ix. of the coffin left behind at the funeral, from *Humphry Clinker*. Charlie's sweetheart has to take a new dress to no less a person than Mrs Jarvie, " the wife of the far-famed Bailie Nicol (chap. xv.). Leddy Grippy compares the lawful and tender affection of Robina and Beenie to the mere " puff-paste love o' your Clarissy Harlots " (chap. lxiv.).

tailor in Dalkeith, written by himself (1828), which had been running for three years in *Blackwood*, signed with the well-known initial " Delta." Delta was David Macbeth Moir (1798-1851), the most affectionate of Galt's friends and afterwards his biographer, and author of the last chapters in *The Last of the Lairds*, which Galt had to leave in his hands unfinished on being suddenly called away across the Atlantic. Moir wrote a quantity of miscellaneous verse, largely of a tender domestic order; and the charm for his readers lay in the sentiment and pathos mingled with his jocularities. In a string of anecdotes rather than a connected narrative, Mansie relates his coming into the world, schooling, apprenticeship, calf love and the chequered bliss of wedded life and fatherhood, his exploits with the resurrection men and misadventures in the volunteering days of 1805; and at the same time pictures the general life of the little town, with its provost and councillors, in a manner that falls a long way short of Galt's *Annals*. But the studied pathos often hits the mark, as in the tale of the prentice lad from the Lammermuirs, who pines for his breezy hills and dies of consumption on his way home. The tailor is not a hero, in any sense of the word, and his conceit of his own pawkiness often makes him a butt. The humour is chiefly of the broad, elementary kind, exemplified in so many of the contributions to "Maga"; such is the yarn about the regimental goat passed off as mutton, or of the cigars handed round by his lordship's flunkeys and supposed by the town councillors to be a sort of sweetmeat, till, when they were all growing seasick, he showed his astonished guests that it was a novel form of tobacco-pipe. But the thin vein of humour is disguised by the richness of the broad Scots, which gives most of the point to the long discussion between Mansie and his wife on what they shall do with their Benjie, and to the gravedigger's reply to the debt-collector:

" He just bad me tell ye, faither, that hoo could ye expect he cou'd gie ye onything till the times grew better; as he hadna buried a living soul in the kirkyard for mair nor a fortnight."

Moir was but one of a crowd of writers, many of them contributors to *Blackwood's Magazine*, now trying to vie with Scott, or following the easier path laid down for them by Galt and *The Miss Ferrier*. The three berserks of "Maga" all attempted the Blackwood historical romance or the Scottish domestic novel, or both. group Lockhart's versatility enabled him to register two successes, in *Adam Blair* and *Matthew Wald*, after his failure in *Valerius* (1821) at a novel of Romano-British history. The Ettrick Shepherd gave up the competition with Scott, after *The Brownie of Bodsbeck* (1818), a tale of the Covenanters; but achieved one powerful story that stands out somewhat incongruously from the rest of the group. John Wilson's contribution was a complete fiasco. The two dozen tales and sketches collected under the title of *Lights and Shadows of Scottish Life* (1822) and *The Trials of Margaret Lindsay* (1823) have more than his wonted sentimentality but little of the truth or the natural humour of the genre. The author of the *Noctes* and the *Recreations of Christopher North* was not a novelist. Moir's friend, Andrew Picken (1788-1833), won temporary applause with his *Tales and Sketches of the West Coast of Scotland* (1824) and a respectable novel of domestic life, *The Dominie's Legacy* (1830), but did not live to improve upon this. Other members of the Blackwood coterie who made a noise at the time with at least one book were the Rev. George Robert Gleig (1796-1888), Captain Thomas Hamilton (1789-1842), and Michael Scott (1789-1835); but their work comes into a different category from the foregoing. Gleig served in the Peninsular War, afterwards becoming chaplain of the forces; and his novel, *The Subaltern* (1828), is fiction compounded out of his own reminiscences. There is more imagination and more thought in Hamilton's rambling and very miscellaneous story, loftily entitled, *The Youth and Manhood of Cyril Thornton* (1827), which also consists in part of reminiscences of the Peninsular War. But the one of the Blackwood set who was hailed by the few who knew his literary prowess as a wizard and a magician, and fit to hold a candle to Sir Walter, was the latter's namesake, Michael Scott.

Moir was impressed by the modesty of the man. Michael Michael Scott stuck to business, as a Glasgow merchant managing big Scott estates in Jamaica, till he was middle-aged. Then he contributed his two novels, *Tom Cringle's Log* and *The Cruise of the Midge*, to the magazine, published them anonymously in 1833 and 1834, and died the following year, his name still unknown to the world of readers, and even, it is said, to the editor of *Blackwood*. But, except in character-drawing, in which they both tried to emulate Smollett, he rivals and in sheer narrative power outdoes Captain Marryat, whose nautical romances had begun with *Frank Mildmay* (1829), and were now in full career. In the course of his business, Scott travelled far and wide, and knew every corner of the West Indies. These two brilliant farragos of adventure are obviously composed of personal experiences, though it is not to be supposed that everything related happened to himself. Tom Cringle goes through the American war and the world struggle of 1813-1814, Benjie Brail in the companion volume has a no less eventful career in the years following. Duels with American frigates, and with pirates, privateers, and slavers, cutting-out expeditions, floods, earthquakes, cyclones, shipwrecks, succeed each other with incredible velocity; but the clear, precise, impetuous narrative compels belief in each incident as it occurs. The most blood-curdling proceedings are retailed with a cold-blooded realism that is positively brutal, alternately with scenes of buffoonery hardly less ferocious. A majority of the characters are grotesque in the manner of *Roderick Random*; many have the same air of personal lampoons. Perhaps Aaron Bang and the Yankee pirate Obediah, in *Tom Cringle*, and the first lieutenant, "Old Bloody Politeful," in *The Midge*, are the most tolerable. Picaresque fiction composed of violent sensation and sheer horseplay is not the most elevated kind of literature; but it is redeemed in this case by narrative and descriptive power equal to Sir Walter's. No one hitherto had thus evoked the glory and magic of the sea, and it is a question whether Pierre Loti or Conrad has outdone him since.

Lockhart's "Adam Blair" Lockhart's two Scottish novels, *Some Passages in the Life of Adam Blair* (1822) and *The History of Matthew Wald* (1824), are much of a piece as tragic studies of remorse, and short enough to have been published later in a single pair of covers. The story of Blair is substantially the same as that of Hawthorne's *Scarlet Letter*: a Calvinist minister is guilty of an act of adultery, and publicly confesses his sin. But Lockhart has none of the lofty poetic symbolism of Hawthorne's masterpiece. *Adam Blair* is simple and austere tragedy, related with austere simplicity. Yet the scene in which Blair enters the chapter-house at Glasgow and quietly admits the charge which is being debated and deprecated by his fellow-ministers is as noble in its bare simplicity as the dramatic avowal in the more famous book. "The secret miseries of a soul prostrate under the sense of spiritual abandonment" are revealed with strength and restraint. Lockhart was an extremely able man, who could have turned out efficient novels as easily as any other article of literature, though his range was limited to that of existing models. *Reginald Dalton* (1823), the novel of undergraduate life at Oxford which immediately followed, mixes farce and uproariousness like that of the *Noctes Ambrosianæ* with some idyllic fancy and some not very profound thought in the Ciceronian style. But perhaps his best work is contained in the desultory and incoherent *History of Matthew Wald*, which Scott described as "full of power, but disagreeable and ends vilely."[1]

The incoherence was intentional; for this is his own account "*Matthew* of the critical episodes in an aimless and wasted life, written *Wald*" down when Matthew had recovered from a period of insanity consequent upon a passionate outbreak. The tale might be called an example of the introspective picaresque, so fortuitous is its course. Lockhart here, as in his other novels, was too clear-sighted to tinker with plots.

Matthew Wald went wrong on the very threshold of manhood, when by an act of meanness he injured the woman whom he loved and who had married another; but it was his own nature that he injured most profoundly. Between him and her there is a spiritual bond, deeper than simple affinity, a bond not dwelt upon by Lockhart, but borne in on the reader's mind with a subtlety that is, no doubt, the psychological power alluded to by Scott. Wald loses his self-respect, and loses his compass; henceforth his life drifts at random, and in the marriage which he makes and the other situations he enters into he feels himself in an alien world. By accident, he discovers that his wife is entitled to a great property. He asserts her claims, and becomes rich. The poor

[1] Andrew Lang's *Life of Lockhart*, i. 346.

woman falls under the sway of fanatical Methodists, and he tries to free her from this malign influence. But his first love has been wronged by her husband. He finds her in the house next door, forces a duel on the noble miscreant, and kills him without witnesses. His own wife, who is with child, dies of the shock. Then come the visions of delirium, and finally the placid old age which Scott thought such a vile ending, overlooking the fact that, as Lockhart put it, " our ' grey-haired man of glee ' . . . was in reality the secret slave of despondency." *Matthew Wald*, in truth, was a fit companion for James Hogg's more terrible history of frenzy and crime, which appeared the same year. Was it mere coincidence that the murder committed by the fanatical Cameronian, John M'Ewan, in Lockhart's story, and the holy exultation of the believer in predestination, are a sort of miniature of Hogg's fearful memoir?

John, in a short speech of his own, expressed his sense of his guilt; but even then he borrowed the language of Scripture, styling himself " a sinner, and the chief of sinners." Never was such a specimen of that insane pride. . . .
" Abuse me—spurn me as you will—I loathe myself also; but this deed is Satan's. . . . He had *once* been right, and he could not be wrong; he had been *permitted to make a sore stumble*! " This was his utmost concession.[1]

"The Con- fessions of a Justified Sinner"   Hogg's extraordinary novel, *The Private Memoirs and Con- fessions of a Justified Sinner* (1824),[2] need not appear so extra- ordinary and hard to construe if it be borne in mind that Hogg and others of his set were ever ready to take up the old Scottish quarrel with the unco guid. To begin with, the story is a belated satire on fanatical Calvinism and the self-righteousness of some of its devotees; Hogg's attitude is the same as in his poem, *The Village of Balmaquhapple*:

> O, blessed Saint Andrew, if e'er ye could pity fo'k,
> Men fo'k or women fo'k, country or city fo'k,
> Come for this aince wi' the auld thief to grapple,
> An' save the great village of Balmaquhapple

---

[1] Chap. xviii.
[2] The novel appeared also under the title, *The Confessions of a Fanatic*, and in an American edition of 1895 as *The Suicide's Grave*.

Frae drinking an' leeing, an' flyting an' swearing,
An' sins that ye wad be affrontit at hearing,
An' cheating an' stealing; O, grant them redemption,
All save and except the few after to mention.

The gibes at Johnny the elder,

Wha hopes ne'er to need ye,
Sae pawkie, sae holy, sae gruff, an' sae greedy;
Wha prays every hour as the wayfarer passes,

and at Bess, "wha delights in the sins that beset her," mark this
as of the same bent as *The Holy Fair*, the *Address to the Deil*,
Holy Willie's Prayer, and the *Address to the Unco Guid*. In the
wilder distortions of that creed, or the worst extravagances
imputed to its votaries, Hogg found a Faust-like theme for a
story more terrible than any sensation-mongering Gothicism.
He developed this theme with so much power, coherence, and
restraint that Saintsbury and others have doubted whether some
more practised hand, perhaps Lockhart's, must not have had a
share, or even have been entirely responsible for the book.[1]
Some pages of *Matthew Wald*, published the same year, show a
similar animus in the resentful account of Methodist exploitation
of religiosity. But it has been placed beyond doubt that Hogg
wrote the book himself[2]; although there is nothing inherently
improbable in the theory that Lockhart had a finger, or at any
rate a word, in the plan and execution. The inner circle in
"Maga" were used to putting their heads together.[3] The *Noctes*,
for instance, were written by Christopher North; but Hogg and
others were none the less his collaborators. The poet of *The
Queen's Wake* had imagination enough for such a feat as the
Memoirs and Confessions, and if he were writing a prose story
he was pretty sure to insert in it some news of the other world.
On the other hand, the Blackwood set, almost to a man, relished
sensationalism, and were very far from contemning the works of
German romanticism, then much in the air. At that very date,
from 1821 to 1829, famous examples were running in the pages

---

[1] Saintsbury discusses the possibilities of Lockhart's authorship or collaboration,
without apparently taking the view that the book is, at any rate in origin, a satire
(*Essays in English Literature, 1780-1860*, " Hogg," especially pp. 55-57).
[2] Elton, i. 223 and 438, note.   [3] In the Chaldee MS. for instance.

of the magazine, those compounds of diablerie, mystery, and horror, afterwards issued in a series of volumes as *Tales from Blackwood*.[1]

The story   The supposed date of the events is some years after that of *Old Mortality*; it is a time when Cavaliers and Presbyterians were still at loggerheads in the Edinburgh streets. This state of incessant feud, breaking out continually in acts of violence, furnishes the setting for the baleful conflict between the two brothers, which resolves presently into the career of the Justified Sinner, in which the possible consequences of a belief in absolute predestination are pushed to their utmost extremity. A gay old laird marries a wife of the strictest religious views, and has two sons, one like himself, the other a born fanatic. The latter is brought up by the mother and a bigoted divine, who instils a venomous hatred of his father and brother and all their works. The first part of the memoirs ends with the murder of the elder brother. Circumstances seem to point to the guilt of one of his boon companions, who flees to the Continent. Some suspicion attaches to the pharisaical younger brother, whose hatred and threats were well known; but, when the father dies broken-hearted, he succeeds to the estates, and sees himself blessed with power and riches as well as the assurance of salvation affirmed by his spiritual director.

The Con-   Now begin the confessions, in which the inner history of the
fessions   foregoing events is set forth. The man explains why he did not become a minister, and preferred to be a champion of the Gospel, to cut off the enemies of the Lord. He had seen the folly and inconsistency of "striving and remonstrating with sinners in order to induce them to do that which they had it not in their power to do."

Seeing that God had from all eternity decided the fate of every individual that was to be born of woman, how vain was it in man to endeavour to save those whom their Maker had, by an unchangeable decree, doomed to destruction.

He was a justified person, and at ease because he knew that he could do no wrong. But the influence of the fanatical minister

---

[1] In twelve volumes, 1858-1861. There were two further series at later dates.

who had brought him up has gradually been supplanted by that
of a mysterious stranger, who makes his way into the young man's
affections, and persuades him at length that he has been appointed
to carry out a great work, one of the firstfruits of which is the
making away of his elder brother. The sinner at first debates
the morality, or rather the Scripture sanction, of some of the deeds
to which he is urged. But his Mephistopheles bears down all
misgivings.

There was no religious scruple that irritated my enlightened
friend and master so much as this. And, the sentiments of our
great covenanted reformers being on his side, there is not a doubt
that I was wrong.

Crime follows crime, and the dupe and his tempter escape the
remotest suspicion. But, suddenly, the convinced believer that he
can do no wrong finds himself charged with horrors of which he
has no knowledge whatever. He is tried and found guilty. More
crimes are discovered, and the wretch takes flight to escape the
fury of the whole country. Naked and destitute, he wanders from
place to place, now deserted and now tempted anew by his evil
spirit, whom at last he begins to recognize for what he is. The
demons rage over any roof beneath which he seeks refuge. He is
turned out into the night, everyone fearing to harbour a man
visibly accursed. He ends the memoirs, which were to be printed
and distributed as a religious pamphlet, and then dies, in a lonely
spot amidst the peat-mosses of the Border. A postscript relates
the final facts, and gives an account of a visit to the suicide's
grave many years later by Mr L——w and Mr L——t,
obviously Laidlaw and Lockhart.

The story may be enjoyed simply as an essay in the macabre, *A satire*
probably more inspired by Goethe's *Faust* than by any other work.
The anatomy of a deluded soul, led on by imperceptible degrees
from one false doctrine to one more monstrous, and in spite of
momentary suspicions convinced in his error, is done on the whole
with sound psychology. As with Shakespeare's ghosts and witches,
the question continually arises whether these are anything more
than the half-materialized projections of a conscience ill at ease.
From either point of view, they are appalling. So too with the

being who haunts and misleads the blinded sinner; he may be taken as the Devil in person, or as the writer's material symbol for the man's evil self now in command of all his actions. But then there is the satire. The new Faust and Mephistopheles were an integral part of this, and no mere afterthoughts. There can be little doubt of Hogg's satirical motive, after such a passage as the old Cameronian Penpunt's account of Satan's plots against the faithful in general and the pious town of Auchtermuchty in particular. The enemy of mankind " was the firmest believer in a' the truths of Christianity that was out o' Heaven; an', sin' the Revolution that the Gospel had turned sae rife, he had been often driven to the shift o' preaching it himsel." Penpunt goes on :

" Gin ever he observes a proud professor, wha has mae than ordinary pretensions to a divine calling, and that reads and prays till the very howlets learn his preambles, *that's* the man Auld Simmie fixes on to mak a dishclout o'. He canna get rest in Hell, if he sees a man, or a set of men o' this stamp, an', when he sets fairly to work, it is seldom that he disna bring them round till his ain measures by hook or by crook. Then, Oh! it is a grand price for him, an' a proud Devil he is, when he gangs hame to his ain ha', wi' a batch o' the souls o' sic strenuous professors on his back."

Satan rejoiced when " the people o' the town o' Auchtermuchty grew so rigidly righteous that the meanest hind among them became a shining light in ither towns an' parishes." Auld Robin Ruthven heard ae corbie speaking, an' another answering him :

" Where will the ravens find a prey the night? " " On the lean crazy souls o' Auchtermuchty," quo the tither. " I fear they will be o'er wrappit up in the warm flannens o' faith, an' clouted wi' the dirty duds o' repentance, for us to make a meal o'," quo the first. " Whaten vile sounds are these that I hear coming bumming up the hill? " " Oh, these are the hymns and praises o' the auld wives and creeshy louns o' Auchtermuchty, wha are gaun crooning their way to Heaven; an', gin it warna for the shame o' being beat, we might let our great enemy tak them. For sic a prize as he will hae! Heaven, forsooth! What shall we think o' Heaven, if it be to be filled wi' vermin like thae, amang whom there is mair poverty and pollution than I can name."

A preacher was sent, who told the people of Auchtermuchty that their town had been delivered over to the Devil for a prey; and the inhabitants were electrified, they were charmed.

They were actually raving mad about the grand and sublime truths delivered to them by this eloquent and impressive preacher of Christianity. " He is a prophet of the Lord," said one, " sent to warn us, as Jonah was sent to the Ninevites." . . . The good people of Auchtermuchty were in perfect raptures with the preacher, who has thus sent them to Hell by the slump, tag-rag, and bobtail! Nothing in the world delights a truly religious people so much as consigning them to eternal damnation.

Strange, that Hogg's critics and editors have taken no notice of the satirical intent so deeply embedded in this grim story, and have been content to regard it as merely a somewhat eccentric specimen of the ordinary novel of terror![1]

[1] For instance, the latest editor, T. Earle Welby (*Campion Reprints*, No. 1), 1924.

SELECT READING AND REFERENCE LIST

GENERAL

DEVONSHIRE, M. G. *The English Novel in France, 1830-1870.* 1929.

ELTON, OLIVER. *A Survey of English Literature, 1780-1830,* vol. i. 1912.
> *Inter alia,* some of the best criticism of Scott.

JOHNSON, R. BRIMLEY (ed.). *Famous Reviews;* selected and edited with introductory notes. 1914.
> Reviews of Hannah More, Jane Austen, Scott, etc.

MASSON, DAVID. *British Novelists and their Styles : being a critical sketch of the history of British prose fiction.* 1859.

MEREDITH, GEORGE. *An Essay on Comedy and the Uses of the Comic Spirit.* 1897.

OLIPHANT, JAMES. *Victorian Novelists.* 1899.
> Scott and Jane Austen, etc.

OMOND, T. S. *The Romantic Triumph.* 1900.

PIERCE, FREDERICK E. *Currents and Eddies in the English Romantic Generation.* 1918.

REYNAUD, LOUIS. *Le Romantisme : ses origines anglo-germaniques.* 1926.

VAUGHAN, C. E. *The Romantic Revolt.* 1907.

WALKER, HUGH. *The Literature of the Victorian Era.* 1910.

WILLIAMS, HAROLD. *Two Centuries of the English Novel.* 1911.

WILLIAMS, ORLO. *Some Great English Novels : studies in the art of fiction.* 1926.
> *Tom Jones, Martin Chuzzlewit, Pendennis, The Egoist, Roxana, Emma,* etc.

CHAPTERS I.-II.—MARIA EDGEWORTH

BUTLER, HARRIET JESSIE and HAROLD EDGEWORTH. *The Black Book of Edgeworthstown and of Edgeworth Memorials, 1585-1817.* 1927.

EDGEWORTH, F. A. *Life and Letters of Maria Edgeworth, edited by her Friends.* 3 vols. 1867.
  Printed but not published, the basis of all the accounts of her life.

EDGEWORTH, MARIA. *Chosen Letters.* Edited F. V. Barry. 1931.

EDGEWORTH, MARIA. *Life and Letters.* Edited by A. J. C. Hare. 2 vols. 1894.

LAWLESS, EMILY. *Maria Edgeworth.* (English Men of Letters.) 1904.

MEAKIN, ANNETTE M. B. *Hannah More.* (Eminent Women.) 1911.

CHAPTERS III.-V.—JANE AUSTEN

AUSTEN, JANE. *Letters to her sister Cassandra and Others.* Edited by R. W. Chapman. 2 vols. 1932.

AUSTEN-LEIGH, JAMES EDWARD. *A Memoir of Jane Austen.* 1926.

AUSTEN-LEIGH, MARY AUGUSTA. *Personal Aspects of Jane Austen.* 1920.

AUSTEN-LEIGH, WILLIAM and RICHARD ARTHUR. *Jane Austen: her Life and Letters, a family record.* 1913.

BAILEY, JOHN. *Introductions to Jane Austen.* 1931.

BRADLEY, ANDREW CECIL. *Jane Austen.* (English Association Essays and Studies, II.) 1911.

CECIL, LORD DAVID. *Jane Austen.* 1935. (Leslie Stephen Lecture delivered 1st May 1935.)

CORNISH, FRANCIS WARRE. *Jane Austen.* (English Men of Letters.) 1913.

KEYNES, GEOFFREY. *Jane Austen: a Bibliography.* 1929.
  Also one by J. L. Edmonds (Chicago Univ. Bulletin). 1925.

MITFORD, MARY RUSSELL. *Recollections of a Literary Life.*
3 vols. 1852.

POLLOCK, WALTER HERRIES. *Jane Austen ; her Contemporaries
and Herself : an essay in criticism.* 1899.

SADLEIR, MICHAEL. *The Northanger Novels : a footnote to
Jane Austen.* (English Association Pamphlets.) 1928.

THOMSON, CLARA LINKLATER. *Jane Austen : a survey.* 1930.

VILLARD, LÉONIE. *Jane Austen, sa vie et son œuvre, 1775-1817.*
1915.
Translated by Veronica Lucas, with a new study of Jane Austen by R. Brimley
Johnson (1924).

CHAPTERS VI.-IX.—SCOTT

ADOLPHUS, J. L. *Letters to Richard Heber, containing critical
remarks on the series of Novels beginning with "Waverley"*
(1821).

BAGEHOT, WALTER. *Literary Studies,* vol. ii. 1905.
"The Waverley Novels."

BUCHAN, JOHN. *Sir Walter Scott.* 1932.

BUTTERFIELD, T. *The Historical Novel : an essay.* 1924.

CANNING, ALBERT STRATFORD GEORGE. *History in Scott's
Novels : a literary sketch.* 1905.
Philosophy of the Waverley Novels. 1879.

CARLYLE, THOMAS. *Critical and Miscellaneous Essays,* vol. vi.
1839. Later edition, 1872.
"Sir Walter Scott."

CECIL, LORD DAVID. *Sir Walter Scott.* 1933.

CHAMBERS, ROBERT. *Illustrations of the Author of Waverley ;
being notices and anecdotes of real characters, scenes, and
incidents supposed to be described in his Works.* 1825. Third
edition. 1884.

CROCKETT, W. S. *The Scott Originals.* 1912.

GRIERSON, H. J. C. (ed.). *Sir Walter Scott To-day : some
retrospective essays and studies.* 1932.

GWYNN, STEPHEN. *The Life of Sir Walter Scott.* 1930.

HUTTON, RICHARD HOLT. *Sir Walter Scott.* (English Men of Letters.) 1879.

LOCKHART, JOHN GIBSON. *Memoirs of the Life of Sir Walter Scott.* 10 vols. 1837-1838.
There is an abridged edition in one volume (1898).

MAIGRON, LOUIS. *Le Roman historique à l'époque romantique : essai sur l'influence de Walter Scott.* 1898.

PHILADELPHIA FREE LIBRARY. *A Descriptive Catalogue of the Writings of Sir Walter Scott.* 1898.

SCOTT, SIR WALTER. *Miscellaneous Prose.* 2 vols. 1841-1847.

    Journal (1825-1832). Edited by W. Knight. 2 vols. 1890.

    Letters, 1787-1814. Edited by H. J. C. Grierson, vols. i.-viii. 1932-1935.

SECCOMBE, THOMAS, and OTHERS. *Scott Centenary Articles.* (Essays by T. Seccombe, W. P. Ker, etc.) 1932.

SENIOR, NASSAU W. *Essays on Fiction.* 1864.
Scott, Col. Senior, Lytton, Thackeray, Mrs Stowe.

VERRALL, A. W. *The Prose of Sir Walter Scott* (*Quarterly Review*, July 1910).

YOUNG, C. A. *The Waverley Novels : an appreciation.* 1907.

CHAPTER X.—OTHER SCOTTISH NOVELISTS

BATHO, EDITH C. *The Ettrick Shepherd.* 1927.

DOUGLAS, SIR G. B. S. *The Blackwood Group* (Famous Scots). 1897.

DOYLE, J. A. (ed.). *Memoirs and Correspondence of Susan Ferrier.* 1898.

GALT, JOHN. *Autobiography.* 2 vols. 1833.

JEFFREY, FRANCIS. *Contributions to the Edinburgh Review.* 1853.

MILLAR, J. H. *A Literary History of Scotland.* 1903.

SAINTSBURY, GEORGE. *Essays in English Literature, 1780-1860.*
1891.
      Hogg, Peacock, Wilson, Lockhart, etc.

SMITH, G. GREGORY. *Scottish Literature : character and
influence.* 1919.

INDEX

INDEX

A

B

M

N

O